The SMART Family Tax Guide

101 Ways to Keep More of What You Earn

By Mike Nie, CPA, CFP, CFA, EA

Owner, Smart 1040 LLC

Chairman, SMART Life Family Foundation

GIFTED BOOKS

The SMART Family Tax Guide:
101 Ways to Keep More of What You Earn

ISBN
978-1-96626-104-9   Paperback
978-1-96626-103-2   E-book

Contents

Disclaimer

The Securities and Exchange Commission disclaims responsibility for any private publication or statement of any SEC employee or Commissioner. This book expresses the author's views and does not necessarily reflect those of the Commission, the Commissioners or other members of the staff.

This book is intended for educational and informational purposes only. It reflects the author's personal experiences and interpretations and should not be construed as specific tax, legal, financial, or investment advice for any individual situation. Readers should consult with qualified tax, legal, and financial professionals before applying any strategies discussed herein.

While every effort has been made to ensure accuracy as of the date of publication, laws and regulations are subject to change, and the author assumes no responsibility for errors, omissions, or changes in applicable laws.

The book mentioned well diversified broad-based stock index (such as S&P 500 index), well-diversified, broad-based stocks with zero dividends, whole life insurance policies, crypto, real estate or other financial assets. The author advises the reader to seek help from licensed professionals regarding these financial assets. These licensed professionals have their respective expertise to suggest and design portfolio based on your family's financial, liquidity, tax and other specific situations.

The rate of return, yield and dividend ratio are as of year-end 2024. Past data does not guarantee future performance. Readers bear their investment risk. The book author and Smart 1040 LLC are not responsible for such investment related risks or losses.

The IRS tax forms are as of 2024, or the latest version available at the IRS.gov website. The tax code-related dollar amounts are as of 2025, many of which are adjusted annually by the IRS. This book also addresses new tax law changes in the One Big Beautiful Bill Act (OBBBA), which adjusts certain limits, caps or phase-out amounts. The book may have incorporated these new tax law changes. Many of the tax rule changes will require the readers to re-evaluate their tax planning strategies.

The hyperlinks used throughout the book may not work if the content owner removes or edits the post.

All names and stories have fictional elements, and are designed for illustration purpose only.

This book and its contents may not be used for training, developing, or enhancing any artificial intelligence (AI) model without the express written consent of the author.

To my beloved SMART family —

Olga, Olesia, Sasha, Chris, and Kevin.

You are my greatest blessing, my inspiration, and the reason I do what I do. Your love, patience, and strength have carried me through every chapter of life and this book. I love you all, deeply, unconditionally, and forever.

Preface

As a Christian father, CPA, and coach, I have long witnessed how the U.S. tax system, while often confusing, offers powerful opportunities for strategic planning. These opportunities are too often overlooked or misunderstood by hardworking families. I wrote this book for **SMART (Strategies to Master Assets and Reduce Taxes)** families because I believe that every family, whether they're earning $60,000 or $600,000 a year, deserves to know the same tax-saving principles and tools used by wealthier individuals and advisors.

As a CPA since 2008, I spent ten years with a Big Four accounting firm specializing in accounting and auditing. Today, I run my own tax planning practice, where I've had the privilege of advising hundreds of families and high-net-worth individuals. Having witnessed their financial triumphs and challenges, often deeply intertwined with my personal family dynamics, I was inspired to write this book and share my insights, real stories, and best practices with you, the SMART family.

This book is not about tax loopholes or exotic schemes. It's about clarity, consistency, and concrete steps. Through real-life examples, simplified explanations, and actionable tips, I hope to clarify the tax code for those who need it most: middle-class families trying to get ahead, save for their kids' college, plan for retirement, and pass something on.

When I began organizing workshops for families and small business owners, I quickly discovered how often people miss deductions, fail to optimize retirement accounts, or neglect simple tools like Health Savings Accounts (HSAs) or Roth IRAs, not because they're careless, but because the system is dense and the advice fragmented. The fact is that most tax resources aren't written for everyday people.

This book aims to fill that gap. It covers 101 tax-saving tips, from everyday moves like adjusting withholdings and tracking expenses to more advanced strategies involving trusts, rental property, and retirement conversions. Each section is designed to stand alone. Whether you read it cover to cover or jump to a chapter that speaks to your life stage, you'll find something practical and actionable.

I also wrote this book for the next generation, with a dream of FLY (financial literacy for youth). Tax planning should be part of financial literacy, not an afterthought. My hope is that parents will use this book to teach their children about the power of compound interest, smart giving, and how taxes affect every major life decision.

Thank you for picking up this book. May it save your family money, spark new conversations, and give you more confidence during every tax season.

Thank you, my numerous supporters and mentors. I appreciate your selfless time and effort spent on my book. I owe you immensely. All errors in the book belong to me.

- Mike Nie, CPA, CFA, CFP, EA

SMART Coach (Strategies to Master Assets and Reduce Taxes)

PART 1:

SMART FAMILY

Chapter 1

A New Buffet(t) of Riches

I still remember the day I stumbled upon Warren Buffett's annual letters.[1] I was not attending a grand conference or taking some fancy finance class. No, I was at my kitchen table with a half-empty cup of coffee in hand, flipping through random articles online. And there it was: a doorway into a whole new way of thinking about money, life, and legacy. A Buffet of riches.

Reading Buffett's words felt like finding a map to a hidden treasure, not of gold, but of wisdom. Simple ideas, not flashy tricks. Patience over greed. Value over hype. Discipline over drama. That morning, something shifted inside me. I realized that true wealth was not about chasing every hot tip or timing the market perfectly. It was about building a solid, resilient financial life, brick by brick.

Learning to build wealth, not chase hot investments

Buffett did not build his fortune by sprinting. He jogged. Steadily, methodically, intentionally. I then realized I needed to do the same.

Instead of chasing stock tips from TV, Instagram influencers, or friends, I simplified. I anchored my family's portfolio around two pillars: the S&P 500 index fund and well-diversified, broad-based stocks with zero dividends, more or less equally distributed. Simple, strong, diversified, low fee or no fee, and with six decades of proven performance.

When my son Kevin turned 18, we sat down together. His Roth IRA had just hit $60,000. I showed him a simple projection: "If you add to this steadily, let it grow untouched, you could have over $9 million by the time you're 60."

His eyes widened. Mine did too. Not because of greed, but because of the possibility that patience could outwork almost anything.

We also discussed diversification beyond stocks. I explained to Kevin how investing in real estate, small businesses, and even personal development could provide other avenues for wealth accumulation. The idea was not to chase returns, but to plant multiple seeds and let them grow over time, with diversified features and performances.

Building family traditions around money

One January evening, I started a new tradition, inspired by Buffett's shareholder letters. [2] I wrote a "family vision board letter." See Case Study 1. In it, I outlined what went well, what mistakes we made, and how we planned to grow. No shame. No blame. Just reflection and planning.

It became an annual ritual. Each letter became a guidepost for our family's journey, like a journal of growth, values, and accountability.

Over the years, these letters became more than financial summaries. They included life lessons, dreams for the future, and even reflections on our failures. Sometimes, we included sections written by my wife and kids, sharing their perspectives. These letters are now a cherished part of our family history, capturing not just numbers but emotions, milestones, and aspirations.

Teaching by doing: Roth IRAs, HSAs, and beyond

When my daughter Olesia turned 18, instead of just wishing her "Happy Birthday," I gifted her a health savings account (HSA). My wife hired Olesia in her personal coaching business. Olesia used her earned money to open a Roth Individual Retirement Arrangement (IRA). See Chapter 15 for more details about the HSA. See Chapter 7 for more details about the IRA.

> 🔍 **Tax term: Health Savings account (HSA)** is a tax-advantaged savings account available to individuals enrolled in a high-deductible health plan (HDHP). Contributions are tax-deductible, grow tax-free, and withdrawals are also tax-free when used for qualified medical expenses. Unused funds roll over each year and can be invested, making the HSA a powerful tool for both healthcare and long-term savings. HSA tax provisions were effective January 2004.
>
> A **High-Deductible Health Plan (HDHP)** is a health insurance plan with lower monthly premiums but higher deductibles than traditional plans. To qualify as an HDHP in 2025, it must have a minimum deductible of $1,600 for individuals or $3,200 for families. HDHPs are required in order to contribute to a Health Savings Account (HSA).
>
> 🔍 **Tax term: Roth Individual Retirement Arrangement (Roth IRA)** is a retirement savings account where contributions are made with after-tax dollars, meaning you don't get a tax deduction up front. The money grows tax-free, and qualified withdrawals in retirement are also tax-free. It's especially beneficial for younger earners or those expecting to be in a higher tax bracket in the future.
>
> The Roth IRA is named after Senator William Roth, who created this type of account as part of the Taxpayer Relief Act of 1997.

"Most people overlook this," I told her. "But it's a triple tax win. You can deduct your contributions, grow them tax-free, and withdraw them for health expenses without paying a dime in tax."

She smiled politely at first. But later that year, after a minor surgery, she saw firsthand how her HSA paid bills without touching her savings-- a lesson more powerful than any lecture.

I also made sure my children earned real income working in our family business. Filing paperwork. Managing client files. Maintaining company website. They earned it, and I paid them fairly. Then we funded their Roth IRAs. Those small deposits are seeds that will grow into towering oaks by the time they are older.

We even set up monthly "finance nights" where we would sit around the kitchen table, look over their savings, discuss investment strategies, and set short-term goals. Watching them set up budgets, track expenses, and choose investments gave me immense joy. It was not about controlling them; it was about empowering them.

The rise of AI and why human resilience matters

When AI burst into the scene, friends panicked: "Jobs are disappearing!"

I stayed calm. Buffett taught me: adapt, do not panic. I encouraged my family to build skills AI cannot replace. Personal care. Tax advice. Real estate investment. Senior services. Businesses built on human trust and presence, not algorithms.

Side hustles became part of our DNA. Multiple streams of income were not just handy but essential.

We brainstormed ideas: tutoring, freelance writing, property management, even teaching music lessons. The goal was simple: build resilience, not dependence. It was not about making millions overnight, but building a safety net strong enough to weather any storm.

Cutting the fat: High fees and bad advisors

One year, I did a deep dive into our retirement accounts. I was stunned. High-fee funds were quietly draining thousands.

I fired our overpriced advisor, shifted everything to low-cost index funds, and rebalanced myself. Every dollar saved in fees became another soldier working for our family's future.

I also started teaching my children how to read a fund prospectus. We reviewed expense ratios, turnover rates, and performance history. It was eye-opening for them, and empowering. Financial literacy is not just knowing how to earn; it is knowing how to protect and grow what you earn.

Learning to love the dips

When markets tumbled, I did not hide. I converted small amounts from traditional IRAs to Roth IRAs. Strategic, steady Roth conversions during downturns became a game-changer.

> 🔍 **Tax term:** Traditional IRA and Roth IRA differ in that traditional IRA contributions are tax deductible from the current year 1040 tax return, but withdrawals are taxed as the ordinary income, whereas Roth IRA contributions are made with after-tax dollars (i.e., no tax savings benefits in the contribution year) but withdrawals (after 59.5) are tax free.

> 💡 **Tax tip: Roth conversion** is a strategy to shift money from a traditional IRA to a Roth IRA, paying taxes at the conversion year but allowing future growth and withdrawals tax free. Roth conversion works best when (1) stock markets drop by a material percentage (10% or more) and rebound afterwards; or (2) your tax bracket is reasonably low (i.e., 24% or lower).

"Buy fear, sell greed," I whispered to myself. Buffett would have smiled.

I also taught my children that market dips are opportunities, not disasters. We treated every downturn as a classroom session: reviewing asset allocation, revisiting financial goals, and checking our emotional reactions. Emotional resilience is as important as financial strategy.

Writing, reflecting, and growing

Today, I still write our family financial letter every New Year's Day. It has become a love letter, in a way to discipline, resilience, and hope.

I also committed to reading ten finance and tax books a year. If Buffett, a billionaire at 94+, still learns constantly, how could I afford to stop?

We even started a small "family library" of the best financial books we have read. Every time a family member finishes one, they add notes and highlights for the next reader. It is our version of passing down wisdom: page by page, lesson by lesson.

Buffett's true gift

Warren Buffett did not just teach me how to invest. He taught me how to live:

- Be patient.
- Stay humble.
- Think long-term.
- Communicate clearly.
- Never stop learning.

That is the legacy I want to leave not just money but wisdom. It is a legacy of mindset, not just material wealth. And it is one that, God willing, will ripple through generations of our family long after I am gone.

Top 10 tax planning tips from this chapter

1. Use Roth IRAs for tax-free growth: Start early and allow decades of compounding to millions.

2. Leverage Health Savings Accounts (HSAs) with triple tax advantages: Tax deductible contributions, tax-free growth, and tax-free withdrawals for healthcare expenses.

---

3. Convert to Roth IRAs during market downturns: Use the market dips to create opportunities for tax-efficient Roth conversions. The taxpayer friendly tax brackets become permanent under the OBBB. Roth conversion makes more sense than ever! Be careful of the possible implication of over-conversion pushing you to the higher bracket.

4. Pay children through a family business: Their wages can fund Roth IRAs and teach them work ethics, with tax benefits in that you shift income from parents' higher tax bracket to child's zero or low bracket.

5. Set up a family foundation: Create a lasting charitable legacy while reducing taxable income.

6. Gift appreciated stock to children in lower tax brackets: Let them sell at little or no tax, avoiding high capital gains rates.

7. Use whole life insurance as a wealth transfer tool: Tax-deferred growth, tax-free loans, and estate planning advantages. Apply the buy, borrow and build strategy frequently.

8. Avoid high-fee funds: Low-cost index funds preserve more of your hard-earned money.

9. Create and review annual family financial reports: Reflection and accountability are essential for long-term success.

10. Borrow against investments for smart opportunities: Use low-cost margin loans or life insurance loans to access cash without triggering capital gains.

Chapter 2:

Creating a SMART Vision Board for Tax-Free Financial Freedom

It all started one New Year's Day morning, when my wife, kids, and I sat around the breakfast table.

Instead of resolutions we knew we would forget, I challenged the family: "This year, let's do something different. Let's create a vision board. Not just any vision board, a vision for tax-free financial freedom."

Kevin, still half asleep, asked, "What's a vision board got to do with taxes?"

That simple question became the start of a transformational journey.

The awakening: Financial freedom Is a FEELING first

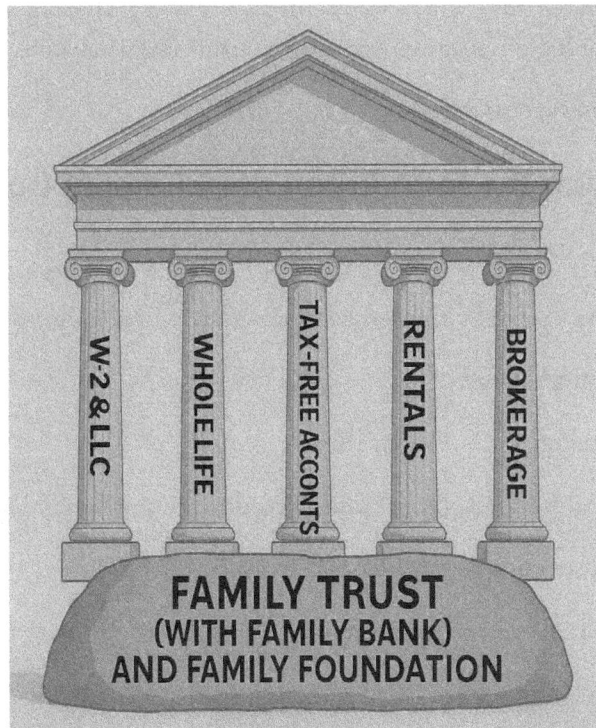

Pillar	Description	Chapters in This Book
1	W-2 (day job) and LLC (side hustle)	4 and 11
2	Cash value whole life insurance	9
3	Tax free or tax advantaged accounts, including 401(K), IRA, 529, and HSA	8, 15, and 16
4	Real estate rentals	17-21
5	Brokerage accounts, including universal minor transfer act (UTMA) accounts	7 and Appendix 5
Base	Family Trust and Family Bank	9 and 10
Base	Family Foundation	22-26

Note: See end of the chapter tax terms and definitions.

Inspired by my mentor, Rev. Jim Webb, author of *"Create A Self-Manifesting Vision Board: Bringing Your Vision Board to Life (The Soul of Prosperity),"* I told my family that realized financial planning is not just numbers; it is an emotional involvement and investment in:[1]

- Security

- Clarity

- Freedom

- Joy

- Legacy

We were not just chasing bigger bank accounts. We were chasing a feeling of complete independence, of living life on our own terms, free from financial stress.

The vision board would be our compass.

Step One: Building the foundation of our vision board

Each family member took a poster board and began crafting:

Pictures of travel dreams (partially funded by business trips or charity-giving activities)

Charts showing zero-debt balances

A savings goal thermometer for our Roth IRAs

Quotes like, "Grow wealth, not tax bills" and "Freedom is our family legacy" [2]

Drawings of rental houses and passive income streams

Colleges representing charitable giving from our future Family Foundation

We made it colorful, joyful, and energizing. Kevin even added "Meme Stocks: Nope!" with a big red X over a GameStop logo. A vision board is not a spreadsheet; it is a blueprint for your dreams.

Step Two: Linking the vision to action

Our vision board was not just decoration. It guided our tax and financial moves all year. We started identifying action items to implement the following:

VB Maxed out Roth IRA contributions every January.

VB Funded HSA accounts aggressively, using them as stealth retirement vehicles.

VB Shifted from mutual funds with hidden fees to super low-cost S&P 500 index funds (e.g., Fidelity 500 Index charges 0.015% fund management fee, equivalent to $1.5 per $10,000 asset balance).

VB Started a small business side hustle to create Solo 401(K) opportunities.

VB Strategically performed Roth conversions during low-income years.

VB Invested in real estate properties eligible for accelerated bonus depreciation. See Chapter 19.

VB Used the Augusta Rule to rent our home to our business for tax-free income. See Chapter 12.

VB Made charitable donations through a family foundation to maximize itemized deductions.

Every strategy tied back to something visible on our board.

To put our vision into action, my family focuses on three fundamental principles:

Low or zero cost. I called "Zero is Hero." Single name stock investment has zero fees or costs. S&P 500 index has annual expense ratio as long as 0.015%. Cash value life insurance can be structured with 10% premium pay (most of them paid to the life insurance agent) and 90% cash value addition. Real estate brokerage fees can be negotiated to the lowest level given the recent legislative moves.

Higher-than-inflation rate of return. The average inflation rate in the past five decades is 2-3% per year.

Diversification among the investment to ensure at any given year, at least one asset produces higher-than-inflation rate with minimal fee. Year 2008 was the most stressful year to the investment model.

The table below outlines the four-pronged asset allocation approach to the SMART goal (*strategies to master assets and reduce taxes*).

Year	ESV / UTMA / Roth IRA / Solo Roth 401(K) / HSA / FF / Family Bank	Roth 401(K) / 529 / IUL / FF	Whole Life Insurance	Real Estate Rental
	Berkshire Hathaway (BRK.B) (1)	S&P 500 Index (2)	Guardian Life Gross Yield (3)	House Price Index (4)
1975	2.5%	37.2%	5.2%	4.7%
1976	129.3%	23.6%	5.5%	10.5%
1977	46.8%	-7.4%	6.1%	14.5%
1978	14.5%	6.4%	6.4%	14.9%
1979	102.5%	18.2%	6.5%	9.4%
1980	32.8%	32.3%	7.1%	5.2%
1981	31.8%	-5.0%	7.2%	0.9%
1982	38.4%	21.4%	7.5%	7.8%
1983	69.0%	22.4%	7.7%	4.4%
1984	-2.7%	6.1%	12.3%	4.6%
1985	93.7%	31.6%	13.3%	6.3%
1986	14.2%	18.6%	13.3%	7.3%
1987	4.6%	5.1%	12.5%	5.0%
1988	59.3%	16.6%	12.0%	5.2%
1989	84.6%	31.7%	11.5%	5.0%
1990	-23.1%	-3.1%	11.0%	1.5%
1991	35.6%	30.5%	10.5%	3.1%
1992	29.8%	7.6%	10.3%	1.7%
1993	38.9%	10.1%	9.8%	3.2%
1994	25.0%	1.3%	9.0%	1.5%
1995	57.4%	37.6%	8.5%	5.2%
1996	6.2%	23.0%	8.0%	2.2%
1997	34.9%	33.4%	8.5%	5.1%
1998	52.2%	28.6%	8.8%	4.6%
1999	-19.9%	21.0%	8.8%	5.8%
2000	26.6%	-9.1%	8.5%	7.7%
2001	6.5%	-11.9%	8.5%	6.0%
2002	-3.8%	-22.1%	8.0%	6.5%
2003	15.8%	28.7%	7.0%	7.4%
2004	4.3%	10.9%	6.6%	11.1%

Year	ESV / UTMA / Roth IRA / Solo Roth 401(K) / HSA / FF / Family Bank	Roth 401(K) / 529 / IUL / FF	Whole Life Insurance	Real Estate Rental
	Berkshire Hathaway (BRK.B) (1)	S&P 500 Index (2)	Guardian Life Gross Yield (3)	House Price Index (4)
2005	0.8%	4.9%	6.8%	10.5%
2006	24.1%	15.8%	6.5%	3.3%
2007	28.7%	5.5%	6.8%	-2.2%
2008	-31.8%	-37.0%	7.3%	-5.8%
2009	2.7%	26.5%	7.3%	-7.0%
2010	21.4%	15.1%	7.0%	-3.4%
2011	-4.7%	2.1%	6.9%	-1.6%
2012	16.8%	16.0%	7.0%	2.2%
2013	32.7%	32.4%	6.7%	4.7%
2014	27.0%	13.7%	6.3%	5.4%
2015	-12.5%	1.4%	6.1%	4.9%
2016	23.4%	12.0%	6.1%	5.3%
2017	21.9%	21.8%	5.9%	6.2%
2018	2.8%	-4.4%	5.9%	4.6%
2019	11.0%	31.5%	5.9%	5.1%
2020	2.4%	18.4%	5.7%	7.5%
2021	29.6%	28.7%	5.7%	19.6%
2022	4.0%	-18.1%	5.7%	8.1%
2023	15.8%	26.3%	5.9%	5.5%
2024	25.5%	25.0%	5.6%	4.0%
Compounded Annual Return (1975-2024)	19.90%	10.40%	8.30%	8.25%

Sources:

(1)   BRK.B return: Berkshire Hathaway Company annual reports, available at https://www.berkshirehathaway.com/reports.html [2]

(2)   S&P   500   index   yield,   available   at https://www.stern.nyu.edu/~adamodar/pc/datasets/histre401(K).xls [3]

(3)   Guardian life insurance yield, available at https://topwholelife.com/whole-life-insurance-dividend-rate-history/. Note: yield disclosed as gross number. Policyholders may receive lower ones after the cost of insurance and other overhead deductions.

(4)   Real estate returns, computed by the author based on Case Schiller Home Pricing Index (HPI) at https://fred.stlouisfed.org/series/csushpinsa.

Diversification is a key component of the SMART strategy. The table below shows the correlation ratios of these four pillars of financial assets. Most notably, the rate of return on cash value whole life insurance policies is remotely related to stock market, and even negatively related to the housing market. In other words, with family assets and tax friendly accounts allocated among these four types of assets, a SMART family achieves at least one, or even all four positive returns in any of the 50 years from 1975 to 2024. The worst performing year was

2008 (the subprime financial crisis). Cash value whole life insurance policy still produced a 7.3% annual return.

Correlation	BRK.B	S&P 500	Guardian Whole Life Insurance	House Price Index
BRK.B	100%	44.3%	12.0%	26.8%
S&P 500	44.3%	100%	4.1%	12.8%
Guardian Whole Life Insurance	12.0%	4.1%	100%	-15.8%
House Price Index	26.8%	12.8%	-15.8%	100%

Four enemies to our financial freedom: We started by naming the enemies threatening working families like ours:

High investment management fees that quietly drain investment returns year after year. We only choose S&P 500 index fund with expense ratio as low as 0.015% per year.

High taxes that reduce our hard-earned savings every April. We use the "Buy, Borrow and Build" approach to avoid the capital gain tax.

Inflation that erodes purchasing power while we put money in a bank checking account with 0.05% interest earned.

Procrastination, which silently kills our financial dreams. The time to plant the tree is NOW.

Naming these enemies helped us see why so many families struggle to reach true freedom. It was not just bad luck; it was lack of proactive, conscious planning.

Disclaimer: The table and any other sections in the book that make references for stocks or stock indexes are for illustration only, by no means constituting investment advice or recommendation. The author strongly advises the reader to consult with qualified financial advisors for securities investment strategies.

Term	IRS Tax-Oriented Definition	Tax Code Effective Year
529 Plan	Tax-advantaged savings for education; earnings and withdrawals are tax-free for qualified expenses.	1997
ESA	Coverdell Educational Savings Account. Investment earnings tax free if used for education expenses.	1998
Family Bank	A **Family Bank** is a private financial resource and system created by a family trust that provides loans, grants or scholarships to family members for approved purposes, such as education, business startup, or major life events). The assets in the Family Bank were managed and distributed prudently with a family bank constitution.	1954
Family Foundation	A **Family Foundation** is a type of private foundation that is typically funded and governed by members of a single family. It is a 501(c)(3) nonprofit organization, often used for charitable giving, estate planning, and legacy building. Family members retain control over grantmaking decisions, and the foundation is required by the IRS to distribute at least 5% of its assets annually for charitable purposes.	1969
Family Trust	A **Family Trust** is a legal arrangement where a trustee (normally the parents and the successor trustee if the parents pass away) holds, manages and distributes assets on behalf of the beneficiaries (usually children, grandchildren and future generations of the family).	1954
HSA	**Health Savings Account.**[4] Tax-deductible contributions, tax-free growth, and tax-free withdrawals for qualified medical expenses.[5]	2004
IUL	**Indexed Universal Life.** Permanent life insurance tied to market indexes; cash value grows tax deferred.	1984
LLC	A **Limited Liability Company** (LLC) is a business structure that combines the liability protection of a corporation with the tax flexibility of a partnership or sole	1997

	proprietorship. Owners, called members, are generally not personally liable for the company's debts or legal obligations.	
Real Estate Rental	Investment income property; allows depreciation, expense deductions, and §199A pass-through benefits.	1954 (Depreciation)
Roth 401(K)	Employer-sponsored Roth account; withdrawals tax-free if age and holding period requirements met.	2006
Roth Conversion	A **Roth conversion** is the process of moving funds from a pre-tax retirement account, like a Traditional IRA or 401(K), into a Roth IRA.[6] You pay income tax on the converted amount in the year of the transfer, but future growth and qualified withdrawals from the Roth IRA are tax-free. This strategy is often used to reduce long-term taxes, especially when done during lower-income years.	1998
Roth IRA	**Individual Retirement Arrangement.** After-tax retirement account; qualified withdrawals are tax-free if conditions are met.	1998
Solo 401(K)	A **Solo 401(K)** is a retirement savings plan designed for self-employed individuals or business owners with no full-time employees other than a spouse. It allows higher contribution limits than traditional IRAs by letting the owner contribute both as an employee and employer. This plan can include Roth and traditional options, and may allow loans and flexible investment choices. **Roth Solo 401(K)** is for self-employed individuals with no employees; grows tax-free, without tax deduction in the contribution years.	2006
UTMA	**Uniform Transfers to Minors Account.**[7] Allows irrevocable gifts to minors, managed by a custodian, taxed at child's rate. To avoid kiddie tax, look for zero-dividend yield, broad-based stocks with a long and strong proved record dated back to 1960s. Avoid selling the investment due to capital gain taxes. Use the "Buy, Borrow, and Build" strategy to access the liquidity.	1986

Whole Life Insurance	Life insurance with fixed premiums, death benefit, and cash value that grows tax deferred.	1800s

> 💡 **Tax tip:** The "**Buy, Borrow, and Build**" strategy has been a SMART approach (strategies to master assets and reduce taxes) for decades. It works in three steps: (1) buy appreciating assets (stocks, life insurance, real estate, or crypto); (2) instead of selling assets that could trigger capital gain taxes, you borrow against the assets as collateral; and (3) build more wealth by reinvesting borrowed in tax preferential account or in business expansions. Some of the interest expense of the borrowed money could be deductible business expense.

Step Three: Meditation, prayer, and visualization

Dr. Webb teaches us that vision boards work best when paired with daily reflection. Every morning, I spent five minutes visualizing:

Tax-free retirement withdrawals.

Family vacations funded by passive income.

Writing donation checks from our Smart Life Family Foundation without worrying about taxes.

Walking my future grandchildren through their own financial vision boards.

These prayers and meditations grounded our ambitions in gratitude and service.

We also kept a "Gratitude Ledger" beside our board, listing five things we were thankful for every week.

Step Four: Overcoming doubts and staying focused

We placed two columns on our vision board:

Left side: Fears ("What if the market crashes? What if we cannot save enough?")

Right side: Solutions ("Long-term investing mindset. Emergency funds. Multiple income streams.")

We even framed setbacks as tests, not failures:

If a tenant moved out? Test.

If the market dipped? Test.

If we fell behind on savings? Test.

Every time fear whispered, we looked right, and remembered we had a plan and faith bigger than any setback.

Step Five: Updating and celebrating wins

Each quarter, we updated our vision boards:

Adding new Roth contributions

Celebrating debt payoffs

Tracking real estate rental income milestones

Documenting new skills learned (like QuickBooks or real estate negotiation)

Even small wins fueled momentum.

We celebrated milestones with simple family dinners, reinforcing that the journey mattered just as much as the destination.

We also started taking "Victory Photos" snapping pictures next to our vision board updates to create a visual history of our progress.

Step Six: Vision boards for the next generation

When Kevin turned 18, we helped him create his own vision board.

Pictures of his dream apartment

A bar chart tracking Roth IRA growth

A checklist for building his first rental property portfolio

Dreams of opening a small business consulting firm

The board was not about flashy cars or huge mansions. It was about freedom to choose, to live, and to give.

Even our younger daughter built one, with unicorns, college campuses, and "Financial Freedom by 30" doodled across the top.

Top 15 ways we built and used our vision board

VB 1. Identify emotional drivers first (freedom, peace, legacy)

VB 2. Name four financial enemies clearly

VB 3. Use images and words that spark real emotions

VB 4. Connect each vision item to a specific tax or financial strategy

VB 5. Incorporate faith, prayer, and daily meditation

VB 6. Write about fears and proactive solutions side by side

VB 7. Celebrate small milestones joyfully

VB 8. Involve the entire family, across generations

VB 9. Update quarterly to stay aligned with changing goals

VB 10. Visualize tax-free wealth daily

VB 11. Teach children the habit of "Dream it, then plan it"

VB 12. Anchor every goal in gratitude and service to others

VB 13. Track skill development alongside financial milestones

VB 14. Frame setbacks as tests, not failures

VB 15. Create "Victory Photos" for motivation and reflection

Final Reflection: A vision board is architecture – not art

In the end, our family learned that vision boards are not wishful thinking. They are architectural blueprints for the life we want to build. Tax-free financial freedom is not luck.

It is vision + faith + action, repeated daily.

Every dollar saved, every tax strategy implemented, and every small victory achieved can all traced back to those early morning moments, staring at our colorful boards, daring to believe. You do not just hope your dreams come true. You build them: one prayer; one plan; and one purposeful step at a time.

Chapter 3

Ten Tax Planning Moves That Fueled My FIRE Journey

When I first heard about FIRE, Financial Independence, Retire Early, I dismissed it as fantasy. Surely it was only for Silicon Valley millionaires or lucky tech wizards, right?

But the more I studied it, the more I realized FIRE was not about retiring young to do nothing. It was about buying back time to serve, time to travel, time to build, and time to be fully present.[1]

The spark that lit the FIRE

I still remember a Saturday morning at the library. I stumbled onto a book about early retirement strategies, and for the first time, FIRE seemed real. Possible. Achievable even for a working-class family like ours. FIRE lays out a roadmap of retiring from a grinding 9-5 job and diving into activities we are passionate about without financial worries, if we plan smartly, use the tax code creatively, and live intentionally.

Move 1: Buying life insurance early

When my daughter Olesia was just 15 days old, I bought her a cash value whole life insurance policy: low premium cost; minimum whole life death benefit and one-year term rider; high cash value paid up addition; no medical exam, and permanent insurability.[2]

That policy quietly grew, tax-deferred, into a financial tool we could later use for college expenses, first business loans, or even down payments.

I realized that insurance, when used right, was not just protection, but an asset.

Move 2: Gifting well diversified broad-based stocks

Every Christmas, birthday, and graduation, instead of gadgets and gift cards, I gift my children shares of no-dividend stock and with decades long of strong, proved return into their UTMA accounts.[3] Such gifting will (1) avoid dividend-caused kiddie tax, (2) avoid long term capital gain tax if selling the shares, and (3) keep the compounding effect uninterrupted. We even host "stock ceremonies" where we celebrate new contributions, review performance, and discuss long-term investments.

Move 3: Using 529s differently.

Instead of dumping money mindlessly into 529s, we focused on aggressive, low-fee equity funds. When market corrections hit, I did not panic. Instead, I funded 529s harder during dips, knowing rebounds would magnify our gains tax-free.[4] During my children's college years when the stock market dropped, I avoided drawing 529 funds (to let the account recover in future years). Instead I borrowed a policy loan against cash value whole life insurance policy to cover the tuition expenses.

We also strategized to overfund some 529s for potential future graduate school or adult retraining because a few family members were residing in California and New Jersey—states which do not allow state tax deductions. But the benefits are that you can invest the best 529 plans nationwide without limiting yourself to the in-state 529 plan that may charge higher fees. I compared the state 529 plan offering S&P 500 index options. The Virginia plan had the lowest expense ratio (0.07% as of 2025), while other states doubled the expense ratio for the same investment option.

Move 4: Embracing Coverdell early

Most people forget Coverdell ESAs exist. We did not.

🔍 **Tax term: Coverdell Education Savings Account (ESA)** is a tax-advantaged account designed to help families save for a child's education expenses. It is named after Coverdell, Mr. Paul Coverdell, a U.S. Senator who pioneered this idea. Contributions are made with after-tax dollars, but earnings grow tax-free, and withdrawals are tax-free when used for qualified education costs, including K–12 and college expenses. Annual contribution limits are low (currently $2,000 per child), and eligibility phases out at higher income levels.

💡 **Tax tip:** Parents can gift $2,000 to a child through a child bank checking account, who uses such money to fund the ESA brokerage account. Given the child's minimal or no current income, he or she will be eligible to fund such an account. The OBBB provides a MAGA account to each qualified child. Such an account works similar to the UTMA but will not factor into the $2,000 annual contribution limit.

$2,000 per year per child as a contribution limit, growing tax-free, with wider investment choices than most 529s. We bought Berkshire stock in Coverdell ESAs and used them flexibly for K-12 expenses when needed.

Small account, mighty impact.

Move 5: Paying children for real jobs and deducting them on your Schedule C or E

At age 7, my children started working in our family business: filing papers. Data entry. Office cleanups.

We paid them reasonable hourly rate, documented their hours, and opened minor Roth IRAs with their earned income. Tax-free retirement growth started before middle school. We deduct the child labor in "Other expenses: outside labor."

> 🔍 **Tax term: A Minor Roth IRA,** also called Junior Roth IRA or Custodial Roth IRA, is a retirement account set up for a child under 18, using their own earned income from jobs like babysitting or part-time work. Contributions are made with after-tax dollars, and the money grows tax-free, with tax-free withdrawals in retirement if rules are met. A parent or guardian serves as the account custodian until the child reaches the age of majority (18 or 21, depending on the state).

By 18, each child had over $60,000 in minor Roth IRA, continuing its compounding quietly for the next 40 years into a multi-million-dollar tax-free retirement fund.

Move 6: Funding HSAs like retirement accounts

Most people use HSAs like glorified savings accounts. We treated them like secret retirement accounts.

We maxed out HSA contributions annually. Invested the balances aggressively. Paid current medical expenses out of pocket. Let the HSA grow untouched.

Someday, those tax-free dollars will cover Medicare premiums, long-term care insurance, or even just boost retirement spending.

Move 7: Never waste a Roth opportunity

During market dips, we executed strategic Roth conversions such as moving traditional IRA dollars into Roths while valuations were low.[5]

Sometimes we "filled up" our lower tax brackets by converting just enough to maximize the 12% or 22% brackets.

> 🔍 **Tax term: Tax brackets** are ranges of income that are taxed at different rates under a progressive tax system. As your income increases, portions of it are taxed at higher rates, but it is only the income within each bracket that is taxed at that rate, not your entire income. In the U.S., there are seven federal tax brackets (ranging from 10% to 37% as of 2025), and the exact thresholds depend on your filing status.

Every dollar converted was a future tax-free soldier in our FIRE army.

Move 8: Capturing every old 401(K)

Every job change was an opportunity.

We rolled over old 401(K)s into low-cost IRAs. We streamlined accounts. We avoided orphaned accounts sitting in high-fee, low-performance plans.

More control. Lower costs. Higher compounding.

Move 9: Mastering Rule of 55 and 72(t)

When I was unexpectedly laid off at 55, we did not panic. Because I had planned ahead, I tapped my 401(K) penalty-free under the Rule of 55.[6] I quickly turned my side business LLC to a main hustle, and fund my Solo 401(K) plan to continue my retirement fund building.

Tax codes are not obstacles. They are opportunities if you learn the rules.

> **Tax term:** The **IRS Rule 72(t)** allows you to take early withdrawals from your company-sponsored retirement account (such as 401(K)) before age 59.5 without the 10% penalty.

> **Tax term:** The **401(K) Rule of 55** allows individuals who leave their job during or after the year they turn 55 (or 50 for certain public safety employees) to withdraw funds from their 401(K) without the 10% early withdrawal penalty. This applies only to the 401(K) from the employer they just left, not IRAs or previous 401(K)s unless they rolled into that employer's plan. Ordinary income taxes still apply to the withdrawals.
>
> 💡 **Tax tip:** Use Code 2 in Box 7 of Form 1099-R. Code 2 = Early distribution, exception applies (other than disability).

> **Tax term: Substantially Equal Periodic Payments (SEPPs)** are a method that allows early withdrawals from retirement accounts like IRAs or 401(K)s before age 59½ without incurring the 10% early withdrawal penalty. Payments must follow strict IRS rules and continue for at least 5 years or until age 59½, whichever is longer. SEPPs are commonly used in early retirement strategies to access retirement funds in a penalty-free way.
>
> 💡 **Tax tip:** File IRS Form 5329 and enter Code 02 for the SEPP exception.

Move 10: Combining real estate and Solo 401(K)s

We launched a family business and opened a Solo 401(K).[7] We maxed out Mega 401(K) contributions, $70,000/year for high-savings years—while using rental properties to generate additional cash flow.

Depreciation, cost segregation, 1031 exchange…each piece added to our arsenal.

Our real estate income covered expenses. Our Solo 401(K)s built retirement wealth. Our tax planning minimized Uncle Sam's cut.

> 🔍 **Tax term: A Mega 401(K),** also called Mega Backdoor Roth 401(K) is an advanced retirement savings strategy that allows high earners to contribute after-tax dollars into their 401(K) plan—beyond the standard $23,500 limit (2025)—and then roll those dollars into a Roth IRA or Roth 401(K). Contribute up to the total 401(K) contribution cap: $70,000 (2025), indexed with inflation, including employee ($23.5K), employer match (up to 25% of salary), and after-tax contributions.

> 🔍 **Tax term: Cost Segregation** is a strategic tax planning tool that breaks down a property into components like land improvements, equipment, and fixtures. This allows investors to depreciate certain parts of the property faster, often over 5, 7, or 15 years, rather than the standard 27.5 or 39 years. For real estate investors, it accelerates deductions and significantly improves early cash flow.

> 🔍 **Tax term: A 1031 exchange,** named after Section 1031 of the Internal Revenue Code, allows real estate investors to defer capital gains tax by reinvesting the proceeds from a sold property into another like-kind property.[8] To qualify, the new property must be identified within 45 days and closed within 180 days. This strategy enables investors to grow their portfolios tax-deferred and preserve capital for future investments.

The real firepower: mindset

FIRE was not about gimmicks. It was about discipline, creativity, and persistence.

We did not drive brand-new cars. We did not chase status. We did not match up with the Jones. We focused relentlessly on freedom to serve, to build, to love, and to live life on our terms.

Every tax move we made was not just about dollars. It was about buying back time.

Today, we are living proof that ordinary families, with planning, faith, and action, can achieve extraordinary freedom.

> ## Top 12 tax planning moves for FIRE
>
> 🔥 1. Buy whole life insurance early: Create a tax-deferred asset for future use.
>
> 🔥 2. Gift appreciated stocks to children: Encourage ownership mentality and avoid wasteful spending.

3. Fund 529s aggressively during market dips: Supercharge tax-free growth.

4. Use Coverdell ESAs for flexibility: Cover K-12 and higher education expenses creatively.

5. Put children on payroll to fund Roth IRAs: Start building their tax-free retirement accounts young.

6. Maximize HSA contributions and invest: Use HSAs as hidden retirement vehicles.

7. Execute strategic Roth conversions: Lock in low tax rates for future tax-free income.

8. Consolidate and rebalance old 401(K): Reduce fees and improve investment options.

9. Use Rule 55 and 72(t) for early withdrawals: Tap retirement funds strategically without penalties.

10. Leverage Solo 401(K)s for high contributions: Max out tax-deferred savings as business owners.

11. Combine real estate depreciation and exchanges: Minimize taxes while growing cash flow.

12. Focus on mindset, not just mechanics: Financial independence is 80% discipline and vision, 20% strategy.

Chapter 4

Turning Layoffs into Liftoffs – How We Navigated an Employee Layoff with Tax Strategy and Resilience

The phone call came on a rainy Thursday afternoon. "Due to restructuring," the voice said carefully, "your position with the XYX company will be ending."

Just like that, after two decades of faithful service, our family's world tilted.

I hung up, sat at the kitchen table, and stared out at the gray drizzle. Fear crept in. What about health insurance? What about college tuition for our kids? Retirement?

But then I remembered something: We had a plan.[1] And Buffett's voice echoed in my mind: "Be fearful when others are greedy and greedy when others are fearful."

This was not necessarily an ending. It could be a new beginning. A liftoff. Being laid off does not have to mean you are worse off.

The first 24 hours: Regaining control

Instead of panicking, we decided to control what we can. That night, my wife and I made a list titled "Immediate Action Items." It gave us direction and hope.

We treated it like a financial fire drill, preparing for the months ahead. Every task we completed felt like regaining a piece of our future.

Step 1: Gather documents, gather strength

That evening, my wife and I sat side by side, pulling together every critical document we could find:

- Most recent 401(K)/403(b) statement (including 401(K) loan balance)
- Employee stock options or RSU vesting schedule
- Annual leave and sick leave balances
- HSA/FSA balances

- Benefit plan documents (health, dental, vision, life insurance)

- COBRA notice and premium chart

- Other benefits included in the severance package

🔍 Tax Terms: **A 403(b) plan** is a tax-advantaged retirement savings account designed for employees of public schools, non-profits, and certain religious organizations. It is similar to a 401(K).

🔍 Tax Terms: **Employer stock options** are benefits that give employees the right to buy company stock at a fixed price within a set timeframe. Incentive Stock Options (ISOs) may qualify for favorable capital gains treatment if holding requirements are met, while Non-Qualified Stock Options (NSOs) are taxed as ordinary income at exercise. Understanding timing, tax impact, and diversification strategies is critical to managing concentrated equity risk.

🔍 Tax Terms: **Restricted Stock Units** (RSUs) are a form of employee compensation where company shares are granted but not received until they vest. Vesting means that employees take ownership of RSUs and are taxed as ordinary income based on the market value at that time. RSUs can be a valuable wealth-building tool, especially when managed strategically for diversification and tax efficiency.

🔍 Tax Terms: A **Flexible Spending Account (FSA)** is an employer-sponsored benefit that allows employees to set aside pre-tax dollars to pay for eligible medical, dental, or dependent care expenses. Contributions reduce taxable income but must be used by year-end (or within a short grace period), or the funds may be forfeited. Unlike an HSA, FSAs do not require a high-deductible health plan and are less flexible for long-term savings.

🔍 Tax Terms: **Consolidated Omnibus Budget Reconciliation Act (COBRA)** is a federal law that allows individuals to continue their employer-sponsored health insurance coverage after losing a job or experiencing a qualifying life event. Coverage can typically be extended for 18–36 months, but the individual must pay the full premium (including the employer portion) plus a small administrative fee. COBRA provides a critical health safety net during transitions but can be expensive.

Before the layoff hit, we had already secured have cash value life insurance for the whole family, opened a home equity line of credit, and unblocked emergency fund CD. We even cancelled our spring break travel to Orlando, Florida.

We even organized them by topics: retirement, health insurance, unemployment benefits, and education aid. We created a binder labeled "Resilience 2025" and filled it with everything we would need.

It felt overwhelming at first. But acting, even with small steps, brought clarity and strength.

Step 2: Unlocking retirement accounts without penalties

I dove into research late into the night. That is when I rediscovered the "Rule of 55" and SEPP (Substantially Equal Periodic Payments).[2] If I separated from service at age 55 or older (either by voluntary or by involuntary resignation), I could access my 401(K) without a 10% penalty. If younger, SEPP allowed structured, penalty-free withdrawals.

We mapped it out carefully, using IRS Form 5329 codes to report correctly. Precision mattered and gave us peace of mind.

We even simulated multiple withdrawal strategies using Blue J Tax AI tools to find the most penalty-free path.

Step 3: Strategic Roth IRA conversions

With our income temporarily lower after the layoff, we had a golden opportunity.

We rolled part of the 401(K) into a Traditional IRA, then executed small Roth conversions each year, maximizing the 12% and 22% tax brackets without triggering tax credit phase outs by higher AGI when the Roth conversion amount is added in. We made larger Roth conversions when stock market was down by 10% or more.

> 🔍 **Tax term: Adjusted Gross Income (AGI)** is your total gross income for the year (wages, dividends, capital gains, and retirement distributions) minus specific deductions such as student loan interest, retirement contributions, and HSA deposits. AGI is a key figure that determines eligibility for many tax credits and deductions, including the American Opportunity Tax Credit, Lifetime Learning Credit, Child Tax Credit, Earned Income Tax Credit, and Premium Tax Credit (Marketplace Health Insurance Subsidy). Lowering AGI strategically can unlock powerful tax-saving opportunities.

We used market dips to convert more shares at lower valuations. Every conversion felt like planting seeds for future tax-free harvests.

We tracked every conversion meticulously with Form 8606 (Nondeductible IRAs).[3]

Step 4: Securing cash flow

Cash is king when life gets unpredictable.

We lined up:

- A home equity line of credit (HELOC) as a liquidity bridge

- Insurance backed line of credit (IBLOC) as an additional liquidity buffer

- Securities backed line of credit (SBLOC)

We created a "Liquidity Ladder" chart, showing which cash buckets we could tap first without margin calls, rate hikes, or tax surprises. This ladder gave us psychological peace, knowing we had 12 months of survival money mapped out.

Step 5: Health insurance without breaking the bank

Instead of paying COBRA's crushing premiums, we pivoted.

We shopped Affordable Care Act (ACA) Marketplace plans and found a silver-level plan with substantial subsidies based on our adjusted income.[4] OBBB allows bronze- or silver-level plan to qualify as high-deductible health plans.

Pairing it with such an HSA-eligible plan meant we kept building tax-free health savings even during transition. We scheduled annual physicals and preventative care while still under our old plan to maximize benefits before the switch.

> 🔍 **Tax term:** The **ACA Marketplace** is a federal or state-run health insurance exchange where individuals and families can purchase subsidized health coverage.

Step 6: Embracing entrepreneurship

Laid off? Fine. Time to bet on ourselves.

We registered with a small consulting LLC. Suddenly, startup cost, organizational cost, office expenses like laptops, rental, and mileage became legitimate tax deductions.[5] An unprofitable LLC for up to two years may reduce our AGI to allow for more Roth conversion.

We opened a Solo 401(K) and started rebuilding retirement savings aggressively, with the flexibility and control self-employment brings.

We also picked up freelance gigs online (such as resume writing, consulting, and tutoring) turning skills into income streams.

Step 7: Real estate as our resilient asset

Real estate became our anchor. We applied for Real Estate Professional status, allowing rental losses to offset ordinary income. We maximized depreciation, took advantage of bonus write-offs, and even experimented with short-term rentals.

One beach rental covered a full year's worth of grocery bills. That changed everything.

OBBB allows for 100% bonus depreciation for properties or equipment acquired and put into service after January 19, 2025. Therefore we used cost segregation studies to accelerate depreciation deductions legally.

> 🔍 **Tax term:** A **Real Estate Professional** (REP) is a special tax status that allows qualifying taxpayers to treat rental real estate losses as non-passive, which means they can use those losses to offset other active income like W-2 wages or business income.
>
> To Qualify as a Real Estate Professional:
> 1. More than 50% of your personal services in a year must be in real property trades or businesses (e.g., development, brokerage, leasing, management, construction).
> 2. You must work at least 750 hours per year in those activities.
> 3. You must participate in each rental activity, unless you group them as one activity.

Step 8: Education and financial aid strategy

With job loss came new opportunities for college aid.

We used our layoff letter and updated financials to file a FAFSA appeal.[6] We coached our children on scholarship hunting like it was a sport. We created "Scholarship Saturdays" where the children spent 2 hours each week applying for grants. We also timed Roth conversions carefully to avoid inflating FAFSA income in critical years.

> 🔍 **Tax term:** FAFSA stands for Free Application for Federal Student Aid. It's a form used by the U.S. Department of Education to determine a student's eligibility for federal financial aid, including grants, loans, and work-study. The FAFSA collects financial information from the student and their family, often pulled directly from IRS tax returns, to calculate the Student Aid Index (SAI), which schools use to offer aid packages.

Step 9: Building psychological resilience

It was not just about money. It was about mindset. [7] We started morning walks, journaling, and weekly gratitude sessions. We talked openly about fears and hopes with the kids. We reframed the layoff: it was not a failure; it was an invitation to redesign our future.

Step 10: Building a new vision board

Instead of spiraling into "what ifs," we created a new family vision board.

- Pictures of places we wanted to visit

- Quotes that inspired our resilience

- Sketches of our dream future

Every day, that board reminded us: This is not the end. It is just a pivot. We updated it monthly, celebrating even the smallest wins.

Bonus Step: Building a layoff playbook

We documented every step, every form, and every resource into a "Family Playbook."[8] This way, if any family member or friend ever faced a layoff, they would not start from scratch. They would have a guide, born from our journey.

Top 12 action steps for W-2 employees facing layoffs

W-2   1. Gather all critical documents immediately

W-2   2. Understand early withdrawal rules (Rule of 55 and SEPP)

W-2   3. Plan strategic Roth IRA conversions during low-income years

W-2   4. Secure multiple cash flow sources (HELOC, SBLOC, and IBLOC)

W-2   5. Shop ACA health plans early and pair with an HSA

W-2   6. Start a small business for tax flexibility

W-2   7. Maximize real estate professional strategies

W-2   8. File FAFSA appeals and optimize financial aid

W-2   9. Prioritize mental and emotional resilience

W-2   10. Create a family vision board for the next chapter

W-2   11. Document your journey to create a family playbook

W-2   12. Turn each setback into a stepping stone for future success

---

Chapter 5

✦

Building Educational Dreams Without Financial Nightmares

I still remember the day my oldest child, Kevin, walked into the living room holding a glossy college brochure. The cover had a picture of ivy-draped brick buildings, smiling students, and big dreams.

"Dad, I want to go here," he said, his eyes shining.

Pride swelled inside me, until I flipped to the tuition page. Sticker shock hit me like a freight train. How were we going to afford this without sacrificing our future or burying him under a mountain of debt?

That night, I stayed up late, notebook in hand, sketching out every strategy I could find. I was not just planning for Kevin. I was building a blueprint for our whole family. It was not about throwing money into a problem. It was about thinking strategically, using every tool available, and keeping our future intact.

Starting early: Laying the foundation

We began with a simple truth: saving early beats saving more later. Even $50 a month, started when Kevin was in kindergarten, could snowball into tens of thousands by the time he turned 18.

We opened 529 plans (tax-advantaged savings plan designed to encourage family saving for future education expenses, including college, K–12 tuition, and apprenticeship and credentialling programs) for our children.[1] Not just any 529. We sought out low-cost options with broad investment choices, such as S&P500 index. I treated their accounts like mini-retirement accounts: disciplined, automatic, and hands-off except for annual reviews.

I taught them to see the 529 not just as "Dad's money" but "our family's investment." They tracked the balances. They celebrated small milestones. Ownership mattered.

Every birthday, instead of a pile of toys, relatives contributed to their 529s. We made it part of our family culture. Financial literacy, we decided, would start before their first day of school.

Maximizing every dollar: Scholarships, credits, and shifts

When Kevin started applying for scholarships, I became his unofficial college financial advisor. We treated scholarship hunting like a part-time job. For every $500 won, it was $500 less we would ever have to pay, and it was often tax-free.[2]

We set up "scholarship Saturdays" at the kitchen table. Two hours, every week, dedicated to filling out applications, writing essays, and gathering recommendation letters. It was not glamorous work, but it paid better than any part-time job.

Meanwhile, we planned around the American Opportunity Tax Credit (AOTC).[3] I coached Kevin to file his own tax return during his four years of college. This way, he captured the maximum $2,500 per year tax credit (including $1,000 refundable credit), a $10,000 total windfall.

Every year, we reviewed our Modified Adjusted Gross Income (MAGI) to stay within credit eligibility limits: single $90,000 and married joint filing $180,000 per IRS Publication 970, subject to annual inflation adjustment). Sometimes it meant timing bonuses or deferring income: small moves, big savings.

> 🔍 **Tax term:** American Opportunity Tax Credit (AOTC) is a federal tax credit designed to help offset the costs of higher education for eligible students during their first four years of postsecondary education. The maximum annual credit is $2,500 per eligible student, including up to 40% of the credit (maximum $1,000) refundable tax credit.

Room, board, and rental properties

College costs were not just tuition. Room and board often added 50% or more to the bill.

That is when I had an idea: why rent when we could own? We used a 1031 exchange to swap a currently owned rental in our home state to buy a modest condo near Kevin's campus.

> 💡 **Tax tip:** A **1031 exchange,** also known as a like-kind exchange, is a tax-deferred transaction under the U.S. Internal Revenue Code Section 1031 that allows real estate investors to swap one investment property for another without triggering immediate capital gains taxes.

He lived in one room and rented out the others to a few classmates. His "rent" came from his 529 plan, a qualified expense as long as he maintains at least half-time student status . The property appreciated. When he graduated, we did another 1031 exchange, tax-deferred and rolled the proceeds into another rental.

We did not stop there. After graduation, we rented the property to Ph.D. students who continued paying rent for three to five years. It became a passive income stream that paid dividends for years. If Kevin's AGI for this graduation year or later years is below $100,000, he could use cost segregation to accelerate depreciation and apply up to $25,000 rental losses against his active income.

It was not just about saving money. It taught Kevin how to manage a property, negotiate leases, and handle responsibility. These skills are worth more than any lecture hall.

Coverdell accounts: Small but mighty

Alongside the 529s, we quietly funded Coverdell Education Savings Accounts.[4]

> 💡 **Tax tip:** A **Coverdell Education Savings Account** (ESA) is a tax-advantaged savings account designed to help families save for a child's education expenses, including K-12 and college costs. While contributions aren't tax-deductible, withdrawals for qualified education expenses are tax-free.

Only $2,000 a year, tiny compared to college costs, but incredibly flexible. We used Coverdell's to pay for laptops, lab fees, and even private school tuition when Kevin needed extra academic support, such as SAT tutoring.

Sometimes small streams create mighty rivers. When you combine a 529 and a Coverdell, you diversify your tax strategies, and open options for the future.

Health and retirement: Playing the long game

Most families only focus on education costs. We thought bigger.

We funded Roth IRAs for our children as soon as they earned their first paychecks. Even small summer jobs meant thousands in future tax-free growth.

We opened Health Savings Accounts (HSAs) for them too, teaching them to invest those dollars aggressively in future medical needs.

Every dollar earned, saved, or invested was not just about college, it was about building lifelong habits. Financial education was not a one-time conversation. It was a thousand small lessons layered over years.

Lessons learned along the way

Not every plan worked perfectly. Markets dipped. Scholarships got delayed. Administrative paperwork sometimes caused headaches. There were frustrating nights on FAFSA deadlines. Scholarship essays that went unanswered. Unexpected tuition hikes that threw off our budget.[5]

But we adapted. We stayed flexible. And most importantly, we kept our eyes on the long game: creating opportunities without destroying our financial stability. When Kevin graduated debt-free, with investments already growing in his name, I realized: it was not just about the money. It was about the confidence, independence, and freedom we had built together. Today, Kevin teaches these lessons to his friends, co-workers, and even his younger cousins. The ripple effect is real.

Top 12 tax planning tips for children's education

EDU 1. Claim the American Opportunity Tax Credit (AOTC): Enjoy up to $2,500 tax credit per student annually to maximize by careful MAGI planning.

EDU 2. Open and maximize 529 plans: Take advantage of early tax-free growth and withdrawals for qualified expenses.

EDU 3. Use Coverdell ESAs for flexibility: Cover K-12 expenses and offers wider investment options than 529s. If parental AGI exceeds the phase-out limit, parents can gift up to $2,000 per year to the child who maintains a bank account and contributes into a Coverdell ESA brokerage account.

EDU 4. Own, don't rent, for college housing: Use 1031 exchange to acquire student housing and leverage tax advantages.

EDU 5. Hire children legitimately to fund Roth IRAs: Fuel earnings early tax-free retirement growth. Be mindful of the reasonable pay rate to hire your child.

EDU 6. Strategically time income to qualify for credits: Manage MAGI through deferrals, deductions, and bonuses.

EDU 7. Understand that scholarship taxation: Tuition scholarships are tax-free; room and board scholarships are taxable.

EDU 8. Use HSA accounts as long-term education support: Enjoy the triple tax benefit for medical needs during college and beyond.

EDU 9. Gift annual contributions strategically: Shift assets efficiently by gifting appreciated stocks into UTMA. When the child ages past 18, he or she can claim the ownership and applies the buy, borrow and build strategy via a securities-backed line of credit.

EDU 10. Think beyond college: Build financial independence early teach children to view education as part of a bigger wealth-building journey.

EDU 11. Reassign 529 funds if needed: Reassign the unused 529 balances to siblings, nieces, nephews, parents, or even yourself.

EDU 12. Document everything for financial aid: Include scholarships, grants, and financial aid.

Chapter 6

Artificial Intelligence and Tax Planning: How to Plan Smarter, Not Harder

It started innocently enough, with an article shared by a friend. "AI will change tax planning forever," it proclaimed.[1]

Skeptical but curious, I decided to experiment. After all, we had spent years building our family's financial house carefully. If there was a tool that could make it even stronger, I wanted to know.

The first encounter: ChatGPT, meet family finance

One evening after dinner, I sat down with my son Kevin and typed into ChatGPT: "Explain my W-2 Box 12 codes." [2]

Within seconds, a breakdown appeared, simple, clear, and accurate. It flagged an overlooked dependent care deduction worth $2,400.

Kevin looked at me, wide-eyed. "Dad, it's like having a mini-CPA at home!"

That was our first "aha" moment.

Building trust: Test, verify, repeat

Before we trusted AI fully, we tested it relentlessly.

- We fed it with complex RSU (Restricted Stock Unit) tax scenarios.
- We asked it to draft Safe Harbor election letters for rental property repairs.
- We simulated Schedule C red flag audits.

Every time, we double-checked outputs against IRS pubs and real tax software.

Sometimes it nailed it. Sometimes it hallucinated with minor errors.

The lesson: AI was a co-pilot, not a replacement for human judgment.

Expanding our AI toolkit

Soon, our family became "AI tool testers."

- BlueJ Tax AI: We used it to predict audit risks based on real court cases.

- Abacus AI: Aggregated outputs from multiple large language models for just $10 a month.

We even ran depreciation schedules for our rental properties through Abacus, saving hours of spreadsheet drudgery.

We also experimented with:

- Auto-GPT workflows: Automating tax tasks like document review and checklist generation.

- TaxGPT AI: Filing simpler 1040 returns automatically with human review add-ons.

Each tool added another layer of efficiency to our family's financial system.

Real-life family wins with AI:

- Kevin discovered he could deduct $800 more in college expenses using Form 8863 guidance.[3]

- We reconstructed missing cost basis for uncovered Tesla stock, saving $4,200 in capital gains taxes.[4]

- My wife's consulting side hustle optimized Solo 401(K) contributions to hit the $70,000 annual cap.[5]

- We generated a polished LLC annual report, perfect for the bank when applying for a business line of credit.

- My daughter used AI to pre-draft her scholarship applications, cutting her workload by 50% while maintaining authenticity.

- We simulated AMT (Alternative Minimum Tax) scenarios to make smarter year-end charitable giving decisions.

AI was not just "cool." It was real savings, real efficiency, real empowerment. Keeping it ethical and safe. Every family meeting, we reinforced three AI commandments:

- Traceability: Always ask, "Where did this advice come from?"

- Explainability: If AI could not explain it clearly, we did not use it.

- Accountability: Humans, not AI, sign tax returns. Final responsibility is ours.

We used encrypted platforms, masked sensitive data, and never shared full SSNs or bank account numbers with AI apps.

We even created "AI Ethics Checklists" for any financial task involving automation.

AI in action: Our family's favorite use cases

- Rental property depreciation: ChatGPT helped create a 27.5-year straight-line depreciation schedule from a messy HUD-1 statement.

- Correcting a late K-1: AI drafted a professional IRS correction memo after we received a late K-1 post-filing.

- Maximizing Tesla EV credits: AI cross-checked EV eligibility based on VIN, battery source, and income phaseouts.[6]

- Generating audit defense letters: We simulated CP2000 notices and practiced writing response memos, calmly and confidently.

- Projected ACA subsidy cliffs: We used AI to model healthcare premiums based on different Roth conversion scenarios.

- Building a "family tax playbook": AI helped draft templates for Schedule C, E, and F best practices to pass down to the next generation.

> 🔍 **Tax term:** The **HUD-1 Settlement Statement** is a standardized form used in real estate closings to provide a detailed breakdown of all costs and fees involved in a property transaction.

> 🔍 **Tax term:** The **EV Tax Credit** refers to a federal income tax credit available to individuals who purchase qualifying electric vehicles (EVs) or plug-in hybrid electric vehicles (PHEVs).

> 🔍 **Tax term:** The **IRS CP2000** (Notice of Underreported Income) is not a bill or audit, but a proposed adjustment notice from the IRS's automated matching system (AUR) when your filed tax return doesn't match income or payment data received from third parties like employers or financial institutions.

> 🔍 **Tax term:** An **ACA subsidy** (Affordable Care Act subsidy) refers to federal financial assistance that helps individuals and families lower the cost of health insurance premiums and sometimes out-of-pocket costs when purchasing coverage through the HealthCare.gov or state-based ACA Marketplace.

> 🔍 **Tax term:** A **K-1** is a tax form issued to owners of pass-through entities—such as partnerships, S corporations, and some trusts or estates—to report each owner's share of the entity's income, deductions, credits, and other tax items.

Future-proofing the family legacy

We realized that AI was not just about saving money today. It was about preparing our children for a future where:

- Knowledge workers use AI as a core skill.

- Tax complexity only grows.

- Speed, accuracy, and adaptability become survival skills.

Kevin is now learning how to prompt, verify, and critically assess AI outputs. Our daughter is exploring AI for scholarship searching, real estate analysis, and even creating small online businesses.

We envision a future where "financial fluency" includes knowing how to use AI tools ethically and intelligently.

Final reflection: Human + AI = unstoppable

Will AI replace CPAs and financial planners? [7]

Maybe some. But the real winners will be those who combine AI speed with human wisdom. Those who can think critically, compassionately, collaboratively, and creatively will thrive in the AI era.

In our family, AI did not replace us. It leveled up. It made us faster, smarter, bolder.

And it gave us a glimpse of a future where financial empowerment is not just for Wall Street: it is for every kitchen table in America.

Top 12 ways we use AI for family tax planning

AI 1. Decode W-2s and spot overlooked deductions

AI 2. Rebuild cost basis for uncovered securities

AI 3. Draft IRS safe harbor election letters and amendments

AI 4. Analyze rental property depreciation and repairs

AI 5. Optimize Solo 401(K) contributions for family businesses

AI 6. Adjust W-4 withholdings proactively

AI 7. Audit proof Schedule C and E filings

AI 8. Cross-check investment advisor fees and performance

AI 9. Professionalize LLC reporting with AI-generated reports

---

AI 10. Decode IRS audit letters and draft responses

AI 11. Plan ACA subsidy management strategically

AI 12. Draft and update a family tax playbook for generational wealth

---

Case Study 1

The NIE Family Vision Board – A Journey Toward Financial Independence and Abundance

Purpose of this case study

This case study explores how my family uses a vision board and annual goal setting to pursue financial independence and abundance. Drawing from our annual letters, it highlights the power of intentional planning, family engagement, and disciplined action in building a life of security, opportunity, and fulfillment across generations. By examining our holistic approach, readers can discover practical strategies for integrating financial, familial, spiritual, physical, and professional growth into daily life.

The NIE family's vision board philosophy

- **Holistic balance:** The vision board is a living document, integrating financial, familial, spiritual, physical, and professional goals. It serves as a compass for the entire family, ensuring that no area of life is neglected.

- **Annual reflection:** Each year, the family reviews accomplishments, sets new targets, and adjusts their vision board to reflect evolving dreams and priorities. This ritual fosters accountability and continuous improvement.

- **Generational mindset:** The vision board is a tool for teaching children about financial literacy, stewardship, and the compounding effect of good habits. It encourages passing down wisdom and values from one generation to the next.

- **Celebration and gratitude:** Achievements are celebrated, and gratitude is practiced daily, reinforcing a positive mindset and resilience in the face of challenges.

Key elements of the NIE Family vision board

1. Financial independence goals

- **Consistent saving and investing:** Maximize retirement contributions (401(K), Roth IRA, HSA, education accounts) for all family members. Automate savings to ensure discipline.

- **Smart asset allocation:** Regularly rebalance investment portfolios, diversify across asset classes, and adjust strategies based on market conditions and family needs.

- **Debt management:** Refinance mortgages to lower rates, pay down high-interest debt, and track spending to avoid lifestyle inflation.

- **Insurance and protection:** Maintain life, health, and long-term care insurance for peace of mind and legacy planning. Review policies annually.

- **Charitable giving:** Operate a family foundation, donating to causes that align with their values. Involve children in grantmaking and volunteering to instill a spirit of generosity.

- **Tax Optimization:** Leverage tax-advantaged accounts, Roth conversions, and strategic charitable giving to minimize tax burdens and maximize after-tax wealth.

2. Family engagement and education

- **Financial literacy for children:** All four children hold tax-advantaged accounts and are involved in budgeting, saving, and investing decisions. Family meetings discuss money openly.

- **Vision board workshops:** The family participates in annual vision board sessions, setting and reviewing goals together. Each member creates personal and shared goals.

- **Celebrating milestones:** Achievements, such as earning scholarships, starting businesses, or winning competitions, are recognized and tied back to vision board intentions.

- **Travel and cultural exposure:** Family trips to multiple continents foster global perspective, adaptability, and appreciation for diversity.

- **Intergenerational bonding:** Visits with grandparents and extended family strengthen roots and reinforce family traditions.

3. Spiritual and personal growth

- **Daily gratitude practice:** Each family member writes down things they are grateful for, fostering a positive mindset and resilience.

- **Faith and service:** Regular Bible reading, prayer, and community service are integral to the family's sense of purpose and abundance. Participation in church and faith-based activities is encouraged.

- **Journaling and reflection:** Keeping journals of gratitude, accomplishments, and lessons learned helps each member grow in self-awareness and wisdom.

- **Mentorship and coaching:** The family seeks guidance from spiritual mentors and life coaches to navigate challenges and deepen their faith.

4. Physical and mental well-being

- **Health goals:** Track body weight, fitness routines, and healthy eating habits as part of the vision board. Set measurable targets for exercise and nutrition.

- **Family activities:** Engage in yoga, sports, hiking, and travel to strengthen bonds and create lasting memories. Participate in challenges and competitions together.

- **Wellness routines:** Practice mindfulness, meditation, and regular health checkups. Encourage each member to pursue activities that promote mental and emotional well-being.

- **Healthy habits:** Adopt family traditions such as meatless dinners, home-cooked meals, and shared fitness goals.

5. Professional and personal development

- **Lifelong learning:** Pursue certifications (CPA, CFA, CFP, FRM, EA), attend workshops, and coach others in public speaking and financial literacy. Encourage curiosity and continuous improvement.

- **Entrepreneurship:** Encourage children to start businesses, take on leadership roles in family and community projects, and explore their passions.

- **Public speaking and communication:** Weekly workshops and coaching sessions help family members build confidence and influence.

- **Career advancement:** Set professional development goals, seek feedback, and celebrate promotions, awards, and new opportunities.

The NIE Family's annual vision board in action

Vision Board Area	Example Actions and Achievements	Impact
Financial	16.2% retirement account growth; all children have Roth IRAs; 24 life insurance policies managed; $47,000+ donated via family foundation	Wealth compounding, security, legacy, generosity
Family	Family travel to China, Iceland, France; Olesia and Sasha met grandparents; Olga's music students won awards; Friday night dinners	Global perspective, unity, achievement, tradition

Vision Board Area	Example Actions and Achievements	Impact
Spiritual	Daily Bible reading, gratitude journaling, prayer with family; use of Parallel Bible; church and community service	Peace, resilience, shared values, spiritual growth
Physical	18 lbs weight loss; 300+ hot yoga sessions; national yoga competition; sobriety challenge; healthy eating	Health, discipline, family bonding, longevity
Professional	300+ CPE credits; new certifications; public speaking coaching; team leadership; tax planning workshops	Career growth, influence, lifelong learning, impact

Expanded vision board practices

Financial mastery

- Multi-generational wealth planning: Establish and update family trusts, revocable living trusts, and estate plans. Teach children about wills, powers of attorney, and the importance of legal protection.

- Investment education: Children learn about stocks, bonds, mutual funds, and real estate. Family discussions include market trends, risk management, and the power of compounding.

- Philanthropy: The family foundation supports nonprofits in the U.S. and abroad. Children participate in site visits, grant evaluations, and volunteer, learning the joy and responsibility of giving.

Family and relationship building

- Quality time: Regular family dinners, game nights, and shared hobbies foster closeness and open communication.

- Personal growth challenges: Each member sets annual challenges, such as learning a new language, mastering an instrument, or completing a fitness milestone.

- Celebrating diversity: Embrace cultural heritage through travel, language study, and family storytelling.

Spiritual and emotional resilience

- Faith-based routines: Attend weekly services, participate in Bible study groups, and volunteer in faith communities.

- Emotional check-ins: Family members support each other through life's ups and downs, practicing empathy and active listening.

- Gratitude and mindfulness: Daily gratitude lists and mindfulness exercises help manage stress and cultivate joy.

Physical excellence

- Fitness as a family: Compete in yoga competitions, run races, and set group fitness goals. Track progress with charts and celebrate achievements.

- Healthy living: Prioritize sleep, hydration, and balanced nutrition. Experiment with new recipes and wellness trends as a family.

- Medical and preventive care: Schedule regular checkups, vaccinations, and screenings. Educate children about health and self-care.

Professional and academic growth

- Certifications and credentials: Pursue advanced degrees and professional designations. Share learning experiences and mentor others.

- Public speaking and leadership: Lead workshops, coach students, and participate in Toastmasters. Encourage children to develop communication and leadership skills.

- Entrepreneurial ventures: Support family businesses, side hustles, and creative projects. Celebrate successes and learn from failures.

The NIE Family's vision board: yearly progress and reflection

Year	Major Achievements	Lessons Learned	Adjustments for Next Year
2019	Yoga competition, career advancement, family travel	Balance is key; celebrate small wins	Add more family workshops
2020	Family dance, children's academic and athletic awards, financial milestones	Consistency compounds results	Increase charitable giving

Year	Major Achievements	Lessons Learned	Adjustments for Next Year
2021	Navigating pandemic, virtual learning, home workouts, 24.7% investment return	Flexibility and gratitude	More focus on mental health
2022	21% retirement growth, Bible completion, national yoga ranking, new certifications	Perseverance through adversity	Expand vision board to include new skills
2023	Launch of family foundation, new business ventures, travel, IRS Enrolled Agent license	Giving back multiplies joy	More intergenerational planning
2024	16.2% retirement growth, $47,000+ donated, all children with tax-advantaged accounts, global travel	Vision board is a living document	Continue to refine and set higher goals

Vision board lessons and takeaways

- Vision boards drive results: Visualizing goals and tracking progress keeps the family focused and motivated. The act of writing and reviewing goals creates accountability and momentum.

- Family involvement multiplies success: Engaging children in financial and life planning builds skills and confidence for the next generation. Open communication fosters trust and shared purpose.

- Balance is key: True abundance comes from integrating financial, physical, spiritual, and relational well-being. Neglecting one area can undermine progress in others.

- Annual reflection fuels growth: Regular review and adjustment of goals ensure continued progress and adaptability. Celebrate achievements and learn from setbacks.

- Generosity and service: Charitable giving and community involvement enrich the family's sense of purpose and connection to the world.

- Lifelong learning: Pursuing new knowledge, skills, and experiences keeps the family adaptable and resilient in a changing world.

Expanded closing reflection

The NIE Family's journey shows that financial independence and abundance are not accidental—they are the result of vision, discipline, and shared purpose. By making their vision board a living, evolving part of family life, they have created a blueprint for generational wealth, happiness, and impact. Their story demonstrates that with intentional planning, gratitude, and commitment to growth, any family can build a legacy of security, opportunity, and fulfillment.

Key takeaways for readers:

- Start your own family vision, covering every area of life.

- Involve all family members in goal setting and reflection.

- Celebrate progress, learn from challenges, and adjust as needed.

- Make generosity and gratitude central to your family culture.

- Remember: The journey to abundance is ongoing, and every step counts

PART 2

SMART RETIREMENT AND LEGACY PLANNING

Chapter 7

How FIRE Changed Our Family's Financial Destiny – Time Freedom Over Tax Burden

One winter night, my CPA Lisa visited us for dinner. Yes! Most CPAs hire a more experienced CPA to handle complicated tax matters. With a glass of red wine, she mentioned to us the FIRE concept: Financial Independence and Retire Early. My son Kevin was present as well, absorbing all wisdom and witty quotes like a sponge.

That night, I made a decision: Our family would pursue time freedom, using tax-smart strategies, small business ownership, and smart health planning; not just for ourselves, but for our children.

The Spark: Kevin's summer job and a $7,000 Roth IRA

We started our FIRE dream with our son, Kevin. At 16, he started working part-time for our small family business, helping with customer calls and bookkeeping. At the end of the summer, I handed him a check: not for spending, but for investing.[1]

"You're getting a Roth IRA," I told him.

He laughed. "I'm too young to retire."

"No," I smiled. "You're just early."

We opened a custodial Roth IRA at Vanguard and funded it with his W-2 wages. [2] I taught him how that $7,000, invested into the S&P 500, could become over $1 million by the time he was 60, even if he never contributed again. If Kevin contributes $7K annually, his FIRE Roth IRA account could snowball into an eye popping $37 million dollar by the age of 60.

FIRE Needs a health plan too

Healthcare is one of FIRE's biggest obstacles, especially if you retire before Medicare eligibility. So, we leaned in hard to the Health Savings Account (HSA).

I told my wife, "This is our stealth IRA. It's triple tax-free."

Every year, we maxed out our HSA ($8,300 family limit in 2024), paid medical expenses out of pocket, and let the HSA grow tax-free in a brokerage account. At age 65, it would act like a Roth IRA for anything, or a medical fund for long-term care, dental, or Medicare premiums.

Hiring family wasn't just smart. It was strategic.

In our FIRE journey, tax efficiency became the engine. I hired both my wife and son in the family business.

Why?

1. I could deduct their health insurance premiums as business expenses (Schedule C, Line 14).

2. I established a Health Reimbursement Arrangement (HRA), reimbursing them for all out-of-pocket medical costs, 100% tax-free.

3. Their wages funded their Roth IRAs, locking in lifetime tax-free income.

It was a win-win. We paid our kids, saved taxes, and built generational wealth.

> 💡 **Tax tip:** The **IRS Family Help Rule** provides tax savings tips in that (1) if you run a sole proprietorship (i.e., single member LLC) or a qualified family partnership (i.e., each partner is a parent of the child), small business owners can avoid payroll taxes for minors: If you hire your child under age 18, you don't have to pay Social Security or Medicare taxes; (2) if the child's compensation is below the standard deduction amount ($15,000 for 2025), you do not need to withhold federal income tax; (3) legitimate earned income qualifies the child to contribute up to $7,000/year (2024) to a Roth IRA; and (4) deduct the child's compensation from his or her actual services on Schedule C or 1065 partnership return.[3]

> 🔍 **Tax term:** A **Health Reimbursement Arrangement (HRA)** is an employer-funded plan that reimburses employees for qualified medical expenses and, in some cases, insurance premiums. Unlike HSAs or FSAs, only the employer can contribute, and unused funds may roll over at the employer's discretion. HRAs are tax-advantaged, meaning reimbursements are generally not taxable to the employee.[4]

FIRE with small business: Deductions, flexibility, and exit plans

Small business ownership wasn't just a hustle; it was a tax shelter.

We structured our LLC to:

- Deduct 100% of our health insurance premiums

- Set up a Solo 401(K) with $70,000 in tax-deferred contributions
- Use business miles, meals, and home office deductions to cut our AGI

And we weren't afraid to pivot.

When business income dropped during the pandemic, we shifted to part-time consulting and used those lower-income years to execute Roth conversions at minimal tax cost: converting pre-tax IRA dollars into tax-free Roth income.

Long-term planning: FIRE Isn't one size fits all

I introduced my CPA Lisa to my friend Liang and Omar at one of my tax workshops. Omar had just retired early from a tech job. Liang wanted to open a home bakery. Together, we mapped a FIRE-friendly plan:

- High-deductible health plan (HDHP) → Maxed out HAS
- Hire Liang as W-2 employee in the LLC → Enable HRA reimbursements
- Switch to ACA silver plan after COBRA ended → Use strategic Roth conversions to stay under the subsidy cliff
- Fund Roth IRAs using taxable brokerage gains

We even ran a FIRE projection. Both Liang and Omar kept their eyes wide open. I saw their fire and desire to achieve their goals as early as possible.[5]

FIRE lessons we taught our kids

We turned FIRE into a family mindset:

- Kevin's Roth grew while he was in high school.
- Olesia put her birthday money into an HSA at age 18.
- Both children tracked their net worth and reviewed their 3-bucket plan: Taxable, Tax-deferred, and Tax-free.[6]

One day, Olesia asked me, "Why don't we just spend less and save more like this forever?"

I smiled. "Exactly. That's FIRE."

10 End of chapter: Top 10 FIRE tax strategies for small business owners

#	Strategy	Tax Code / Tool
1	Fund Roth IRA for children with earned income	§408A, Custodial Account
2	Max out HSA contributions & invest it	§230 triple tax advantage
3	Deduct family health premiums via Schedule C	Schedule C, Line 14
4	Use an HRA to reimburse out-of-pocket costs	§105 HRA
5	Hire spouse in the business	W-2 employee + HRA
6	Contribute to Solo 401(K) (up to $70,000/year)	§401(K)
7	Execute Roth conversions in low-income years	Tax Bracket Optimization
8	Use ACA marketplace subsidies with income planning	IRS Pub 974
9	Claim small business health tax credit (Form 8941)	For <25 employees
10	Track deductions for meals, travel, and home office	IRS Pub 535

Top 12 Inspiring and FIRE Financial Strategies

1. Anchor Investments in low-fee S&P 500 index funds and broad-based stocks with zero dividends

2. Write annual family financial letters

3. Praise by name, criticize by category

4. Open Roth IRAs early for children and fund consistently

5. Use HSAs as triple tax-advantaged accounts

6. Diversify across stocks, real estate, businesses, and insurance

7. Embrace humility and lifelong learning

8. Plan Roth conversions during market dips

9. Invest for multiple generations, not just yourself

10. Define retirement as freedom, not inactivity

11. Use side hustles and multiple income streams to build liquidity

12. Prioritize wisdom and character over instant gratification

Chapter 8

John and Jane's Retirement Revolution: How They Mastered the 401(K) to Build a Dream Life

It was a snowy January evening when John Smart, a 42-year-old FedEx truck driver, took off his uniform and trudged into the kitchen. His $65,000 annual salary did not stretch that far after all the costs from food, utilities, and mortgage.

Jane, his wife of 15 years, sat at the kitchen table surrounded by a messy stack of unopened 401(K) statements, bank notices, and a crumpled electric bill.

She looked up, exhausted. "John, we work so hard. Why does it still feel like we are drowning?"

That night, something shifted. Not in their bank accounts yet, but in their minds.

They decided, right there with the broken toaster humming and the dog whining for scraps, that they would take back control of their future.

This was the beginning of their SMART Family Retirement Revolution.[1]

Rewriting their story: Dream first, dollars second

The first thing they did was not financial. It was emotional.

They grabbed an old corkboard, scissors, and magazines from the basement and built their retirement vision board. They were inspired by the vision board exercise sponsored each January by the SMART Life Family Foundation in Vienna, VA. Visit SmartLifeUSA.org for details.

No numbers yet; just pictures of:

- A cozy log cabin tucked near Shenandoah.

- A golden retriever by a roaring fireplace.

- Passports filled with stamps from Iceland, Ireland, and New Zealand.

- A scholarship letter awarded in their family's name to a local high schooler.

It was not about "How much do we need?" It was "Who do we want to become?"

From that night forward, every decision was filtered through their Dream Board.

Key move:

🎯 Vision leads, action follows.

They were not saving for retirement. They were saving for a life worth living.

The retirement pyramid: Building from bedrock, not sand

At a Saturday morning seminar at the local library (yes, with free burnt coffee and all), they heard about the "Retirement Plan Pyramid".

- **Bottom layers: Stability and protection (emergency funds, employer matches).**
- **Middle layers: Growth (401(K)s, IRAs).**
- **Top layers: Freedom (real estate, taxable investments, fun projects).**

They realized they had it all upside down.
John had been chasing hot stocks. Jane kept cash under the mattress.

Together, they flipped their strategy:

- **John boosted his 401(K) to grab 100% of his employer match: free money they had been leaving on the table for years.**
- **Jane opened a Solo 401(K) at E*Trade (with a loan feature), setting automatic drafts from her salon income.**
- **They built a $20,000 emergency fund: sleeping easier every night.**

🔍 Tax term: A Solo 401(K) is a retirement savings plan designed for self-employed individuals or business owners with no full-time employees other than a spouse. It allows higher contribution limits than traditional IRAs by letting the owner contribute both as an employee and employer. This plan can include Roth and traditional options, and may allow loans and flexible investment choices.[2]

Key move:

🏛 Build the pyramid from the ground up: protection first, growth second, dreams third.

Tax bracket kung fu: Winning by playing defense

The first year John received a fat bonus, they celebrated, until tax time came.

Their excitement turned into anger when they saw their bonus pushed them into a higher tax bracket, wiping out much of the gain.

That night, Jane said something that changed everything:
"It is not just about what you earn. It's about what you keep."

They learned Tax Bracket Management:

- **John split his 401(K) contributions between Traditional and Roth to diversify their future withdrawal options.**
- **During years when Jane's salon income was lower (thanks, COVID), they performed Roth conversions at the low S&P index level and locked in the low tax rates. They repeat this strategy when the broad market index drops by 10% or more.**
- **They used tax planning software to project the next 30 years of income streams and RMDs.**

They began thinking like a chess master, not just for this year, but three moves ahead.

🔍 **Tax term: Required Minimum Distribution (RMD)** refers to the minimum amount that must be withdrawn each year from certain retirement accounts once you reach a specific age. For most people, RMDs begin at age 73 (if you turn 72 after Jan 1, 2023). A few strategies are available to reduce or minimize the taxes caused by the RMD.

Key move:

♟ Don't play tax checkers. Play tax chess.

Investing like the pros: Four streams of freedom

Jane's sister, a financial planner, introduced them to a new mantra:
"Assets create freedom. One income source is not enough."

Together, they built Four Income Streams:

- Stocks: Broad-based index funds like Fidelity 500 (expense ratio as low as 0.015%). Use the buy, borrow and build strategy to access funds without the capital gain tax.

- Small business LLC: active income with legitimate business expense deductions.

- Real estate: Buying a duplex: living on one side, renting out the other.

- Cash value whole life insurance: A small piece for ultra-conservative growth and future tax-free loans. Given the investment nature of whole life insurance companies, the cash value compounding within a life insurance policy is a proxy of a bond index fund portfolio without paying interest income or capital gain taxes.

Each stream brought not just money but confidence.
Confidence that no matter what Washington D.C., Wall Street, or Main Street threw at them, they would be okay.

Key move:
🛡 Diversification is the armor of true wealth builders.

The great Roth vs. traditional debate, and why they chose both

They used to think it was a choice:

- Roth = Pay tax now.

- Traditional = Pay tax later.

Simple, right?

Wrong.

What they learned blew their minds:
Future taxes may be even higher, because of the rising deficits, changing tax laws, and rising healthcare costs.

So instead of picking one, they built both:

- **John contributed into his Roth 401(K) at work up to the company matching, which normally ranges between 3% and 8% of base salary.**
- **Jane split her Solo 401(K) 50/50 between Roth and traditional.**
- **They funded Roth IRAs every January like clockwork.**

Their future selves would have tax-free options and taxable options, and the freedom to pivot no matter what Congress decided.

Key move:

🌼 Multiple buckets = maximum flexibility and minimum regret.

Hidden landmines they stepped around (just in time)

They avoided some costly traps:

🚫 No high-fee target-date funds.[3]
🚫 No off-the-shelf investment packages they did not understand.[4]
🚫 No annuities with fat commissions unless the math absolutely made sense.

Instead, they built their own low-cost, simple, intelligent portfolio:

- 45-55% Fidelity 500 index fund

- 20-25% cash value whole life insurance

- 20-25% Real Estate

- 0-5% crypto

Key move:

⚡ Understand every dollar you invest. If you cannot explain it to your kids, do not buy it.

Secret weapon: The Solo 401(K)

Jane's Solo 401(K) became their wild card:

- Contribution limits of $70,000+ (if Jane's business is highly profitable and she issues herself a W-2 salary of up to $350,000.
- Roth + Traditional options.
- No complicated brokerage restrictions.
- Backdoor Roth IRA access.[5]
- Full control over investments.

- Loan feature up to $50,000.

Even when her salon had a slow year, Jane kept contributing what she could, because she knew even small deposits compound into massive results.

Key move:

🚀 If you have a side hustle or small business, the Solo 401(K) is your tax and growth superpower.

Beyond money: The true wealth they built

Jane and John accumulated family wealth prudently and filed tax return efficiently. Now they had something magical happen along the way: They stopped worrying about money. They slept better and argued less. They started talking about dreams with their grandchildren. They had the comfort and confidence to live their retirement life with gratitude.

🆗 They planned trips instead of tax bills.

🆗 They discussed giving (through their own family foundation), not just spending on necessities and nagging children.

🆗 They volunteered at a local mentorship program for young entrepreneurs.

They realized:

💡 Wealth is a tool to expand who you are, not just what you have. Their Retirement Vision Board, once full of magazine clippings, was now full of memories.

John & Jane's 20-step retirement freedom checklist

Strategy	Action Taken
1. Create a vision board	Emotional and financial clarity
2. Maximize employer match	Grabbed every matching dollar
3. Open Solo 401(K)	For Jane's self-employed income
4. Build an emergency fund	$20,000 for peace of mind (could be a policy loan within a whole life insurance policy)
5. Master tax brackets	Smoothed taxes across 30 years
6. Build three tax buckets	Pre-tax, tax-free, and taxable

Strategy	Action Taken
	Taxable account applies the buy, borrow and build strategy
7. Perform Roth conversions	During low-income years and during stock index down time
8. Diversify across four assets	Stocks, crypto, real estate, and life insurance
9. Annual rebalancing	Prevented portfolio drifting away from the optimal asset allocation percentage
10. Low-cost index funds	Cut fees, boosted returns
11. Open and fund Roth IRAs (as early as seven and as long as 70s, if earned income)	Regular contributions, no hesitation
12. Avoid high-fee products	No target-date funds (401(K), 529s, or other accounts), no bad annuities
13. Fund life insurance wisely	For future flexibility
14. Buy income-producing real estate	Duplex strategy
15. Plan for healthcare inflation	Fund HSA account (self and adult-aged child)
16. Simulate withdrawals	Stress-tested plans under different scenarios
17. Involve family	Talked about money openly with kids
18. Celebrate small wins	Every year they hit a milestone
19. Volunteer and mentor	Give back while living richly
20. Always think: "What would future us thank us for?"	Take the last week of December each year for a family retreat to reunite, reflect and recharge

Closing reflection:

John and Jane did not wait for Washington to fix their future. Nor did they win the lottery. Instead, they built it themselves: They won the discipline game. And you can too.

Finally, retirement is not an age. It is a choice, one smart move at a time.[6]

Top 10 tax tips from John & Jane's 401(K) journey

1. Max out employer matches first: Always contribute enough to your 401(K) to capture the full employer match. It is free, untaxed money you are giving up otherwise.

2. Use Roth and traditional buckets together: Don't bet everything on one tax strategy. Build both Roth (tax-free) and Traditional (tax-deferred) accounts to stay flexible in retirement.

3. Roth conversions during low-income years: When income dips (job change, business slowdown, semi-retirement), seize the chance to convert Traditional IRAs/401(K)s into Roth accounts at a lower tax cost. Use life insurance policy loan to pay the additional taxes.

4. Solo 401(K)s for Self-employed and side hustlers: If you have self-employed income, even small, open a Solo 401(K) to shelter tens of thousands of dollars tax-advantaged every year.

5. Avoid high-fee target-date funds: many employer plans default you into expensive, underperforming target-date funds. Choose low-cost index funds whenever possible.

6. Manage tax brackets proactively: Use tax software or a CPA to map out how much you can withdraw (or convert) each year without jumping into a higher tax bracket.

7. Use HSAs for triple tax advantage: If available, fund a Health Savings Account (HSA): you get a deduction, tax-free growth, and tax-free withdrawals for medical expenses.

8. Defer RMDs strategically: Plan early to minimize Required Minimum Distributions (RMDs) by drawing down Traditional IRA accounts before age 73 or hiring through family businesses to defer.

9. Turn real estate into tax efficiency: Rental income offers depreciation deductions and tax breaks. [7] John and Jane's real estate professional or short term rental created rental losses offsetting W-2 income and tax advantages.

10. Do not forget state taxes: State income tax rates can drastically impact your retirement withdrawals. Think ahead if you might move across state lines after retirement.

Chapter 9

Building Multigenerational Wealth with Cash Value Life Insurance: A Family Legacy Story

I still remember the day we signed our first life insurance policy. Kevin was just a toddler, and our daughter was barely walking. Sitting across from our financial advisor, the paperwork felt heavy, pages of unfamiliar terms and fine print.

At the time, it seemed simple: protect the family if the worst happened.

But what we did not realize was that properly structured cash value life insurance would become one of the most powerful financial tools in our family's entire legacy plan.

The awakening: Insurance as a living asset

Years later, as I dove deeper into financial strategy books, and after attending a seminar by a wealth strategist from IBC Global, a lightbulb went off: Life insurance was not just a death benefit. It was a living, breathing financial asset.

It could serve as:

- A tax-advantaged savings account (with 4-5% annual return, low volatility, or no early withdrawal penalty)

- A source of emergency liquidity (with no credit approval requirement or intrusive lender requirements)

- A family bank to fund real estate, education, or business ventures [1] (with interest deducible if funds are used in an income producing business or property)

- A generational wealth anchor shielded from probate and creditors (with family privacy and well-protected privileges)

That realization changed everything.

Designing policies with intention

We were not interested in "off-the-shelf" policies. We wanted blueprints customized for:

- Maximum cash value early

- Flexibility for loans

- Minimum insurance cost for maximum cash value accumulation

Our strategy:

- Base whole life component (~5-10% of annual pay into premium)

- One-year term rider to boost initial death benefit affordably (~5-10% of annual pay into premium)

- Heavy cash value funding, aka paid-up addition (~80-90% of annual pay)

This design turned our policies into turbocharged savings engines.

> 🔍 **Tax term:** The **One-Year Term Rider (OYTR)** on a Cash Value Whole Life Insurance policy is an optional add-on that provides temporary term coverage for one year, usually to boost the death benefit in a cost-effective way. Adding extra death benefit for one year does not significantly increase the premium.

Starting early: the gift of time

One of our biggest wins?

Buying policies young, in our 30s for ourselves, and even earlier for our children.

Every year that premiums were paid, the cash value snowballed. The policies compounded quietly, unaffected by stock market chaos.

Today, Kevin's policy, started at age 10, already has a five-figure cash value. At retirement, it could easily exceed six figures, without ever stressing about age 59½ early draw penalty, RMDs, market crashes, or capital gains taxes.

Using cash value as our "family bank"

When we needed capital for home repairs, car purchases, or business opportunities, we tapped policy loans. No credit checks. No lengthy approvals. No invasive questions. We were aware of the taxable event risk caused by over-borrowing policy loans (i.e., modified endowment contract). We frequently paid back loan interest to our insurance companies.

Just tax-free access to our own money, while the policy continued compounding untouched. We even taught Kevin to use his policy as a "launchpad" to help fund his first rental property someday.

Diversifying across trusted companies

We spread policies across top-rated mutual insurers:

- New York Life [2]

- Northwestern Mutual [3]

- Guardian Life [4]

- MassMutual [5]

Each company had:

- Solid dividend histories (170+ years)

- Strong financial ratings (same credit rating as U.S. treasuries)

- Flexible loan provisions (borrowing cost pegged at AAA-rated corporate bond yield)

This diversification protected us from over-relying on any one institution.

Trusts and foundations: Building a true legacy

Rather than naming individuals directly, we made our family trust the beneficiary (shown in the vision board of Chapter 2).

Why?

- **Asset Protection:** Shielding proceeds from lawsuits, divorces, and spendthrift family members.

- **Control:** Managing how and when heirs access funds, governed by the family bank constitution.

- **Continuation:** Using the death benefits to fund future generations' education, businesses, and philanthropy.

We created a modest Family Foundation to eventually own some of the policies, combining wealth building with charitable giving. [6]

Practical wins for family planning

FAFSA & financial aid: Cash value did not count as "assessable assets" for college aid formulas.

Retirement flexibility: Using tax-free loans to supplement future retirement income without triggering taxes on social security benefits or Medicare premium hikes. [7] OBBB provides $6,000 senior deduction per person, but it has an AGI phase-out clause. A policy loan can reduce the 401(K) withdraw needs and make the senior deduction available to retirees.

Emergency fund: We could access funds without selling stocks at a market low.

Business financing: Policy loans funded equipment purchases for our consulting side hustle, interest payments went back to our own policies, not banks. Interest expenses could be deducted as business expenses.

Comparing to other investments

We never saw life insurance as replacing stocks or real estate. It complemented them.[7]

- Stocks = Growth engine (high return but volatile)

- Real Estate = Cash flow (property management intensive)

- IRAs/401(K)s = Tax deferral (but RMD risk)

- Life Insurance = Stability + Liquidity + Tax-Free Access

Each played a role. But during market crashes, life insurance felt like a warm blanket on a freezing night.

Teaching the next generation

Now, we involve the Gen Z.

- Reviewing annual statements

- Discussing loan strategies

- Reinforcing that "banking on yourself" is a superpower

Kevin jokes, "Most children get toy cars. I got a financial Ferrari growing up."

Final reflection: More than insurance, it is legacy engineering

Cash value life insurance was not just an expense. It was one of the smartest, most resilient financial decisions our family ever made. It gave us peace of mind. It gave us liquidity. And most importantly, it gave us a platform to teach our children how to steward wealth wisely, for their children and for their children's children.[9]

Real wealth is not what you leave behind. It is what you pass forward. [10]

Top 12 Cash Value Life Insurance Strategies We Use

1. Buy early to maximize compounding and minimize age-driven insurance premium

2. Use minimal base death benefit with one-year term riders to boost cash value

3. Diversify across multiple top-rated mutual insurers

4. Borrow via policy loans, not withdrawals, to keep growth compounding

5. Use policies as a private family bank

6. Integrate policies with family trusts for protection and control

7. Leverage policies for FAFSA advantage in college aid

---

8. Supplement retirement income tax-free

9. Finance business ventures using policy loans

10. Mitigate estate taxes using irrevocable life insurance trusts

11. Blend charitable giving by funding a family foundation

12. Use long-term care riders for future health needs

Chapter 10

Guardians of the Legacy: How We Built a Family Trust to Protect Dreams, Not Just Dollars

It was something deeper, an overwhelming desire to make sure that everything we built, every sacrifice, every lesson, every dollar, would serve not just our children, but generations beyond us.

My wife and I did not start planning because we were afraid of death.

We started because we believed in life beyond ourselves.

That night, sitting with mountains of estate planning documents spread across our kitchen table, we decided to stop putting it off. We would create something lasting. Something living. Something loving.

Thus began The SMART Family Trust and Family Bank, our greatest investment in the future. SMART, the acronym of Strategies to Master Assets and Reduce Taxes, works perfectly in the context of family trust and family bank.[1]

Step 1: The myth of "too small to matter" — broken

At first, we hesitated.

"Are we really big enough for all this paperwork?"
"Do regular families even need a trust?"

Lisa, our CPA and her husband, an estate attorney, smiled knowingly.

"If you own a home, have kids, or care about what happens to your life's work, you need a trust."[2]

👪 Protect minor children if something happens to you.

👪 Bypass expensive and public probate courts.

👪 Ensure your life savings are managed wisely, not squandered.

It was not about wealth. It was about responsibility. The trust was not just for us.

- It was for Olesia's future college fund.
- It was for Kevin's dream of launching a business.
- It was for Sasha's vision of helping underserved artists.

Key mindset shift: You do not need to be rich to need a trust. You just need to be wise enough to love someone more than you love the IRS.

Step 2: How a trust became our family compass

We realized that a trust could do far more than split assets.

A properly built trust could:

👪 Protect against lawsuits if descendants faced divorce or bankruptcy.

👪 Allow phased inheritance to teach financial maturity.

👪 Create incentives tied to education, entrepreneurship, or philanthropy.

👪 Build multi-generational wealth by preserving assets inside protected structures.

Most of all, it could preserve family unity, because money can bring out the best or the worst in people.

And we decided early: "Our trust will be a source of blessing, not a source of battles."

Key Lesson: A family trust is a moral compass disguised as a legal document.

Step 3: The family bank — investing in dreams, not just dollars

We did not just stop at a trust.

We dreamed bigger.

We created The SMART Family Bank, a living financial institution inside the trust.

Purpose?

- Fund college degrees (with GPA requirements!)
- Seed new business startups (after formal application review and approval by family bank committee comprised of adult family members)
- Help first-time homebuyers (primary residence only)
- Offer emergency loans for true financial crises

But no handouts. No entitlement.

Loans required:

📋 Written requests.

📋 Business plans.

📋 Repayment schedules.

The Family Bank was not a piggy bank. It was a launchpad. [3]

Key strategy: Use your trust to fund opportunity, not foster dependency. Creating and updating a family bank constitution is a critical step to govern family wealth. All family members will meet and vote at least once a year to promote the family value and mission.

Step 4: Life insurance — planting money trees for the future

Lisa shared the secret sauce of ultra-wealthy families:

- They do not pass on taxes.
- They pass on tax-free cash, through life insurance owned by family trusts.

So, we:

- Purchased permanent life insurance policies while we were young and healthy. [4]

- Named the SMART Family Trust as beneficiary. [5]

- Structured policies with flexibility: borrowing features, cash value growth, tax-free death benefits. [6]

For pennies on the dollar, we could guarantee millions to future generations, without the IRS getting a bite.

Key strategy: Life insurance in trusts is how you plant money trees your great-grandchildren can harvest.

Step 5: Choosing trustees without ruining thanksgiving

Choosing a trustee was brutal.

Family? Too emotional. Too risky. Too biased. Too attached.
Friends? Even worse, friendships die faster than families when money is involved.

We went professional:

☑ Corporate trustee (bank trust department) with strict fiduciary duties.
☑ Advisory board of family elders and financial advisors (e.g., a professional with a Certified Financial Planner (CFP) credential) to oversee trustee actions.

Built-in oversight.
Built-in continuity.

Because when you are managing your family's future, you cannot leave it to chance, or to Uncle Sam's judgment.

Key strategy: Use independent trustees and family bank committee to preserve fairness and professionalism.

Step 6: Tax planning inside the trust — fighting the silent killer

Taxes are stealthy thieves of generational wealth. Without careful planning, your heirs might lose 40%+ of their inheritance to taxes at the federal level, plus 5-10% at the state level. Not ours.

We structured:

🏛 Generation-skipping tax (GST) protection clauses.[7] Use your GST exemption to create a multigenerational trust that avoids estate and GST tax for decades or even permanently. Under the OBBB, such GST lifetime exemption amount is $15 million, indexed with inflation.

🏛 Annual exclusion gifts to fund insurance premiums (up to $19,000 per child in 2025, and indexed with inflation in future years).

🏛 Investments inside the trust with minimal taxable events (e.g., S&P 500 index fund with management fee as low as 0.015% per year).

🏛 Lifetime exemptions locked in early while limits were high. The OBBB gives us a wonderful opportunity to lock in such a high exemption amount ($15 million per person, indexed with inflation).

We were not just thinking about taxes this year. We were thinking 100 years ahead. We use family bank assets smartly by applying the "buy, borrow, and build" strategy: (1) access fund from a securities backed line of credit (SBLOC) or insurance backed line of credit (IBLOC); (2) provide financing to family member's business initiative with an interest rate published at the IRS website; (3) purchase more life insurance policies of younger family members; and (4) use death proceeds to pay off the SBLOC or IBLOC loans.

> 🔍 **Tax term:** The **Generation-Skipping Transfer Tax (GST Tax)** is a federal tax imposed on transfers of wealth, either gifts or inheritances, to someone who is at least 37½ years younger than the donor, typically a grandchild or great-grandchild, skipping the donor's children.[8]

Key strategy: The enemy is not just bad investments; it is poor tax planning. Plan for future laws, not just today's rules.

Step 7: Preparing our children to handle inheritance

Sasha once asked: "Will I get a million dollars on my 21st birthday?"

We laughed, and explained. No. Our trust would not just hand over piles of money.

Instead, she would:

- Attend financial education classes.
- Earn staged distributions based on age and milestones (such as graduation, professional licenses, or major life events).
- Submit and present financial plans for major business requests.

We were not trying to control her. We were trying to equip her. We understand that money without wisdom is a curse, not a blessing.

Key principle: Money without maturity is a time bomb. Build character before cutting checks.

Step 8: Mistakes we almost made—and how you can dodge them

⊖ Forgot to title real estate into the trust (critical!).

⊖ Forgot to coordinate life insurance beneficiary designations (trust must be listed).

⊖ Named siblings as trustees (potential war zone!).

⊖ Skipped annual reviews (life changes; trusts must too).

Fixing these early saved us years of heartache and headache.

Key Warning: In estate planning, small mistakes cost millions. Triple-check everything.

Step 9: Communication—the true wealth transfer tool

Once a year, we now host **The SMART Family Summit.** No secrets. No mysteries. No ticking time bombs.

During our annual family retreat, we share:

- Trust goals.

- Investment performance.

- Education milestones.

- Changes in family structure (births, deaths, marriages).

Transparency breeds trust. Silence breeds suspicion. We chose transparency.

Trust creates harmony. Harmony produces peace. Peace builds a strong family.

Key Rule: If you cannot talk about wealth openly, you cannot pass it wisely.

Step 10: The final secret—your trust is a living document

A trust is not a time capsule. It is a living thing.

It needs:

- **Annual reviews with a CFP or other competent and objective financial advisor.**
- **Updates after marriages, births, divorces, deaths, or other material life events.**
- **Refreshes as tax laws evolve, including the state laws.**

Our rule? "If life changes, the trust changes." Simple. Vital.

Key lesson: An updated trust is a powerful shield.[9] A stale trust is a legal landmine.

Top 20 family trust & tax tips from our journey

Tip	Why It Matters
1. Create a trust early	Death or disability does not make appointments.
2. Think beyond inheritance	Build opportunity to nurture family members, not just give them cash gifts.
3. Fund a family bank	Controlled loans beat chaotic gifts. Responsible borrowing avoids the trust fund dependency syndrome.
4. Buy life insurance inside the trust	Tax-free wealth creation.
5. Hire a corporate trustee	Impartial, professional, reliable, competent.
6. Plan for changing tax laws	Exemptions may shrink, so plan accordingly.
7. Use GST protection	Skip generations, skip double taxation.
8. Title assets properly	Unfunded trusts = useless.
9. Review annually	Life evolves, documents must too.
10. Equip children financially	Knowledge before inheritance.
11. Host family meetings	Transparency produces harmony.
12. Align beneficiary designations	Ensure consistency across all accounts.
13. Educate through examples	Share real case studies (good and bad).
14. Think three generations ahead	True wealth is multi-generational. Imitate the Rockefeller family.
15. Protect heirs from themselves	Spendthrift clauses save lives.
16. Balance fairness and flexibility	One size does not fit all heirs.
17. Invest trust assets tax-efficiently	Minimize taxable income. Avoid holding real estate in the trust due to high property taxes and maintenance costs.
18. Celebrate milestones	Reward achievements, not just birthdays.
19. Communicate early and often	Secrets destroy families.
20. Remember: trusts are love letters	Your real legacy is your values, not just your valuables.

Final Reflection: A trust is not just a financial document.

It is a love letter. It is a blueprint. It is a lifeboat you launch into the future.

With it, you give your family the most precious gift of all:
the freedom to dream, to achieve, and to thrive — protected and prepared.

Case Study 2

The Retiree Tax-Saving Blueprint: Jack's Story

Purpose of this case study:

This case study is designed to illustrate how a thoughtful, multi-layered tax strategy can dramatically improve financial outcomes for retirees facing large Required Minimum Distributions (RMDs). By following Jack's journey, readers will see how proactive planning, leveraging real estate, charitable giving, and tax-advantaged accounts can not only reduce tax burdens but also protect assets, optimize lifetime tax rates, and create a lasting family legacy. The goal is to provide actionable insights and a blueprint for retirees and their advisors to navigate complex tax challenges and turn retirement into a period of financial empowerment and purposeful wealth transfer.

Situation:

At 73 years old, Jack faced a tax puzzle: his $2 million traditional IRA/401(K) was about to trigger large Required Minimum Distributions (RMDs). As a retired tech executive with multiple rental properties and $60,000/year in Social Security benefits, Jack did not need his retirement money, but he would be forced to withdraw and pay heavy taxes soon.

Task:

Jack needed to find ways to:

- Reduce his RMD tax burden

- Take advantage of the $6,000 senior deduction (2025-2028)

- Protect his retirement assets

- Optimize his lifetime tax rate

- Leave a legacy for his family

Action:

Jack took a series of layered smart moves:

A: **Initially, Jack withdrew RMDs ($82K/year)** — but realized too late that early Roth conversions would have reduced future burdens.

B: **In hindsight, younger Jack could have converted $55K/year to Roth** — minimizing RMDs and building tax-free retirement assets.

C: **Jack earned Real Estate Professional status (REP)** — using cost segregation studies to generate large passive losses, offsetting other income.

D: **Jack invested in a Delaware Beach Airbnb rental** — strategically creating real losses to offset RMD income and enable further Roth conversions.

E: **Jack's son established a family foundation (FF)** — Jack donated 30% of AGI to the FF and served as a compensated senior advisor.

F: **Jack drew a W-2 salary from the Foundation** — activating the "still-employed" rule to defer additional RMDs past age 73.

Result:

By combining all these strategies, Jack achieved:

- $237K total income (Roth, rentals, salary)
- Only $26K federal tax owed (11% effective rate)
- Deferred extra RMDs into future lower-tax years
- Protected investment growth
- Supported family charitable giving
- No state income tax on rental profits in Delaware

Jack secured a financially independent retirement and built a philanthropy-driven family legacy. He lived a fulfilled and joyful life.

Top 20 Retirement Tax Saving Tips from Jack's Playbook

Tip	Why It Matters
1. Start Roth conversions early	Lower lifetime RMDs and tax costs
2. Maximize 24% bracket fill	Strategic Roth conversions smartly capped
3. Real estate professional status (REP)	Active loss offsets income so that the AGI is low enough to enjoy the $6,000 senior deduction under OBBB
4. Cost segregation studies	Accelerated depreciation boosts losses. OBBB allows for 100% bonus depreciation for properties acquired and rented out in 2025 and later.
5. Short-term rentals strategy	Large rental losses usable without REP
6. Establish family foundation	Maximize giving + board advisor salary strategy
7. Still-employed rule	Defer RMD past 73 if earning W-2
8. Delaware rentals	No sales income tax advantage
9. Stack rental losses	Shield Roth conversion tax
10. Monitor Medicare premiums	Avoid IRMAA surcharge traps
11. Time donations strategically	Max out 30%-60% AGI charity deductions
12. Roth conversion laddering	Spread tax hits over years smartly
13. Leverage QCDs after 70½	Charitable IRA distributions to lower RMD
14. Use multiple income buckets	IRA, Roth, W-2, Rental to smooth income
15. Relocate to tax-friendly states	Eliminate extra tax burdens
16. Bunch deductions when needed	Maximize itemized deductions intermittently
17. Family charitable engagement	Involve next generation in giving plan
18. Preserve step-up basis	Strategic holding of appreciated assets
19. Track AGI thresholds	Maximize credits and minimize phase-outs
20. Stay nimble	Review tax plans annually, adjust dynamically

> 💡 **Tax tip:** A **Qualified Charitable Distribution (QCD)** is a tax-free donation made directly from a traditional IRA to a public charity, typically used by individuals subject to the required minimum distribution amount.

> 🔍 **Tax term**: The **Step-up in basis** is a tax provision that adjusts the value (basis) of an inherited asset to its fair market value (FMV) on the date of the original owner's death, which can significantly reduce capital gains tax when the heir sells the asset.

Closing Reflection: Jack's story proves that retirement is not the end of smart tax planning — it is the opening of Act Two. When you combine strategy, structure, and stream of income into legacy building, you do not just preserve wealth. You transform retirement into a mission.

PART 3

SMART SMALL BUSINESS

Chapter 11

How I Turned My Small Business into a Tax Planning Powerhouse

When I started my first side hustle (tax planning and tax consulting), I never imagined it would become one oft the most powerful engine for tax savings and wealth building in my life. I just wanted to make a little extra cash. Instead, I discovered a secret hidden in plain sight: the U.S. tax code favors small business owners.[1]

The accidental entrepreneur

My first business was humble and simple: consulting on weekends and preparing tax returns during evenings. I operated from my basement study room, armed with a laptop, printer, and a head full of dreams.

But from the very beginning, I treated it like a "real" business. Separate bank accounts. Accounting software. Contracts and invoices. Websites. Email distribution list. Business credit card.

That mindset shift made all the difference.

Tip 1: Choosing the right structure – from sole prop to S-Corp

At first, I ran everything as a sole proprietor, easy and simple.[2] But by year two, the self-employment tax bill hit me like a ton of bricks.

After careful cost benefit analysis, I formed an LLC and elected S-Corp status.[3]

> 🔍 **Tax term:** An **S Corporation (S Corp)** is a type of business entity that combines LLC's limited liability protection of a corporation with the pass-through taxation of a partnership or sole proprietorship.

Now, I could:

- Pay myself a "reasonable salary" (subject to payroll taxes)

- Take distributions (not subject to self-employment tax)
- Fund solo 401(K) plan
- Save thousands every year

That one paperwork decision accelerated my FIRE timeline by years.

Tip 2: My home became my boardroom

I did not rent an expensive office. I formalized a dedicated workspace at home: 12.3% of my home was exclusively used for business (321 square feet office in a 2,610 square feet primary residence).

Every month, I deducted:

- 12.3% of mortgage interest, real estate taxes
- 12.3% of utilities
- 12.3% of home insurance
- 12.3% of internet and security costs
- 12.3% of home repairs
- 12.3% of depreciation (subject to depreciation recapture, up to 25% tax rate when you sell the house)

And I took photos, kept floor plans, and documented everything. Be audit-ready.

Tip 3: Turning my car into a business tool

I tracked every business mile using MileIQ.

At the end of the year, I had over 8,210 business miles, worth nearly $5,747 in deductions. Parking and tolls for business related activities are deductible too.

When it came time to buy a new car in 2025, I qualified for bonus depreciation. (See Chapter 19 for more discussion of bonus depreciation.)

$35,000 deduction in year one. A game-changer.

Tip 4: Hiring my children – family business, family legacy, and family wallet

As soon as my children were old enough, I hired them legitimately.

Filing, shredding, scanning, and other errands were all documented and paid through my business bank account to their personal account. If a child is under age 17, issuing a W-2 or 1099 NEC would be optional because they are not subject to FICA taxes. If their annual earned income is below standard deduction amount ($15,000 in 2025), income tax would be zero as well. [4]

In summary, no payroll taxes under the family business rules. Their income funded Roth IRAs and built financial literacy from the ground up.[5]

Tip 5: Mastering business travel and meals

Whenever I traveled for conferences or client meetings, I carefully:

- Scheduled business activities on Fridays and Mondays
- Turned weekends into deductible trips ("sandwich rule")
- Documented meeting notes, agendas, invitations, and receipts

I enjoyed vacations, while legally deducting airfare, hotels, meals, and even Uber rides.[6]

Tip 6: The Augusta rule – renting my home to my own business

This was one of my favorite discoveries. Under IRS rules, I rented my home to my business for 14 days a year for planning meetings. The business tax return deducted the rent. I received the rental income, tax-free and not required to report on my personal return.

Again, I used the market comparable rent, sent out meeting invites and flyers in advance, took meeting notes and pictures, and followed up with my clients or vendors after the home meetings. It felt like printing money within the law.

Tip 7: Safe harbors as my shields against audits

I used every IRS safe harbor available:

- Expensed equipment under $2,500[7]
- Used the simplified home office deduction when appropriate
- Took 100% bonus depreciation or section 179 deduction when available, under OBBB

I kept impeccable digital records: receipts scanned into Google Drive, mileage logs, and categorized bank statements.

Tip 8: Business credit and leverage

I built business credit early.

- Use separate business credit cards[8]
- Obtain business loans based on revenue, not personal credit
- Maintain vendor accounts to establish payment history

By year three, I had access to over $100,000 in business lines of credit: available for growth, emergencies, or opportunities. More business loan interest can be deducted by using the earnings before interest, taxes, depreciation, and amortization (i.e., EBITDA) formula under OBBB.

Tip 9: Succession planning – thinking beyond myself

Finally, I created a succession plan:

- Set up a revocable living trust
- Named my children as contingent business owners
- Created detailed standard operating procedures for my operations

- Purchased company-owned life insurance policy against key executives of the business. The death benefits could pay off business loans and recruit qualified professionals to continue the business operations.

A real business is not just about you; it is about the legacy you leave behind.

🔍 **Tax term:** A **Revocable Living Trust** is a legal entity created to hold and manage your assets during your lifetime and distribute them after your death — all without going through probate. **Probate** is the legal process through which a deceased person's will is validated and their assets are distributed under court supervision.

Tip 10: The startup cost and organizational cost safe harbor

When launching my business through a single member LLC, I put the IRS "safe harbor" provisions to work by:

- Deducting up to $5,000 each in start-up and organizational costs for my first year of actual business.
- Recording all research, pre-opening, and organizational expenses before opening day—think marketing, training, professional fees, and entity formation charges.
- Calculating total costs for each category: If either start-up or organizational expenses exceeded $50,000, I reduced my $5,000 immediate deduction by the extra amount and amortized the remainder over 15 years.
- Making sure to elect the deductions on my very first business tax return. See Appendix 6 for a template election letter.

This safe harbor enabled me to recover a chunk of my investment right away, reducing my taxable income and freeing up cash to reinvest in my new venture. Don't confuse this safe harbor with the *de minimis* rule for small equipment purchases, which is a separate deduction.

Top 12 small business tax planning strategies

1. Elect S-Corp status for tax savings: Split income between salary and distributions to reduce self-employment taxes.

2. Deduct a home office legally: Exclusive, regular use allows deductions on a percentage of home costs. Any percentage over 25% may cause higher audit risk.

3. Track and deduct business mileage: Use apps to document every trip—huge savings at tax time.

4. Buy qualifying vehicles over 6,000 pounds: Leverage bonus depreciation for immediate deductions.

5. Hire your children and fund their Roth IRAs: Shift income within the family legally and build generational wealth.

---

6. Leverage business travel deductions: Plan trips around business activities to maximize deductions.

7. Apply the Augusta rule: Rent your home to your business for meetings and receive tax-free income.

8. Use *de minimis* safe harbor for equipment: Expense small purchases immediately instead of depreciating over years.

9. Build business credit early: Separate personal and business finances for better leverage and protection.

10. Create a succession plan: Protect your business and your family for future generations.

11. Maximize retirement contributions Solo 401(K)s: Allow massive tax-deferred savings opportunities.

12. Document, document, document: Treat recordkeeping as essential armor against IRS audits.

Chapter 12

How a Tiny Home Office Saved Our Family Thousands: Smart Home, Smart Savings

It started with a small desk in the corner of our guest bedroom. Nothing fancy—just a simple IKEA table, a laptop, and a printer perched on a filing cabinet.

I did not think much of it at first. After all, wasn't a "real" office supposed to have glass walls, a receptionist, and a city view?

But one conversation with my CPA, Lisa, turned everything upside down.

Step 1: The conversation that changed everything

We were going through my taxes when Lisa asked casually, "Are you using any space at home exclusively for business?"

"Well," I hesitated, "I have my desk, but it's in the guest room."

Lisa leaned forward. "Is that space used only for your business? No personal stuff?"

I thought about it. No TV. No laundry baskets. Just my desk, work files, and an office chair. It hit me.

"Yes," I said, surprised at my own answer.

"Perfect," she said, smiling. "You're leaving serious tax savings on the table."

Step 2: Unlocking the hidden value in my home[1]

That afternoon, we walked through what I needed to do:

- Take photos of the office space (to prove exclusive business use).
- Measure the square footage carefully.
- Choose between two methods: the Simplified Method ($5 per square foot, up to 300 sq ft) or the Actual Expense Method (proportion of mortgage, utilities, insurance, HOA fee, depreciation, and property taxes).

Lisa explained both.

The simplified method was, well, simple. No fuss. But the actual expense method could save me way more because of my higher mortgage and utility costs. Lisa further explained that home office expenses are disallowed if the business is not profitable. But these expenses can carry forward to future profitable years to deduct.

We crunched the numbers together, and the choice was clear: the actual expense method could save me almost $3,200 more that year.

It was like finding a secret bank account filled with cash... right inside my own house.

Step 3: The "exclusive and regular" rule

Lisa emphasized two golden rules:

1. Exclusive Use: The space must be used only for business (no video games, no overnight guests, no golf club).

2. Regular Use: I had to use it consistently for my work, not just occasionally.

As long as I kept these sacred, my home office deduction was rock solid—even if the IRS ever knocked on my door.[2]

Step 4: Turning my commute into a tax deduction

Then Lisa dropped another bombshell: having a home office turns your car trips into business miles!

Before, I assumed driving to FedEx, Office Depot, postal office, or a client meeting was just a normal expense. Now, those trips were business mileage—and fully deductible.

I started logging every trip religiously. Over the year, those miles alone shaved another $1,500 off my taxes.

Step 5: Documenting like a pro

I got serious about documentation:

- Snapped pictures of my workspace every January.

- Kept a simple floor plan showing my office's square footage.

- Saved all utility bills, property tax statements, and internet invoices.

- Logged my business mileage using a simple app (such as NEAT Receipt) on my phone.

It was not glamorous, but it was gold when tax season rolled around.

Step 6: Expanding the strategy: Beyond one business

A year later, I started a small consulting side hustle alongside my main business. Could I claim a second home office? Lisa said no—you can only have one home office per taxpayer.[3] But I could allocate the same home office expenses between my two businesses, as long as the math made sense and was clearly documented. If my wife and I each had separate businesses, we could deduct two different rooms as home offices on our respective Schedule C forms.

It felt like learning to play a hidden level in a video game—another layer of smart tax moves most people never knew existed.

Step 7: Home office and depreciation: the good, the bad, the truth

When we first discussed depreciation, I got nervous.

Lisa explained: "If you claim actual expenses, you're also claiming depreciation on part of your home. That's awesome now, but remember—when you sell, you'll have to recapture it at a tax rate up to 25%."

At first, I considered skipping it.

But then she smiled and said, "Whether you claim it or not, the IRS assumes you took it. So, you might as well take the deduction now."

Smart. Very smart.

We documented the depreciation properly, calculated based on 39 years because my home office took up more than 20% of the total house space.

Step 8: Lessons from fellow entrepreneurs

In one of Lisa's tax workshops, I met Ted, an eye doctor who ran a YouTube channel about vision health.

He asked if he could claim his piano room where he sometimes filmed videos.

Lisa's advice was a cautionary tale: mixed-use spaces are dangerous. Unless the piano room was exclusively for business, no deduction.

Ted learned the hard way—and so did I: do not get greedy. Stay clean, stay eligible.

Step 9: Special hacks we used

1. **Renters** can deduct, too: Even if you rent, you can still claim a home office deduction based on your rent payments.
2. **Modular home offices:** Some people buy tiny houses or sheds and dedicate them 100% to business—writing off the entire structure.[4]
3. **The 14-day rule:** You can rent your home to your business for 14 days per year tax-free under the Augusta Rule—hello, extra deductions!

> 🔍 **Tax term:** The **Augusta Rule** allows business owners to rent out their primary residence for up to 14 days per year without reporting such rental income on your tax return, as long

as the property is rented for 14 days or fewer and used personally for more than 14 days that year. Business owners can deduct such rental expenses on the business tax return.

Step 10: When the home office saved our dream vacation

That first year after setting up everything, the combined home office deduction, mileage, utilities, depreciation, and other write-offs slashed nearly $7,800 off my taxable income.

That meant an extra $2,300 refund.

We used that refund for something unforgettable: a family trip to Yellowstone National Park. Hikes. Campfires. Bison herds. And memories that no accountant could ever put a price tag on.

Every time I stood in that tiny home office after that, I smiled. It was not just a desk in a corner.

It was a portal to freedom.

Top 12 home office tax tips I wish I knew earlier

🏠 1. Take photos every January to document exclusive business use.

🏠 2. Measure carefully and choose the method (simplified vs. actual expenses) that saves more. You can switch each year depending on the business profitability.

🏠 3. Log mileage religiously for any business-related trips.

🏠 4. Depreciate responsibly, because the IRS assumes it whether you do or not.

🏠 5. Document internet and utility bills in a dedicated "tax file."

🏠 6. Do not claim mixed-use spaces—exclusivity is non-negotiable.

🏠 7. Apply deductions proportionally if running multiple businesses.

🏠 8. Use a mileage app to automate tracking.

🏠 9. Set up a modular office if you want a fully deductible workspace.

🏠 10. Rent your home for 14 days using the Augusta Rule.

🏠 11. Plan for depreciation recapture when selling your house.

🏠 12. Review your deduction annually to adjust for new expenses or changes in space usage.

Chapter 13

My Deductions on the Wheels: How I Turned My Car into a Tax Tool

It hit me during a meeting with my CPA, right after I bought a new hybrid for work.

I asked, "So… can I write this off?"

He smiled and slid IRS Publication 463 across the table.

"You can—but only if you follow the rules."

That was the moment I realized my car was not just a vehicle, it was a business asset. And with the right strategies, it could drive thousands of dollars off my tax bill each year.

Lesson 1: Choose your path—mileage or actual expenses

The IRS gives us two main paths:

1. **Standard mileage rate** (67¢ per mile in 2024; 70¢ per mile in 2025; and maybe higher in future years) [1]

2. **Actual expense method**

I started with mileage because it was simple. Just track your business miles and multiply.

But once I started driving a luxury SUV for client visits, I switched to actual expenses—and the deductions soared. Once you switch, you must keep using the actual method in future years.

Here is how I compare them each year:

Deduction Method	Best For
Standard mileage	Fuel-efficient cars, lots of short trips
Actual expense	Luxury cars, EVs, high annual costs

Lesson 2: Mileage tracking is non-negotiable

The IRS does not care if you "think" it was a business trip. You need logs.

I use MileIQ. Some friends use QuickBooks or a simple Excel sheet.

Each log should include:

- Date

- Starting and ending location

- Purpose of the trip

- Miles driven

Bonus tip: Take a photo of your odometer on January 1 and December 31 every year. I save mine in a "Mileage" folder on Google Drive. To improve the credibility, do your oil change around year end and keep the odometer reading record.

Lesson 3: Do not forget about parking and tolls

Even if you are using the mileage method, parking fees and tolls are still deductible. I once missed $300 worth of receipts one year because I did not log them.

Now, every time I pay a toll or garage fee, I forward the receipt to my "Car Expenses" email folder.

Lesson 4: Home office = more mileage

Once I qualified for a home office deduction, everything changed.[2]

Now, my drive to the bank? Deductible. The trip to pick up office supplies? Deductible.

A qualified home office turns many previously nondeductible commuting miles into business miles (such as miles from your 9-5 work location to Costco or Home Depot when you buy business or rental supplies).

Lesson 5: Electric vehicles (EV) and the $7,500 credit

In 2023, I bought a Tesla. Not just for the autopilot, but for the tax incentives.[3]

If your AGI is under $300K (married) or $150K (single), you may qualify for a $7,500 tax credit for a new EV.

> 💡 **Tax tip:** The OBBB terminates **EV tax credit** starting September 30, 2025. Tax strategies around Tesla purchase will change significantly. Visit Smart1040.us for more update on this matter.

I also deducted:

- Charging station installation costs [4]

- Part of my electric bill (via home office allocation)

- Depreciation, because it was used 70% for business

I even taught my client how to gift the car to his 18-year-old son and lease it back—legally turning it into a business deduction.

Lesson 6: Depreciation—the power of front-loading

Section 179, Bonus Depreciation, MACRS—sounds like a CPA's alphabet soup. But these tools let you front-load your tax write-offs.

In 2024:

- Section 179 allows an immediate write-off of $28,900 [5]

- Bonus Depreciation = business % uses of vehicles acquired and used in business in 2025

- MACRS spreads deductions over 5 years

The year I made $300K in net profit, I bought a 6,500-lb SUV, used it 80% for business, and wrote off $38,000 in year one.

> 🔍 **Tax term: MACRS** stands for Modified Accelerated Cost Recovery System, the depreciation system used by the IRS to recover the cost of tangible property over a specified life.

Lesson 7: Leasing vs. buying

When I started my business, leasing felt safer—lower payments, fewer surprises.

But buying gave me:

- Bigger depreciation

- Equity in the vehicle

- Long-term tax flexibility

The trick is knowing your cash flow and income outlook. High income year? Buy. Need to conserve cash? Lease.

> 💡 **Tax tip:** A gift and lease back strategy may work if (1) you fully depreciate your car in prior years; (2) you gift it to your child (if market value below $19,000); (3) you lease back from your child with lease payment as business expense; and (4) your child report lease income in his or her tax return (assuming his or her tax bracket is lower than yours).

Lesson 8: Multi-car strategy

By my third year in business, I had two cars:

- A Tesla for local errands (mileage method)

- A luxury SUV for client meetings (actual expense method, as long as 50% or more business uses)

The IRS lets you use different methods for different cars if they are tracked separately.

I created:

- A log for each vehicle

- A usage sheet showing % business vs personal

This combo approach gives you the best of both worlds.

Lesson 9: Car loans and interest deductions

I used to think loan interest was personal—until I learned that if your car is used for business, a portion of the interest is deductible.

I calculated my business use percentage (70% that year) and deducted that % of loan interest. Every dollar counts.

Lesson 10: Do not deduct these!

The IRS is generous—but not with everything.

🚫 **No deduction** for:

- Fines and tickets

- Personal use portion of gas or repairs

- Commuting to your 9-5 job location

My rule of thumb: If it feels personal, it probably is. If it serves the business, track and deduct it.

Final thoughts: Treat your car like a business tool

After five years of running a business, my car is not just transportation, it is part of my tax strategy. [6]

Here is my routine:

- Quarterly review of mileage and expenses

- Annual log cleanup

- Compare deduction methods every January

- Buy or lease strategically based on income year

Your vehicle is on the road anyway—why not make it work for your wallet?

Top ten tax tips for this chapter

🚙 **1. Track your mileage every single day**

Use an app like MileIQ or QuickBooks to log your business miles.[7] The IRS requires contemporaneous records, and sloppy logs can mean denied deductions during an audit.

🚙 **2. Choose the right deduction method annually**

Compare standard mileage vs. actual expenses each year. Mileage is simple and predictable. Actual expenses often yield bigger deductions—especially if you drive a heavy SUV or EV. Once you chose the actual method, you cannot switch back to standard mileage. If your business use falls below 50%, you face the tax consequence of prior year depreciation recapture.

🚙 **3. Odometer photos are proof gold**

Take a photo of your odometer on January 1st or December 31st. Save these in a digital folder labeled by year. It is one of the best ways to substantiate mileage totals. The national average of driving millage is 13,000 per year. Use your judgement based on your business nature and needs.

🚙 **4. Use a home office to boost mileage eligibility**

Having a qualified home office turns many formerly nondeductible trips (like to the post office or supply store) into legitimate business miles.

🚙 **5. Do not miss parking, tolls, and charging costs**

Even when using the standard mileage method, you can still deduct business-related tolls and parking fees. EV charging costs are also partially deductible under the actual expense method (to terminate by 2025 under the OBBB).

🚙 **6. Buy smart: heavy vehicles and bonus depreciation**

Vehicles over 6,000 lbs qualify for bonus depreciation. In 2024, you can deduct up to 80% of the business-use portion in year one. Great for high-income years.

🚙 **7. Allocate loan interest based on business use**

If your vehicle is financed and used for business, you can deduct the proportional interest paid each year. Track your business use % carefully. It works well if the $10,000 auto loan interest deduction under OBBB is phased out due to your high AGI.

🚙 **8. Use different deduction methods for different cars**

You are allowed to use mileage for one car and actual expenses for another—if you track each separately and do not switch method from actual method back to standard method midstream without the IRS rules.

🚚 9. EVs can earn you a $7,500 tax credit

If your income is under the threshold, buying a new electric vehicle may qualify for a federal tax credit—plus potential state incentives and deductible business usage expenses. This credit will go away after September 30, 2025 as a tax code change in the OBBB.

🚚 10. Do not deduct personal use or penalties

The IRS disallows deductions for:

- Commuting (if no home office)

- Fines, speeding tickets

- Personal gas or maintenance

Be honest, document clearly, and only deduct what truly supports your business.

Chapter 14

Miles, Meals, and Mindfulness: How We Mastered Business Travel Deductions

It all started innocently enough.

John and Jane were packing for their very first "business + pleasure" trip to San Diego, a conference for John's work and a few days of vacation for themselves. They booked fancy hotels, upgraded to first-class seats using points, scheduled spa days, and even planned a private city tour.

They thought: *"It is a business trip. Surely, it is all deductible!"*

It was not.

Their CPA, Lisa (yes, the same Lisa I hire for my family tax matters), delivered the hard truth over coffee: "Guys, business travel deductions are powerful, but there are rules—and IRS agents aren't exactly 'just let it slide' types." [1]

At first, John and Jane felt defeated. But their disappointment turned to optimism when they realized this was their chance to turn one of life's best activities—*travel*—into a smart tax strategy. [2]

Step 1: Dream big, plan smarter

First, they rewired their thinking.

They learned that every trip could fit into one of three categories:

- **Pure business travel:** Maximum deductions.

- **Mixed business & personal:** Careful allocations needed.

- **Pure vacation:** No deductions allowed.

They decided, *"If we're going to travel, let's travel intentionally and mindfully."* [3]

They started planning trips **around** business activities:

- Conferences and expos.
- Client meetings.
- Site visits.
- Speaking engagements.
- Real estate property scouting.

Suddenly, trips were not just vacations—they were strategic missions.

Key mindset shift: Use travel as a business growth strategy, not just a reward.

Step 2: The sandwich strategy (and other little-known gems)

Lisa, a recognized CPA for John and my own family tax matters, introduced them to her favorite secret weapon: The Weekend Sandwich Strategy.

- Fly out Thursday night.

- Attend a conference Friday.

- Stay the weekend.

- Meet a client Monday.

Result:

☑ Flights, hotel for the weekend, meals—all deductible. [4]
☑ Even some ground transportation and tips.

They also learned:

- **Extended stays** (past business events) = prorate expenses.

- **Business days** include setup and takedown days at events.

- **Temporary work assignments** (under 1 year) = full deductions.

They realized that tax law rewards the organized.

Key tactical move: Anchor travel with business on both sides of the weekend.

Step 3: Every receipt tells a story

Lisa's Rule: *"Imagine every trip as a mini audit rehearsal."*

They did the work:

☑ Created digital folders for each trip.
☑ Saved receipts for flights, hotels, taxis, meals, even tips.
☑ Snapped photos of badges at conferences and events.
☑ Kept email chains confirming meetings.
☑ Used a dedicated business travel credit card.

Jane even went a step further:

- Sent herself summary emails after each client meeting.

- Jotted down quick meeting notes on her phone.

- Created simple Excel logs for mileage and incidentals.

If the IRS ever came knocking, they would have a full movie, not just snapshots.

Key tactical move: Treat travel documentation like a Netflix documentary on your business life.

Step 4: Mastering meals and entertainment Rules

John was shocked when Lisa told him:

- Meals tied directly to business? 50% deductible. [5]

- Fancy sightseeing tours? ⊘ Nope.

- Broadway tickets? ⊘ No chance.

They learned:

☑ Meals with clear business purpose (discussing projects, closing deals) were fair game.

☑ No receipts needed if meals were under $75 (but keep good notes).

☑ Meals alone on business trips? Still deductible!

Jane loved finding new local restaurants for meetings—it turned every meal into a memory *and* a deduction.

Key tactical move: Business meals = YES. Entertainment = NO. Remember: If it is fun, it is probably not deductible.

Step 5: Family matters (but the IRS does not care)

On a trip to Orlando, Jane's sister wanted to tag along. So John asked Lisa: *"Can we deduct her flights if she helps set up the booth at the expo?"*

Lisa asked, *"Is she a legitimate employee of your business?"*

No, she was not.

Verdict: ✗ No deduction.

However, when John's teenage son helped manage sign-ins at a real estate event—and received a W-2 or 1099 NEC for his work—his travel costs became deductible. [6]

They realized:

☑ Family member expenses = Deductible ONLY if they are doing **real work.**

☑ Must document duties, hours, employment contract, and pay them reasonably.

Key tactical move: Hire family legally if you want travel costs to be deductible.

Step 6: International travel, the higher stakes game

In 2026, John scored a speaking gig in London so they decided to turn it into a 12-day adventure.

Lisa warned:

- Trips 7 days or less = easy rules (at least 50% business related, deductible).

- Trips longer than 7 days = stricter rule (75% of time business related, otherwise allocate expenses between business and personal).

So, they carefully structured:

☑ Business meetings packed into the Monday to Friday.
☑ Personal sightseeing and tours over the weekend.
☑ Schedule the last business meeting on Monday. Flights deducted in full since primary purpose was business.

Every day was scheduled and documented.[7]

Key tactical move: International = Plan like a chess grandmaster. Do not wing it.

Step 7: Little wins add up

John and Jane found dozens of small ways to legally maximize deductions:

- Paid their brother for guesthouse lodging—with a receipt.

- Used airport lounges (thanks to business credit card perks).

- Chose Uber rides directly tied to business meetings.

- Used TSA PreCheck fees reimbursed by their Amex Business card—and wrote off the difference.

Even dry-cleaning during trips became a deductible expense! It was not flashy. It was smart.

Key tactical move: Stack small wins until they become major tax savings.

☑ John & Jane's ultimate business travel tax checklist [8]

Strategy	Action Taken
✈ 1. Anchor trips with business on both sides of weekends	Used the Sandwich Strategy
✈ 2. Separate personal vs business activities	Clear schedules, invites, and receipts

Strategy	Action Taken
✈ 3. Hire family members legally	If age over 17, issue W-2 or 1099 NEC for legitimate business tasks
✈ 4. Maximize per diem rates when applicable	Used GSA meal allowances for simplicity. Remember the 50% rule
✈ 5. Document every client interaction	Emails, meeting notes, itineraries
✈ 6. Keep a digital folder per trip	All receipts and proof in one place
✈ 7. Pay family for lodging if staying at homes	Create formal receipts from the hosting family
✈ 8. Use travel cards for perks + deductions	Business cards only for business trips
✈ 9. Track mileage for local business transport	Simple apps and logs
✈ 10. Allocate properly on long international trips	Pro-rated personal vs business days

Closing reflection:

Business travel is not just a trip, it is a story you write for the IRS, with every receipt, every meeting, and every mile. John and Jane did not just master the art of travel deductions. They built a lifestyle where travel, business, and financial freedom intertwined beautifully.

And now, every plane ticket feels like another step toward independence.

Chapter 15

Smart Health: Medical Tax Planning for Small Businesses

In our family, tax planning was a dinnertime conversation. That night, it was my teenage son Kevin who asked, "Dad, if you're self-employed, who pays for your health insurance?"

I smiled and replied, "We do, son. But the trick is making Uncle Sam help us pay for it."

What followed was a deep dive into one of the most underutilized areas of tax strategy for small business owners: healthcare and medical expenses. This chapter is not just about saving money but about securing your health, your family's future, and your retirement through smart tax planning. Let me walk you through the lessons, case studies, and tips that transformed how our family and clients approached this challenge.

Step 1: The self-employed medical tax trap—and the escape route

Meet Janice, a self-employed artist who earns $90,000 per year painting murals for offices and schools. She pays $12,000 annually for a private health insurance policy. Like many sole proprietors, Janice was unsure how to deduct this cost.

She learned the key: IRS Schedule 1, Line 17. It allowed her to deduct 100% of the premiums for herself, her spouse, and her dependents, as long as she had net business profit. [1] Her $12,000 deduction dropped her AGI to $78,000, potentially lowering her marginal tax rate and eligibility for credits.

However, she could not deduct her $2,000 in co-pays and prescriptions.

The fix? Janice opened a **Health Savings Account (HSA).** She contributed the max: $8,300, the family limit in 2024. That amount was tax-deductible, grew tax-free, and covered her medical costs tax-free. [2]

Total tax savings: Over $3,000.

Step 2: How hiring your spouse can turn your health costs into deductions

Now meet Omar, a landscape designer running an LLC. His wife Tiffany helped with scheduling but wasn't on payroll. Their accountant suggested a change: formally hire Tiffany with a W-2.

Why? As an employee, Tiffany qualified for full benefits—including a **Health Reimbursement Arrangement (HRA)** that reimbursed all out-of-pocket medical costs for the family. [3]

Tiffany's salary was $18,000, which was reasonable for her role. The business deducted:

- $18,000 salary (deductible)

- $12,000 family premiums (deductible through Schedule C, Line 14)

- $5,000 in medical reimbursements via the HRA

The strategy turned $17,000 of previously non-deductible personal costs into tax-deductible expenses. The couple saved $4,500 in federal and self-employment taxes.

Step 3: When S-Corp makes (and doesn't make) sense for health deductions

Ted was an online tutor with $60,000 in profit. He converted his business to an S-Corp to save on self-employment tax. But then he got stuck: health insurance costs had to be included in his W-2 wages.

The deduction was still available—but on **Schedule 1**, not Schedule C. Worse, his S-Corp had to file payroll, pay FICA taxes, and follow strict HRA rules.

Lesson: S-corps are great for reducing FICA, but they complicate health deductions. If your profits are under $40K, stick with Schedule C and LLC. Over $40K? Consider S-Corp for overall savings, but plan for payroll costs.

Step 4: HSAs, the stealth retirement account

Kevin, age 19, opened his own HSA with $4,300, the individual max. [4] We gifted him the amount. He invested in S&P 500 index fund with a fund expense ratio as low as 0.015% per year.

"Let it grow," I told him. "Never touch it unless you really need to."

If he adds the max from age 19 to 65, his HSA could exceed $1.2 million—tax-free for medical needs and penalty-free for anything after age 65. Unlike Flexible Spending Accounts (FSAs), there's no "use it or lose it."

Step 5: HSAs + HRAs double wins for families

Liang and her husband own a dental clinic. She's on a high-deductible health plan and funds an HSA. Her husband is an employee and gets reimbursed via a family HRA for out-of-pocket costs.

The strategy allowed them to:

- Deduct $8,300 via the HSA

- Reimburse $6,000 in out-of-pocket costs through the HRA

- Cover premiums through the business as an employee benefit

Combined savings: Nearly $6,000 in taxes, plus long-term HSA growth.

---

10 Tax Tips for small business medical planning

💲 1. Use Schedule 1, Line 17 to deduct health insurance if you're self-employed with profit.

💲 2. Open an HSA if you have a high-deductible health plan. Max contributions annually.

💲 3. Hire your spouse to unlock HRA reimbursements.

💲 4. Use HRA to cover co-pays, dental, vision, and prescriptions.

💲 5. Avoid mixing S-Corp and HRA unless you're ready for complex compliance.

💲 6. Deduct health premiums via Schedule C if you hire family as W-2 employees.

💲 7. Gift HSA contributions to adult children for triple tax-free medical planning.

💲 8. Invest HSA funds in S&P 500 instead of spending. Treat it like a retirement account.

💲 9. Use the Small Business Health Care Tax Credit (Form 8941) if eligible.[5]

💲 10. Document everything. Keep receipts, plan documents, and W-2s for IRS compliance.

In the world of small business, every dollar counts, and every strategy compounds. Mastering the medical deduction game doesn't just save you money. It protects your family, funds your retirement, and reinforces your independence.

Chapter 16

Small Business Retirement Planning – Our Family's Blueprint for Freedom

As a tax accountant, one of the most frequently asked questions is: "If I run my own business, how do I retire?" Most small business owners do not just need to "retire." They need to engineer their own freedom.

That is exactly what we set out to do as a family.

The eye-opener: Traditional retirement does not fit entrepreneurs

Reading Warren Buffett's shareholder letters and attending tax planning workshops taught me a vital truth: [1]

Step 1: Corporate pensions are disappearing

For small business owners, retirement security depends 100% on what we build ourselves.

- There is no pre-set employer matching your 401(K) automatically.
- No HR department managing investment choices or compliance.
- No pensions falling into your lap at age 65.
- If we wanted financial independence, we had to design it, brick by brick, decision by decision.

Step 2: Choosing the right vehicle: why Solo 401(K) became our MVP

After deep research, comparing SEP IRAs, SIMPLE IRAs, and Solo 401(K)s, we landed on one clear winner: [2]

Solo 401(K)

Why?

- Highest contribution limits ($69,000 per person in 2024, $70,000 in 2025; maybe higher limit in future years)
- Ability to contribute both as "employee" and "employer"

- Roth option for tax-free growth

- Loan feature (borrow up to $50,000 if needed)

- Mega Backdoor Roth strategy possible (for advanced users)

- Greater flexibility than a SEP IRA (which only allows employer contributions)

The Solo 401(K) was not just a savings account. It was a launchpad for freedom.

🔍 **Tax term:** A **SEP IRA (Simplified Employee Pension Individual Retirement Account)** is a retirement plan that allows self-employed individuals and small business owners to make tax-deductible contributions to retirement accounts for themselves and their employees. The drawback is an employer-funded only account: employees cannot contribute.

🔍 **Tax term:** A **SIMPLE IRA (Savings Incentive Match Plan for Employees Individual Retirement Account)** is a tax-advantaged retirement plan designed for small businesses with 100 or fewer employees. The drawback is the lower employee contribution limit ($17,000 in 2025) than the solo 401(K) limit ($23,500).

🔍 **Tax term:** The **Mega Backdoor Roth** is an advanced retirement strategy that allows high small business earners to contribute up to $70,000 in three parts: (1) employee elective deferral $23,500 ; (2) employer contribution, up to 25% of w-2 salary; and (3) after-tax (non-Roth) contributions. Then convert those funds into a Roth IRA or Roth 401(K), enabling a large tax-free growth beyond standard Roth limits.

Step 3: Setting up our family Solo 401(K)s

We opened ours with E-Trade, a simple online process with no setup fees and strong customer service. Most importantly, it offers a loan feature in the Solo 401(K) or Roth Solo 401(K) plan, up to the lesser of $50,000 or 50% of plan assets. As a plan administrator, my small business can decide the loan term and loan interest rate.

Our plan allowed us to:

- Make employee deferrals ($23,500 or $30,500 age 50+)

- Make employer profit-sharing contributions (up to 20% of net profit as an LLC, or 25% as an S Corp W-2 employee)

- Convert after-tax contributions to Roth tax-free annually

- Roll in old 401(K) and IRA balances for consolidation

We even set up a second Solo 401(K) for my consulting LLC—keeping track of contribution limits across all plans carefully. Out of sudden, I can have two loan features from two Solo 401(K) plans.

Managing two Solo 401(K)s made us more disciplined, more strategic, and more aggressive about securing our future. Ensure the combined employee contribution cannot exceed the $23,500 annual limit.

Step 4: Hiring the family and doubling the opportunity

Once our business grew, we officially hired my wife and teenage kids.[3]

Each family member:

- Earned a W-2 wage

- Contributed to my wife's own Solo 401(K). The children set up Roth IRA accounts with their earned income.

- Built up retirement savings fast

Hiring family is not just about cutting taxes. It is about teaching responsibility, work ethic, and long-term planning.

One year, between employee 401(K) contribution (funded from W-2 salary) and employer matches, our family tucked away nearly $150,000—sheltering it from current taxes while building tax-deferred and tax-free buckets. [4]

Even during slower revenue years, we prioritized these contributions just like paying the mortgage.

Step 5: Understanding the Solo 401(K) mega backdoor Roth

This strategy blew our minds.

- Max employee pre-taxes or Roth contribution: $23,500

- Add employer contribution (20%-25%) of W-2

- Then add after-tax contributions up to the $70,000 cap

- Immediately roll after-tax contributions to a Roth Solo 401(K) or Roth IRA

Result? Massive Roth savings without income limits.

We called it "turbocharging" our retirement, building a mountain of tax-free money while friends struggled with contribution caps.

Step 6: S-Corp vs. LLC planning for retirement efficiency

When our businesses matured, we switched from LLC to S-Corp to optimize:[5]

- W-2 salary (for retirement contribution calculations and 25% of employer matching)

- K-1 distributions (to reduce self-employment tax)

Example:

- Salary: $70,000

- Max employee Roth 401(K) contribution: $23,500

- Employer 25% match: $17,500

Total contribution = $41,000 annually, with flexibility for additional after-tax funding.

Moving to an S-Corp also opened smarter health insurance deductions (see Chapter 15) and home office reimbursement strategies (see Chapter 12).

Step 7: Special strategies for business owners

1. Set reasonable salaries to maximize employer matches while minimizing payroll taxes.
2. Use multiple businesses (consulting, rental property management, e-commerce) to diversify income streams and plan contributions creatively.
3. Rollover balances to IRAs before reaching $260K Solo 401(K) balance to avoid mandatory Form 5500-SF filing and $500 CPA filing fee.
4. Leverage Solo 401(K) loans for emergencies or opportunities instead of raiding Roth IRAs or cash savings.
5. Explore Defined Benefit Plans if income spikes and you want to defer even more (up to $300,000+ annually).

Step 8: Real-world wins in our family

We funded Solo 401(K) accounts even during slow years by using distributions carefully.

We rolled over old employer 401(K) plans into our Solo 401(K)s—consolidating assets for better control.

We used Solo Roth 401(K) balances to secure real estate deals without penalty using non-recourse lending structures. It is a self-directed retirement plan feature.

We layered Mega Backdoor Roth conversions every year during market dips—supercharging future tax-free income.[6]

We maximized catch-up contributions once we crossed age 50—adding an extra $7,500 annually to each spouse's account if over age 50.

Step 9: Teaching the next generation

Our children now understand:

- Why starting retirement savings early matters

- How tax deferral boosts compounding

- Why Roth money is golden in retirement

- How owning your business gives ultimate control over retirement outcomes

- How to calculate safe withdrawal rates and plan distributions smartly

- How to pay yourself first

We created "Family Financial Summits" twice a year to walk through Solo 401(K) statements, investment performance, and future projections.

Top 15 small business retirement planning strategies

1. Start with a Solo 401(K) for maximum flexibility and contributions

2. Hire your spouse and children to double or triple savings [7]

3. Use S-Corp structure to reduce FICA and increase match potential [8]

4. Execute mega backdoor Roth contributions if possible

5. Use 401(K) plan loan features wisely to maintain liquidity

6. Roll old employer plans into Solo 401(K)s or IRA for consolidation and saving fees

7. Balance pre-tax and Roth buckets for future tax flexibility

8. Roll over balances to IRA before $260k to avoid Department of Labor 5500 requirements

9. Document W-2 salaries carefully for compliance

10. Treat retirement contributions as fixed expenses, not optional

11. Use market dips to accelerate Roth conversions

12. Educate family members early on the power of tax-advantaged compounding

13. Explore defined benefit plans for high-income years

14. Structure annual bonuses to maximize retirement funding

15. Integrate retirement savings with business exit planning

Final reflection: Freedom is built, not given

Owning a business gave us freedom. Mastering small business retirement planning ensured we could keep that freedom for ourselves, our children, and generations yet to come. It was not just about saving money.

It was about building a future where no boss, no stock market crash, no economic downturn could take away what we created together.

The best retirement plan is not just funded with dollars. It is funded with wisdom, action, and vision.

Case Study 3

Small Business Tax Savings: Olga and Mike Tax Saving Strategies

Purpose of this case study

This case study demonstrates how small business owners, whether running a piano teaching studio or a CPA tax planning practice, can use proactive tax strategies to maximize deductions, reduce tax burdens, and build long-term financial security for themselves and their families. By following Olga and Mike's journey, readers will discover practical, actionable steps for leveraging the tax code, organizing business finances, and turning everyday business decisions into powerful tax-saving opportunities.

Story 1: Olga's studio upgrade — the *de minimis* safe harbor

Olga, a self-employed piano teacher, needed a new digital piano for her studio. She found one for $2,400, including delivery and setup. Unsure if she could deduct the full cost in one year, she consulted her CPA husband, Mike Nie.

Mike explained:

- The IRS allows the *de minimis* **safe harbor election** for tangible property purchases under $2,500 per item or invoice.

- By making this election, Olga could immediately deduct the full $2,400 as a business expense, no depreciation required.

Takeaway: Small business purchases under $2,500 per item can often be fully deducted in the year of purchase, streamlining record-keeping and maximizing cash flow. See Appendix 1 for IRS cover letter template.

Story 2: Olga's family business boost

Olga decided to hire her 17-year-old daughter, Sasha, to help with her studio: organizing music, setting up for recitals, and managing social media. She paid her $18/hour, a fair market rate for teen labor.

Mike advised:

- As long as Sasha's work was real, hours were documented, and pay was reasonable, Olga could deduct her wages as a business expense on her Schedule C.

- Sasha, having earned income, was eligible to contribute to a Roth IRA—even as a minor.

By year-end, Sasha proudly made her first Roth IRA contribution, setting the stage for lifelong tax-free growth.

Takeaway: Paying children for legitimate work in a family business is smart—just keep rates reasonable and document everything. Their earned income can fund a Roth IRA, giving them a powerful head start.

Story 3: Olga's double deduction strategy

Encouraged by Mike, Olga:

- Deducted Sasha's wages on her Schedule C (piano teaching business).

- Helped Sasha contribute her earnings to a Roth IRA.

Results:

- Olga reduced her taxable business income.

- Sasha began building a tax-free retirement nest egg.

Takeaway: Turning a child's earned income into Roth IRA contributions is one of the best financial gifts a business owner can give their kids. If a person contributes $7,000 annually to a Roth IRA from ages 17 to 60, invested in the S&P 500 index with a 0.015% fee, it could grow to a whopping $3 million by age 60, completely tax-free.

Story 4: Mike's CPA practice — business travel done right

Mike, running his own CPA tax planning firm, attended a national tax conference in Las Vegas. He scheduled client meetings on Friday and Monday, with the weekend in between.

- Because business activities were scheduled immediately before and after the weekend, Mike could deduct the entire trip's airfare, hotel, and 50% of business meals.

- Any personal sightseeing or entertainment expenses remained non-deductible.

Takeaway: For mixed personal/business travel, always anchor trips with legitimate business activities before and after weekends to maximize deductions.

Story 5: Mike's vehicle deduction decision

Mike purchased a new hybrid car for client visits. He wondered whether to use the standard mileage rate or actual expenses.

- Mike tracked both methods for several months.
- He chose the method that yielded the highest deduction for his business mileage, knowing that the first-year choice would lock in his options for future years.

Takeaway: First-year vehicle deduction choices matter: standard mileage is simple, actual expenses may yield bigger savings. Always project before you elect, because once you elect the actual expense route, you cannot switch back to the standard mileage approach. Your record-keeping burden could last for years.

Story 6: Olga's home studio: the home office deduction

Olga converted a spare room into a dedicated teaching studio.

- She measured the square footage and calculated the percentage of her home used exclusively for business.
- She deducted a portion of her rent, utilities, and insurance as a home office expense.

Takeaway: A dedicated home office can unlock valuable deductions for small business owners—just ensure the space is used regularly and exclusively for business.

Story 7: Mike's entity optimization

As Mike's CPA practice grew, he evaluated his business structure.

- He considered switching from sole proprietorship to S-Corp to reduce self-employment taxes and optimize retirement contributions.
- After consulting with a tax advisor, he restructured his business, resulting in significant tax savings and improved retirement planning options.

Takeaway: Choosing the right business entity can dramatically impact taxes, retirement savings, and long-term financial health.

Quick Lessons from Olga & Mike's Stories

Person	Strategy	Lesson
Olga	*De minimis* safe harbor	Small business purchases under $2,500 can be fully deducted.
Olga	Hiring family	Pay fair wages, document hours, deduct properly.
Sasha	Roth IRA	Earned income allows minors to contribute to Roth IRAs as early as age 7.

Person	Strategy	Lesson
Olga	Home office deduction	Dedicated space unlocks valuable deductions.
Mike	Business travel	Anchor trips with business activities for full deduction.
Mike	Vehicle deduction	First-year choice: mileage vs. actual expenses—project before you elect.
Mike	Entity optimization	The right structure can slash taxes and boost retirement.

Final Reflection

Smart tax moves aren't just for big corporations: they're for every small business owner, music teacher, and CPA. With careful planning, diligent documentation, and the right strategies, you can turn everyday business decisions into powerful tax advantages, building wealth and security for your family and your future.

PART 4

SMART REAL ESTATE

Chapter 17

The Real Estate Game: How I Turned Tax Law into My Wealth-Building Tool: 100 Tax Planning Tips for Real Estate

Part 1: The first house that changed everything

When I bought my first house, I did not think like an investor. I just wanted a place of my own. It was a modest three-bedroom in a quiet suburb. While not flashy, it was mine. I scraped together a 20% down payment and signed the loan documents with sweaty palms and a racing heart.

Fast forward two years, and I was married with our first child on the way. We needed more space. While looking into selling, I stumbled upon something in a blog post that changed my entire financial outlook: *the Section 121 exclusion.*[1]

> 🔍 **Tax term: Section 121** of the Internal Revenue Code provides a capital gains exclusion for the sale of a primary residence. You can exclude up to $260,000 of capital gains if you're single, or $500,000 if married filing jointly. To qualify, you must have (1) owned the home for at least 2 out of the last 5 years, and (2) lived in it as your primary residence for at least 2 out of the last 5 years before the sale.

I brought it up with my CPA friend, Lisa, over coffee.

"Wait, let me get this straight," I asked, furrowing my brow. "You're telling me I can sell my home, and the first half a million dollars in gain… is completely tax-free?"

Lisa smiled. "If you and your wife lived there for two out of the last five years, absolutely. And you can do it again after a few years. It is one of the best-kept secrets in the code." [2]

That was the moment I stopped being just a homeowner and became a tax-aware real estate investor. [3] I walked out of that café with a fire lit under me. I sold that house for a tidy profit, reinvested the gains into a duplex, and began my journey into the world of rental income.

Part 2: From renter to landlord: the Schedule E master [4]

Managing rental property is not for the faint of heart. My first tenants were a pair of college students who paid rent on time but threw wild parties every other weekend. I learned quickly: always screen your tenants, and always keep documentation.

But even with the headaches, I saw the bigger picture. My duplex paid for itself, and every year when tax season rolled around, I was amazed at the deductions I could claim.

Mortgage interest, property taxes, insurance, auto mileage, business meals, repairs, management fees—it all went on Schedule E. I still remember the first time I realized I was not just making money—I was saving it too.

"Did you know," I told my son, Kevin one day, "that the IRS lets me deduct depreciation on this place? Even though it is going up in value?"

He raised an eyebrow. "Isn't that cheating?"

"Nope," I laughed. "It's tax law."

That deduction was powerful—thousands of dollars shaved off my taxable income every year. And when I learned about *cost segregation* studies, it got even better. I hired a cost segregation specialist to analyze the building and separate the HVAC, cabinets, flooring, and fixtures from the structural value. That let me write off those components faster, front-loading my tax benefits. [5]

Part 3: Playing the long game with 1031 exchange

As my portfolio grew, I faced a big question: Should I sell one of my rentals and cash out?

That is when Lisa introduced me to the 1031 exchange.[6]

"You can sell your property," she explained, "and roll the gains into a new one—tax-deferred. But you have got to follow the timeline. Identify a new property in 45 days. Close in 180."

It sounded stressful. But I did it.

I sold a triplex I had held for five years and rolled it into a six-unit building in a growing college town. I paid no capital gains tax. That exchange let me increase my cash flow and property value without losing a dime to the IRS.

Over the next few years, I repeated that strategy again and again. Like a game of chess, I planned every move with intention. Each sale led to something bigger. Each property brought in more income.

During my retirement stage, I will continue to materially participate in my rental business, claim a real estate professional status, and use bonus depreciation to reduce my AGI to a low level to avoid taxation on my social security benefits or Medicare premium surcharge.

When I die, my children inherit my rentals at a step-up basis based on my last will inheritance clause. They will sell the rentals with no capital gain taxes or depreciation recapture taxes.

Part 4: Making it a family business

I started to see real estate not just as a path to wealth, but as a legacy.

When my son Kevin graduated from high school, I did not just send him to college—I helped him *buy* a house near campus.[7]

"You'll live upstairs," I told him. "Rent the basement to two roommates. I will co-sign, and you will run it like a business."

Kevin was hesitant at first, but once he saw that the rent covered the mortgage, and he could deduct expenses as a property manager, he was in.

We even educated Kevin's college friends to use their 529 plan funds to pay rent (totally legitimate under IRS publication 970), as long as they maintained a half-time or full-time student status. We deducted travel costs when we visited our rental (and visit Kevin of course). He gained financial skills most college students never learn. And I got to help without just writing a check.

I hired my younger daughter to clean my other rentals during turnovers. She made honest money, and I got a business expense deduction. She funded her minor Roth IRA. It was a perfect example of keeping wealth *in the family*—and making the IRS help pay for it.

Part 5: Real estate and retirement: my hidden superpower

As I approached my 50s, retirement planning took center stage. But instead of just loading up a 401(K), I turned to real estate.[8]

One year, I used my Solo 401(K) to purchase a rental property directly. The rent went back into the account, growing tax-deferred. Another year, I borrowed against my life insurance policy—$50,000 in cash value—to fund a deal, all tax-free. Besides, the policy loan interest may be deductible in rental Schedule E in line "Other Interest," because by the IRS interest tracing rule, borrowing cost may be tax deductible if the fund is used in income producing property or business.

> 🔍 **Tax term:** A Solo 401(K) is a retirement savings plan designed for self-employed individuals or business owners with no full-time employees other than a spouse. It allows higher contribution limits than traditional IRAs by letting the owner contribute both as an employee and employer. This plan can include Roth and traditional options, and may allow loans and flexible investment choices.

My CPA warned me: "Just make sure your policy doesn't lapse."

"Don't worry," I said. "The rent covers the interest."

I realized something profound: real estate gave me flexibility, and life insurance gave me tax-free liquidity. While my peers were waiting until 59½ to touch their IRAs, I was building cash flow now—buying freedom with every closing.

I even explored gifting strategies with my elderly parents. A couple transferred a high-value property into their names, and when they passed, the step-up in basis erased decades of gains. That one move saved the couple over six figures in taxes. Such a "gift up and inherit back" strategy has been mentioned in a few well published tax planning books or articles. To avoid the audit risk, one should seek tax professional advice, draft an arm's-length agreement, and use the market comparable valuation.

Part 6: The lessons I share now

Now, I host workshops for young investors and working families. I tell them what I wish I knew earlier:

- Live in your homes long enough to use the Section 121 exclusion, then move and do it again.

- Keep detailed records: receipts, mileage logs, everything.

- Hire your children (and pay them reasonably). Check the IRS rule on employing family members.

- Do not ignore depreciation: claim it every year, or you will regret it at sale time.

- Use 1031 exchange like chess pieces. Think five moves ahead.

- Understand your local market better than anyone. AI will not save you here.

- Use leverage wisely. Other People's Money (OPM) is a powerful force when managed well.

> **Tax tip: Other people's money (OPM)** is a strategy where you use borrowed or invested funds from others, rather than your own, to build wealth or finance a project. Interest expenses are generally deductible from the business tax return.

People laugh when I call real estate one of the "five pillars" of financial freedom, alongside stocks, life insurance, and small business ownership. But I stand by it.

Why? Because people will always need homes. Markets rise and fall. AI can do a lot, but it cannot build trust, walk a property, or negotiate a deal. This business still belongs to people who *show up*, who *study the code*, and who *play the game smarter*.

And after all these years, I am proud to say I am still playing.

> Top 10 tax tips in this chapter
>
> 1. Use the Section 121 exclusion
>
> - If you live in a home for 2 out of the last 5 years, you can exclude up to **$260,000** in capital gains (or **$500,000** if married filing jointly) when selling.

- Tip: Strategically move into investment properties before selling to qualify for a Section 121 and 1031 combo.

2. Leverage 1031 exchange to defer capital gains

- Use **Section 1031** to swap one investment property for another without paying capital gains tax.

- Tip: Follow the **45-day identification** and **180-day closing** rule strictly.

3. Maximize depreciation and cost segregation

- Depreciate residential rental property over **27.5 years**, reducing taxable income annually. Cost segregation and bonus depreciation work extremely well in one of four scenarios below: (1) real estate professional; (2) short term rental; (3) self-rental; or (4) AGI below $100,000.

- Tip: Conduct a **cost segregation study** to accelerate depreciation on specific assets like HVAC, appliances, or flooring.

4. Hire family members legitimately

- Pay your children for legitimate work (e.g., cleaning, maintenance, bookkeeping) and deduct their wages.

- Tip: Keep records and pay through payroll to qualify for deductions.

5. Deduct home office expenses

- Deduct a portion of your home expenses (utilities, insurance, mortgage interest) if you use space **exclusively and regularly** for real estate business.

- Tip: Choose either the simplified method or actual expense method.

6. Deduct travel and meals related to property management

- Track **mileage, meals, and lodging** when traveling for rental property management or real estate business.

- Tip: Use a **contemporaneous mileage log** and document purpose of each trip.

7. Utilize real estate professional status

- If you or your spouse spend **750+ hours/year** and **more than half your working hours** in real estate, you may qualify as a real estate professional. Use an REP app to track your hours.

- Tip: This lets you deduct **unlimited passive losses** against active income.

8. Use self-rental and business structuring smartly

- Rent a property you own to your business to generate legitimate deductions while converting income types.

- Tip: Ensure rent is at **market rate** and avoid self-rental loss recharacterization traps.

9. Convert primary residence to rental

- Move out of your primary residence, turn it to a rental property for two or three years, and then sell it through a 1031 exchange to benefit from **Section 121 exclusion.**

- Tip: This hybrid strategy maximizes tax-free gains while deferring the rest.

10. Offset capital gains with passive losses

- Use passive losses from rentals to offset other passive income or active income if below income thresholds.[9]

- Tip: **$25,000 allowance** applies if AGI is under $100,000 and you are actively participating.

Chapter 18

A Journey into Real Estate Tax Mastery: The Six-Week Shift That Changed My Financial Life

Week 1: A new vision of financial freedom

It started in a room full of whiteboards, spreadsheets, and faded coffee mugs. I remember standing in front of the class I was teaching. Forty investors staring back at me, most of them juggling jobs, families, and financial stress. I told them, "By the end of six weeks, you'll see real estate not just as an asset, but as a lifeline."

My journey started when I realized that earning six figures was not enough if half of it went to taxes. That is when I discovered the three-income model (Trifecta):

Income Source	Description
W-2 or Active Income through an S-Corp	The 9-5 job or business income
Portfolio Income	Dividends, interest, capital gains
Real Estate Rental Income	Cash flow from rental properties

> 💡 **Tax tip:** The **"Trifecta"** strategy was invented by Mark J. Kohler, a nationally renowned tax attorney and CPA. It is a three-part legal + tax structure designed to help business owners and real estate investors: (1) LLC taxed as an S-Corp for Business with a W-2 reasonable compensation, used on the left side of the triangle; (2) LLCs for real estate investments, used on the "right side" of the triangle to shield real estate or other holdings from personal liability; and (3) portfolio income in tax deferred or tax free accounts, positioned in the middle of the triangle. Finally, at the bottom is a revocable living trust, a central planning tool for legacy, privacy, and probate avoidance.

> 🔍 **Tax term:** A **Revocable Living Trust** is a legal document that allows you to control and manage your assets during your lifetime and ensure a smooth transfer of those assets after death, without going through probate.

This model was not just theory. I applied it in my own life—starting with a small duplex I purchased in a college town. With every rent check that came in, I could see a shift in how I thought about money. I realized I was not just earning; I was building.

Add in some powerful tax strategies, and suddenly the financial picture changed entirely. I showed my students how their W-2 income was just a tool, not a trap. We mapped out income funnels and built personal freedom roadmaps together.

Week 2: Two homes, twice the deduction

Most people do not realize you can deduct mortgage interest and property taxes on two primary residences, including vacation homes or secondary properties. They all count if you structure them right.[1]

The diagram below shows the bifurcation of deductions:

First 6 Months	Second 6 Months
Schedule A (Primary residence deductions)	**Schedule E** (Rental expenses)

I shared how I let my parents live in my second home for free while still retaining the mortgage and claiming interest on my taxes. That opened a discussion about leveraging family ties in a tax-smart way.

We also discussed the SALT cap and how you can choose to deduct sales tax instead of state income tax to maximize that $40K limit (for those states with no state income tax). I shared a student success story: Alex, who bought a car in a no-income-tax state to maximize deductions.

> 🔍 Tax Term: The **State and Local Tax (SALT)** deduction cap is an itemized tax deduction limit for high income taxpayers. The cap increased from $10,000 under the Tax Cuts and Jobs Act to $40,000 under the One Big Beautiful Bill Act (OBBB), subject to AGI phase out.

> 💡 **Tax tip:** Given that the SALT cap is significantly raised under the newly passed OBBB, with a cap phasing out by income levels. Readers should consult a tax advisor for a possible change of the sales tax deduction strategy.

Tip table: Primary residence deductions

Strategy	Tax Form	Key Benefit
Two-home interest deduction	Schedule A	Increased deductible mortgage interest (up to $750,000 mortgage loan balance). Do not forget the mortgage points and primary mortgage insurance premium
Bifurcating property deductions	A & E	Maximize deductions through transition
Sales tax vs. income tax choice	Schedule A	Optimize under $40K SALT cap [2]

We role-played conversations with CPAs and realtors. One woman in the class realized she had overpaid in taxes for four years.

Week 3: Depreciation – The hidden goldmine

"My fourplex made money every month, but on paper, it looked like a loss."

That is the magic of depreciation.[3] Add a cost segregation study, and it gets even better.[4] I taught them how to file Form 3115 to correct depreciation mistakes and capture missed years.[5] A few people pulled out laptops mid-class to email their CPAs.

The math works as follows:

- Net rental income minus
- Depreciation deduction, which equals
- Adjusted taxable income (showing net loss)

We broke down myths about passive losses. I explained why showing a paper loss is not a red flag, but a strategy.

Case Study: Sarah, a retired teacher, had three rental properties. With cost segregation and depreciation, her AGI dropped below $30K, unlocking near-zero tax liability and healthcare expense deduction (over 7.5% of AGI), SALT up to $40,000, and $6,000 senior deduction under the OBBB.

Week 4: Real estate professional status (REP)

Kevin and Rachel's story was a showstopper. Kevin is a surgeon. Rachel manages rentals full-time. They met the REP requirements:

Requirement	Threshold
Time in real estate	750 hours/year
% of total work	More than 50% in real estate
Minimum rental properties	5+ recommended
Materially participate in rental	Regular, continuous, and substantial

Benefit: Unlimited passive loss deductions against Kevin's W-2 income.[6]

We did mock scheduling exercises to help attendees hit the 750-hour mark. I showed them how to group properties, maintain logs, and prepare for IRS scrutiny.[7]

We also covered self-rental strategies, renting property to your own S-Corp business for even more deductions.[8] Attorneys, dentists, therapists in my class lit up when I showed them how to split their practice and real estate for dual savings. Make sure to attach the self-rental election letter to your tax return.

Week 5: 1031 exchange + swap & drop

I wrote on the whiteboard:

"NEVER SELL. ONLY SWAP."

We broke down:

- 45-day property ID window
- 180-day closing deadline
- Role of the Qualified Intermediary (QI)

Then came the swap-and-drop: Keep swapping until you pass, then your heirs get a step-up in basis so no tax is owed. We analyzed a real deal: a $350K condo swapped for a $700K duplex, then swapped again into a $1.2M triplex. The tax savings? Over $140,000 deferred.

Table: 1031 exchange essentials

Element	Rule
Replacement ID Period	45 days after sale
Exchange Completion	180 days after sale
Step-up in Basis	Eliminates deferred gains at inheritance

Week 6: Retirement and AGI planning

We talked about the retiree who used rental losses to drop his AGI below $100,000: unlocking a Roth conversion with a taxable amount fully absorbed by rental losses (up to $25,000).

Flowchart

- Rental Losses → AGI Reduction

- AGI < $100K → Roth Conversion Window

- Roth → Tax-Free Growth → full control of Roth IRA withdrawals regardless of the RMD age requirement → after your death, Roth IRA inherited by your children to enjoy the tax free 10-year distribution.

I also showed how families could purchase rental properties near a college campus: rent to their child with 529 money; paying their child reasonable compensation from property management; and deduct travel costs.

We wrapped up with a case study of a couple living off $60K in rental cash flow but only paying tax on $4,200 due to depreciation and careful income layering.

Final blueprint: Real estate tax playbook

Strategy	Purpose
🏠 1. Cost segregation studies	Accelerate depreciation
🏠 2. Real estate professional status	Convert passive to active losses
🏠 3. Swap-and-drop 1031 exchange	Defer taxes, pass assets tax-free
🏠 4. Bifurcating property deductions	Maximize Schedule A + E benefits
🏠 5. Sales Tax vs. State Tax Choice	Optimize under SALT cap
🏠 6. Home office deductions	Deduct business use from residence
🏠 7. Rental property for college use	Offset child's tuition with deductions
🏠 8. Self-rental	Deduct rent paid to personally-owned assets

🏠 9. Roth conversion using losses	Tax-free retirement funding
🏠 10. Estate planning via real estate	Step-up in basis eliminates capital gains and depreciation recapture. The OBBB raises the lifetime exclusion to $15 million per person, providing more capacity for estate and legacy planning.

Conclusion:

Real estate is not just bricks and rent checks. It is a tax strategy. It is also retirement income and legacy.

With education, planning, and the right tools, anyone can transform their financial life through real estate. Just like I did.

The only thing standing between you and financial freedom is knowing how to play the game.

Here are ten tax planning tips:

RE **1. Deduct mortgage interest on two homes:** Take advantage of IRS rules that allow deductions on two residences. This includes vacation homes or properties gifted to parents, if you retain the mortgage.

RE **2. Bifurcate deductions between Schedule A & E:** When transitioning a primary residence into a rental, claim mortgage interest and taxes on Schedule A before tenants move in, and switch to Schedule E once it is rented out.

RE **3. Substitute sales tax for state tax (SALT cap hack):** If you are limited by the SALT cap (either capped at $40,000 or restricted by a high AGI), choose to deduct sales tax instead of state income tax, especially if you live in a no-income-tax state.

RE **4. Use depreciation to create paper losses:** Even profitable rental properties can show losses on your taxes due to depreciation, significantly reducing your adjusted gross income (AGI).

RE **5. File Form 3115 to catch up on missed depreciation:** If you have failed to take depreciation in the past, Form 3115 lets you claim a large one-time deduction without amending previous returns.

RE **6. Qualify for real estate professional status (REP):** Spending 750+ hours/year on real estate and making it your primary work allows unlimited passive loss deductions, even against spousal W-2 income and other active income.

RE **7. Leverage self-rental for business owners:** Business owners can rent personally owned properties (like offices) to their own businesses, turning rent into a deductible business expense, and using rental losses to offset S Corp profit.

RE **8. Use a 1031 exchange + swap-and-drop to avoid capital gains:** Defer taxes by exchanging properties rather than selling them. Keep swapping until death, and your heirs inherit with a step-up in basis, eliminating tax on decades of gains.

RE **9. Lower AGI to enable tax-free Roth conversions:** Use bonus depreciation and real estate losses to reduce your AGI below $100K, unlocking the ability to convert traditional IRAs into Roth IRAs tax-free at a low 22% tax bracket.

RE **10. Buy college rentals for tax planning:** Use 1031 exchange to near campus rental. Draw 529 money to cover your child's room and board.

🔍 **Tax term:** The **Student Aid Index** (SAI) is a number used by the U.S. Department of Education and colleges to determine a student's financial need when awarding federal student aid. It replaced the Expected Family Contribution (EFC) starting with the 2024–2025 FAFSA.

Chapter 19

How I Turned Math into Money: My Depreciation Masterclass: Cost Segregation Primer

Back in the day, the word "depreciation" made me uneasy. It sounded complicated, like something only CPAs and IRS agents needed to understand. I was wrong—dead wrong.

My breakthrough moment happened at a coffee shop in D.C., sitting across from my accountant, Lisa. I was frustrated. "Lisa," I said, "I am making decent money from my rentals, but my tax bill is still brutal. Is there something I am missing?"

She smiled and pushed a spreadsheet toward me. In bold letters, it read: DEPRECIATION SCHEDULE.[1]

"This," she said, "is your tax superpower."

And she was not exaggerating.

That moment started my journey toward understanding one of the most powerful (and underutilized) tools in real estate: depreciation. And this chapter is my attempt to walk you through that same journey, from confusion to clarity, from fear to relief.

Lesson 1: Not all parts of a property are created equal

I used to think the entire purchase price of a rental property was deductible. But here is the first secret I learned: Land does not depreciate.

When I bought my third property for $400,000, I assumed I could depreciate the full amount. Lisa corrected me: "Check the property tax record. You will usually see land separated from the building. You can only depreciate the structure."

In Fairfax County, VA, the land value on one of my homes turned out to be 20-30% of the total assessed value. That meant only $280,000 of the $400,000 purchase was depreciable—big difference!

> 💡 **Tax tip:** Ask your seller or your county assessor's office for the breakdown of land vs. building value when filing depreciation.

To take it further, I even explored using a land lease trust structure by hiring a good real estate attorney. By creating a trust to hold the land and leasing it to my rental LLC, I turned otherwise non-deductible land into a tax-deductible lease payment.

It takes planning, but when done right, it works.

Lesson 2: The closing statement gold mine

The next big lightbulb came when reviewing my closing documents. "Don't ignore that 100-page closing disclosure," Lisa said. "Some costs go directly to your depreciation base. Others can be deducted immediately."

She pointed out line items like title insurance, escrow fees, and appraisal charges. Some of these went toward my adjusted cost basis, which I would depreciate over time. Others were immediate write-offs.

Today, I tell every investor:

Scan your HUD-1 or CD and ask ChatGPT: "Which of these are capitalizable? Which are deductible?" [2]

Example Table:

Expense	Deduct Now?	Add to Basis?
Appraisal Fee		✓
Title Insurance		✓
Attorney Fee (closing)		✓
Prorated Property Tax	✓	
Survey Fees		✓

Doing this gave me nearly $1,800 in year-one deductions that I would otherwise have missed.

Lesson 3: Unlocking real power with cost segregation

When I discovered **cost segregation**, it felt like finding buried treasure.

Instead of depreciating everything over 27.5 years, I hired a specialist to separate the components into categories:

- **5-year property:** Appliances, carpets, cabinetry (bonus depreciation applicable)

- **15-year improvements:** Landscaping, fences, driveways (bonus depreciation applicable)

- **27.5-year structure:** Walls, foundation, and roof

The first time I did this, I got $52,000 in first-year deductions thanks to bonus depreciation on the 5-year assets. I paid $800 for a desktop cost segregation study, and it paid me back tenfold in tax savings.

> 🔍 **Tax term: Bonus depreciation** is a tax incentive that allows businesses to immediately deduct a large percentage (up to 100%) of the cost of qualifying assets in the year they are placed in service. This accelerates tax deductions, reducing taxable income and lowering the tax liability. [3]

> 💡 **Tax tip:** In 2024, bonus depreciation is 60%, meaning you can write off 60% of 5- and 15-year assets immediately. Bonus depreciation will be permanently set at 100% under OBBB for properties acquired and used in 2025+. Tax filers will enjoy a full bonus depreciation.
>
> **Bonus Tip:** If you are a Real Estate Professional (REP), these losses become active, not passive, allowing you to deduct them against W-2 or business income.

Lesson 4: I forgot to depreciate—now what?

Believe it or not, I forgot to claim depreciation on one of my properties for *four years*.

When I realized the mistake, I thought I was doomed. But my CPA said, "Relax. We will file Form 3115 and catch up all the missed depreciation in one shot."

It worked. I claimed $49,000 in one-time catch-up deductions and avoided amending multiple years of tax returns.

> 💡 **Tax tip:** Always attach a cover letter explaining your intent. "Dear IRS, I forgot to depreciate. Here is my one-time correction." That level of transparency goes a long way.

Lesson 5: Depreciation is a double-edged sword

Depreciation is amazing—until you sell. That is when the IRS shows up with something called depreciation recapture. It says: "You saved money deducting this depreciation. Now we want a piece back."

If you depreciated \$131,000, the IRS can tax that portion of your gain up to 25%.[4]

But here is the trick:

Do not sell at your peak income time. Instead, plan to sell during a gap year, early retirement, or after a job change, when your taxable income is lower and your ordinary tax bracket is below 25%.

Even better? Use a 1031 exchange and defer all taxes by reinvesting into a new property.[5]

Or my favorite strategy: Die with the property and let your heirs inherit it with a step-up in basis. No capital gains. No recapture. Nada. The step-up in basis is a tax provision that adjusts the value (basis) of an inherited asset to its fair market value (FMV) on the date of the original owner's death, which can significantly reduce capital gains tax when the heir sells the asset.

Lesson 6: The stock market tie-in

One year, I had \$100,000 in long-term capital losses from a market dip. That same year, I sold a rental with a \$187,000 gain.

Thanks to the losses, I only paid tax on the net gain: \$87,000. This works especially well when you rebalance your portfolio from RSU, or single-name stocks to S&P 500 index funds.

Lesson: Use stock losses to offset real estate gains strategically.[6]

Another year, I harvested some stock gains to offset prior-year passive rental losses.

Lesson 7: Real estate professional status (REP) is the key to the vault

All the fancy strategies (cost segregation, loss carryforwards, catch-ups) only work their full magic if you are a Real Estate Professional.[7]

To qualify:

- 750+ hours per year on real estate

- More time on real estate than any other job

- Good documentation (logs, schedules)

One year, I grouped my properties into one activity (under IRS guidelines) to pass the test. Then I changed my job title on my tax return: "Occupation: Real Estate Professional."

Lesson 8: Timing the exit strategy

If you do have to sell, work with your CPA and simulate the taxes first.

One couple I worked with was planning to sell a duplex during their highest-income year. I ran the numbers and showed them they would pay \$71,000 in taxes.

I suggested they delay until retirement, when their bracket would drop from 35% to 15%. That one move saved them over $30,000.

> 💡 **Tax tip:** Never rush to sell a property without running a simulation.

Lesson 9: Using AI to decode depreciation

I started uploading closing statements and asking ChatGPT to separate costs into categories:

- Deduct now
- Add to basis
- Amortize over loan period

It was not perfect, but it saved hours of sorting through a 100-line settlement statement. Today, I teach my clients how to use AI to double-check tax software and catch human mistakes.

Lesson 10: Build the habit, reap the rewards

Now, every time I buy a rental, I follow a checklist:

- Get tax assessment split
- Upload closing docs to AI
- Confirm depreciation categories
- Decide on cost segregation
- Update occupation on tax return
- Track REP hours weekly

It sounds tedious, but it is not. It is wealth-building on autopilot.

Final thought:

Depreciation is not just math; it is money. And once you understand it, you will never look at your tax return the same way again.

Real estate offers more than cash flow and appreciation. It offers control. Depreciation is how you legally shift thousands from the IRS's pocket to your own.

You just have to learn the game. And play it smart.

Top ten tax planning tips for this chapter:

1. Separate land from building for accurate depreciation: Only the building portion of your property can be depreciated. Get the land/building value split from your county tax assessment to avoid over- or under-depreciating.

2. Capitalize or deduct closing costs strategically: Some closing costs (e.g., title insurance, survey fees) should be added to basis and depreciated, while others (e.g., appraisal fees, prorated taxes) can be deducted immediately.

3. Use cost segregation to accelerate deductions: Instead of depreciating everything over 27.5 years, identify shorter-life assets (like appliances and landscaping) and use bonus depreciation for big first-year write-offs.

4. File Form 3115 to catch up on missed depreciation: If you forgot to depreciate in prior years, do not panic. Use IRS Form 3115 to catch up all missed deductions at once without amending past returns.

5. Plan around depreciation recapture before selling: When you sell a property, depreciation is "recaptured" and taxed up to 25%. Avoid this by timing the sale in a low-income year or using a 1031 exchange to defer taxes.

6. Offset real estate gains with stock market losses: Use capital losses from stocks to offset taxable gains from real estate sales. This strategy can slash your tax bill if timed well.

7. Qualify as a real estate professional (REP): If you meet the 750-hour rule and spend more time in real estate than any other job, your rental losses become fully deductible against active income like your spouse's W-2 wages.

8. Run tax simulations before selling: Always project your gain, bracket, and depreciation recapture before a property sale. A simple timing change, like waiting until retirement, can save tens of thousands.

9. Use AI to categorize expenses and maximize basis: Upload your settlement statement or closing document to AI tools to sort out which expenses are deductible, capitalizable, or amortizable. This saves time and ensures no line item is wasted.

10. Follow a systematic depreciation checklist: With each purchase, follow a checklist: get your land/building split, analyze closing costs, consider cost segregation, and update your REP logs to stay audit-ready and maximize savings.

Chapter 20

$$\sim\!\!\!\curlyvee\!\!\!\sim$$

REP Changed Everything: How I Made the IRS Work for Me: REP dos and don'ts

I still remember my feeling of frustration on a busy tax season day when I learned I could beat the passive loss rule. [1]

I was staring at my tax return, once again seeing thousands in real estate losses just sitting there, disallowed because of the passive activity rules. My rentals were cash-flowing, but my wife's W-2 income was too high to use those losses.

"Unless you're a real estate professional," Lisa, my CPA said casually.

That was the spark. The phrase sounded official, mysterious, like a title I was not qualified for. But as I started reading, researching, and calling every investor I knew, I realized something: REP status was not just possible. It was attainable.

Once I unlocked that door, the floodgates opened. And what I found behind it was the secret weapon of real estate taxation.

Lesson 1: Four Paths To Escape the Passive Loss Trap

Before REP, I had no idea that rental losses were not always usable. I thought losses just meant refunds. Instead, the IRS treats most rental income as passive, meaning losses are trapped, unless you meet exceptions.

Here is what I uncovered:

1. **Real estate professional (REP):** Lets you convert losses to active if you also materially participate.

2. **Up to $25,000 active participation allowance:** If AGI is under $150,000 (phases out from $100,000) and you materially participate in the rental.

3. **Short-term rentals (Airbnb, VRBO):** Often considered active businesses, and may not follow passive activity rules.

4. **Self-rental**: Renting a property to your own business can make losses deductible against active income.

Choosing REP was not just about taxes. It was about legitimacy. It meant I was taking my real estate operation seriously—as a business.

Lesson 2: 750 Hours and Half Your Life—REP Math 101

I started journaling every hour I spent on real estate. What surprised me was not how hard it was, but how easy it was to lose track.

The IRS requires:

- 750 hours per year in real estate activities
- More than 50% of your total working time in real estate

Here is the kicker: commuting does not count. Education hours do not count. Travel time might not count unless it is directly tied to the work.

So, I restructured my entire workflow. I stopped doing freelance web design. I began managing my rentals completely hands-on. No property manager. No shortcuts—just effort and logs.

Lesson 3: The logbook became my lifeline

At first, I wrote things down on sticky notes and Google Docs. That got messy quickly.

Then I switched to a proper logging spreadsheet with:[2]

- Property address
- Task type
- Time spent
- Date and time
- Proof (receipts, texts, calendar entries)

I used the MileIQ app for mileage, and Google Calendar for activity history. Every month, I exported everything into a folder labeled "REP Audit Ready."

"You do not prepare your taxes. You prepare for your audit."

That quote became my mantra.

Lesson 4: Do Not Trigger the Red Flags

My tax advisor sat me down and said, "There are red flags that instantly trigger an audit defense."[3]

Here is the list we built together:

- W-2 job that is clearly full-time, yet claiming 750 REP hours

- Property management companies handling all your units
- No receipts, no travel logs, no lease agreements [4]
- Logging time for "thinking" or "research"

So, I adjusted. I cut hours from my tech gig and started self-managing two new properties. I created folders for every tenant file, lease, maintenance invoice, and repair log.

My motto became: "If you can't prove it, you didn't do it."

Lesson 5: The Grouping Election that Saved Me

After claiming REP status, my CPA called me one day in April. "You filed as a REP, but you didn't file a grouping election."

My stomach dropped.

The IRS assumes each property is a separate activity unless you elect to treat them as one. Without the election, I could not meet material participation hours across all of them. [5]

So, I fixed it just in time. Now I file this with every return:

> **Tax tip:** Attach an election cover letter to your tax return:
>
> "Pursuant to Treasury Reg §1.469-9(g), I elect to treat all interests in rental real estate as a single activity."

Simple sentence—lifesaver.

Lesson 6: Married Filing Strategically—The Spouse Hack

My wife did not work a W-2 job, but she was smart, organized, and better at managing tenants than I ever was.

We sat down and planned it: she would become the REP.

She tracked her hours. Took calls. Handled cleanings. Supervised landscaping. Filed everything into our Google Drive system.

Because we file jointly, her REP status let us deduct $47,000 in passive losses against my business income that year.

> **Tax tip:** Only one spouse needs to qualify for REP if you file jointly. He or she does not need to be a licensed real estate agent or broker. You do not have to claim REP each year. Use this to your advantage.

Lesson 7: Traveling Smart = Deducting Wisely

I love to travel. But I also learned the IRS loves to ask questions.[6]

So, when I fly to Miami to visit my rental there, I:

- Schedule inspections and repairs in advance

- Book meetings with my property insurance agent

- Snap photos of the property both inside and outside

- Attend local real estate meet-up meetings

- Save all receipts and emails

Now my trips serve double duty: rest and deduction, but only because I document everything.

Lesson 8: REP + Cost Seg = Tax Firepower

The year I did my first cost segregation study. I saved more than I made: a $420,000 rental produced a $114,000 paper loss in year one thanks to bonus depreciation. Because I was a REP, it offset every dollar of my other income. I reinvested that tax refund into another down payment. Rinse and repeat.

Lesson: REP status transforms paper losses into real tax refunds.

Lesson 9: Audit-Proofing with Purpose

Every January 1, I:

- Rebuild my time log template for the new year

- Review last year's entries for gaps

- Reorganize receipts into property folders

- Check grouping election language

- Recertify my REP strategy with my CPA

I also do a dry run: "What would I show an IRS agent if they called today?" The more I treat my rentals like a business, the less I worry about audits.

Lesson 10: What I Teach Every Client Now

REP is not for dabblers. It is for real estate professionals who treat this like their livelihood. When you do so, it rewards you with tax sheltering powers most people cannot imagine.

If you are thinking about it:

- Log every hour, every week

- Audit your own records quarterly

- Build a repeatable system

- File your grouping election on time

- Use apps, folders, and real advisors

And most importantly: do not wait until tax time to start acting like a pro.

Final Thought:

REP status is not just a tax designation. It is a business model.

Once you qualify, the tax code opens wide. You are no longer at the mercy of the passive loss rules. You control the timing, the deductions—and ultimately, the game.

And when that control kicks in, so does the confidence.

Do not fear the IRS: instead, outlog them.

Here are ten end-of-chapter tax planning tips based on your expanded REP status chapter:

1. Qualify for REP to convert passive losses to active: If you spend 750+ hours and more than 50% of your working time on real estate activities, you can deduct rental losses against W-2 or business income, unlocking massive tax savings.

2. Always file a grouping election: To combine time across multiple properties, you must file an election (under Reg. §1.469-9(g)) with your tax return. Without it, each property is treated separately, and you may fail the material participation test.

3. Keep detailed, contemporaneous time logs: Track your hours as you go, not after the fact. Use spreadsheets, calendar entries, or time-tracking apps, and include dates, property names, tasks, and supporting evidence like receipts and emails.

4. Avoid IRS red flags: Do not claim REP if you:

- Have a full-time unrelated job

- Use a property manager

- Lack documented hours

- Fail to match activity with mileage or expenses

Stay proactive and audit-proof your status.

5. Leverage REP as a couple: If filing jointly, only one spouse needs to qualify for REP status. This allows high-income households to use passive losses to offset active income from the working spouse.

6. Strategically deduct business travel: Travel to inspect or manage your rentals can be deductible if you document the business purpose. Keep receipts, create a trip itinerary, and log miles and expenses.

7. Stack REP with cost segregation studies: Use REP status to unlock full benefits of cost segregation and bonus depreciation. Losses that would otherwise be suspended become immediately deductible against your non-passive income.

8. Conduct an annual REP self-audit: Each January:

- Review logs and hours

- Verify you still meet REP thresholds

- Check for any gaps or audit risks

- Ensure grouping elections are filed (this annual review keeps you compliant and prepared)

9. Treat REP Like a business designation

Change your mindset. REP is not just a tax box; it is a business role. Update your occupation on your tax return if applicable: treat real estate like your primary trade.

10. Build a REP binder

Create a folder (physical or digital) with:

- Hour logs

- Receipts

- Tenant files

- Grouping election letter

- Travel logs

- Lease agreements

This is your IRS audit defense kit.

Chapter 21

Real Estate Answers I Wish I Knew Earlier

I did not always have answers. When I bought my first rental, I was googling terms like "depreciation" and "report cash rent." I wish someone had handed me a guide: something real, not generic tax code jargon.

That is what this is—my journey, shaped around 40 questions I have been asked as a CPA (and asked myself). I have lived these lessons. Paid for a few mistakes. Earned the rest with experience. Let us walk through them together.

1. What are the main tax advantages of owning rental properties?

I call real estate "the legal cheat code" of the tax system. Between depreciation, mortgage interest deductions, and a 1031 exchange, I shaved tens of thousands off my tax bill—while my W-2 friends paid full freight.

It is not just about avoiding taxes. It is about shifting how you earn, how you grow wealth, and how you protect it.

2. How does depreciation impact my tax liability?

The first year I claimed depreciation, I was confused why my tax software said I had a "loss" when I made money every month. Then I realized: depreciation lets you deduct phantom losses—**tax savings without losing cash.**

That is when I started to fall in love with spreadsheets.

3. What is the deal with passive vs. active income?

One year I could not use my losses. The next year, I qualified as a **real estate professional**—and suddenly, those losses wiped out my freelance income. Understanding the IRS's income buckets changed how I managed time, filings, and strategy.

4. Can I deduct rental losses against W-2 income?

Only if you meet any of the three tests: (1) your income is under $150K, (2) you conduct a short-term rental; or (3) you qualify as a REP. I missed this my first two years. Now, I structure everything—time logs, spouse roles, and tax plans—so I can use every dollar of loss.

5. Is cost segregation worth it?

I paid $1,200 for my first study. It gave me $48,000 in bonus depreciation. That refund funded the down payment on my next property. Easy answer: *yes*.

6. What are the biggest tax mistakes I have made?

I've:

- Misclassified improvements as repairs.

- Lost receipts.

- Forgot to depreciate a property for three years.

Mistakes happen. But good systems (and learning from FAQs like this) help avoid them next time.

7. What expenses can I deduct as a landlord?[1]

Everything from insurance to landscaping, management fees, utilities, and professional services. The key? *Track everything.* I use Neat Receipt, and keep digital folders by property and year.

8. Schedule E or Schedule C?[2]

I once used Schedule C for a long-term rental. Red flag. The IRS expects Schedule E unless you are operating like a hotel (short-term rentals + substantial services). I amended my return and learned to keep it clean and clear.

9. What is a repair vs. an improvement?[3]

A repair fixes a problem that already occurred. An improvement upgrades the property or prevents a problem. I keep a cheat sheet in my tax binder and check every invoice before I file.

Rule of thumb: If it lasts more than a year or adds value, it is likely an improvement.

10. Can I deduct travel for my rentals?

Yes—but only if it is primarily *for business*. I used to snap photos of inspection visits, email contractors ahead of trips, and print Zillow screenshots to prove intent. Keep a mileage log. Save boarding passes. It adds up.

11. What triggers audits?[4]

Red flags include:

- Huge travel deductions

- No reported rental income

- Inconsistent forms

- REP claims without logs

I do not fear the IRS—but I prepare for them like a client meeting.

12. How do I avoid audits?

Three rules:

1. Do not be sloppy.

2. Do not be greedy.

3. Do not be vague.

I keep folders labeled by year, property, and deduction type. I also do a "mock audit" every January.

13. Best way to keep records?

Go digital.[5] I use the NEAT Receipt app to scan and save into the cloud (by type of expense). NEAT App has a set of predefined expense types (such as car, medical, charity, travel, and more). You can create your own expenses as well. Monthly folder. Auto backups. No more shoeboxes.

14. TurboTax desktop or online?

Desktop, always. It is more powerful, more customizable, and has better audit support. I use it every year—and export backups just in case.

15. What's REP and why does it matter?

Real Estate Professional status saved me more money than any investment course. It lets rental losses offset **active income**. If you qualify, it is the key to unlocking massive deductions. [6]

🔍 **Tax term: Active income** refers to income that is not from a passive activity or from portfolio sources. Active income is subject to Federal Insurance Contributions Act (FICA) and Medicare taxes. It typically includes:

- Wages, salaries, and other compensation for personal services;
- Income from a trade or business in which the taxpayer materially participates; and
- Income from self-employment.

---

16. How do I report a sale?

You will need Form 4797 and Schedule D.[7] Track your depreciation, adjust your basis, and calculate gains. The first time I did it myself, I spent six hours—but learned more than any book could teach me.

17. What's depreciation recapture?

It is the IRS saying, "We gave you a break—now we want some of it back." When you sell, the depreciation you have claimed is taxed up to 25%. That is why timing your sale—or doing a 1031—is critical. Pick the right time to sell your rental when your marginal tax bracket is 10%, 12% or 22%. Otherwise delay the taxable gain with a 1031 exchange.

18. What is a 1031 exchange?

It is like rolling your profits forward **tax-free**. I did one in 2022, trading a 3-unit into a 6-unit. No tax owed, bigger cash flow. Just make sure you follow the 45- and 180-day rules.

19. Short-term vs. long-term capital gains?

If you buy a stock, hold it for a year. That's it. Holding longer turns a 35% tax into 15% or 20%. This one rule has saved me thousands. A better way is never sell: use the buy, borrow, and build approach to let your securities compound forever.

20. What if I have no receipts?

Log everything you can. Reconstruct with emails, text messages, social media posting, calendar events, bank statements, or credit card statements. It is not ideal, but it is better than silence. I once rebuilt an entire year using Venmo screenshots and Google Maps history. Remember: credit card statements alone do not constitute a valid record in the eyes of the IRS auditor.

21. Can I deduct home office expenses as a landlord?

Yes! It is more powerful than you might think.

When I first started managing my rentals from the dining room table, I did not realize I was missing out on a legitimate deduction. Then I learned that if you use a specific part of your home exclusively and regularly for managing rentals such as filing paperwork, doing bookkeeping, and scheduling repairs, you can deduct a portion of your home expenses. Any mixed-use space would disqualify.

That includes:

- Utilities

- Insurance

- Mortgage interest

- Internet and phone (partial)

The square footage rule means you deduct the percentage of your home used for business. If you have a 321-square-foot office in a 2,610-square-foot home, that is 12.3% of your bills, deductible (321 divided by 2,610 equals approximately 12.3%).

I now have a designated "landlord HQ" in my spare room: with a locked file cabinet, a desk, and proof in photos and calendar logs.

22. Should I own rental property in my name or through an LLC?

This is one of the most misunderstood questions in real estate.

When I started, everything was in my name. Then I got nervous: "What if someone sues me?"

LLCs offer liability protection, only if structured properly. If a tenant sues for a slip-and-fall, your LLC can shield your personal assets. But here is the truth:

- For single-member LLCs (reported in Schedule C), tax filing is almost the same as owning it personally.

- You must maintain financial information separate from your personal account: bank accounts, credit card statements and purchase receipts.

- Transferring property to an LLC after purchase can trigger transfer taxes in some states. Rentals under an LLC may complicate a future-year 1031 exchange. Some states charge high annual fees for an LLC.

I use LLCs only when the equities are over a large amount (such as $500,000), but I set them up before closing and insure each one properly (such as tenant insurance and umbrella insurance). And I talk to my CPA and attorney before making any structural changes.

23. How do I handle ownership changes in an LLC?

I learned this the hard way.

When my partner wanted out of our duplex deal, we updated the operating agreement but forgot to file new ownership records with the state. That caused a reporting issue at tax time.

Here is what to do:

- Amend your operating agreement immediately.

- Notify your Secretary of State.

- Update your EIN records with the IRS (use Form 8822-B).

- Issue the right K-1s if it is a multi-member LLC.

Even if no money changes hands, document everything as if it did: paper trails protect you.

24. What is a self-directed IRA and can I use it to invest in real estate?

Yes…but it comes with a maze of rules.

A self-directed IRA lets you invest your retirement savings in alternative assets, including real estate. But you cannot:

- Live on the property

- Let relatives use it

- Pay yourself or your business to manage it

I opened one to buy a vacant lot, then had to learn that every expense, including property repairs and taxes, had to be paid from the IRA. Every deposit had to go back into it—no shortcuts.

It is powerful, but it is not for beginners. Use a custodian who understands real estate rules.

> **Tax tip:** A **Self-Directed IRA (SDIRA)** can unlock powerful tax-deferred (traditional) or tax-free (Roth) growth on alternative investments (such as real estate, private companies, precious metals (like gold), cryptocurrency, tax liens, and private lending (notes, loans)). Be aware of the IRS penalties for prohibited transactions and high fees by some SDIRA custodians.

Using a self-directed IRA to buy rentals has a few unexpected consequences: (1) your time spent on the rental cannot count toward the 750 hour requirement as a real estate professional; (2) bonus depreciation becomes less useful because of the tax-deferral nature of your IRA; and (3) Roth conversion becomes infeasible if you worry about the RMD requirement.

25. How do I pay state income tax on rental income?

Owning properties in multiple states means multiple returns.

Each state wants a slice of the income earned within its borders. For example, I live in Virginia but own rentals in Florida and Maryland.

- Florida has no state income tax.

- Maryland requires a nonresident return and local income tax.

- Virginia still wants a full return, with credit for taxes paid to other states.

I use professional tax software and file electronically for each state. If you are managing multi-state income, get a pro to help the first time.

26. What is the homestead exemption and do I qualify? [8]

Your primary residence can save you money every year through property tax exemptions.

In Texas, Florida, Georgia, and many other states, you can file a homestead exemption to:

- Reduce your assessed value

- Cap future increases

- Protect against creditors (in some states)

You must:

- Live on the property as your primary home

- File the exemption form (once or annually, depending on the state)

Rentals do not qualify. But remember to claim this on your new homes.

27. How do I calculate my real estate tax bill?

Your bill = assessed value × tax rate.

That sounds simple, but localities add:

- Special district taxes

- Local surcharges

- School district taxes

I use my county's online property tax estimator tool, check my annual assessment, and appeal it if I think it is too high. In 2023, I won a reassessment challenge that lowered my tax bill by $1,300.

Never just accept your bill. Check it. Challenge it. Know what you are paying for.

28. What is the difference between a primary residence and rental for taxes?

Your primary residence lets you:

- Deduct mortgage interest

- Exclude capital gains on sale (up to $260K single / $500K married)

- Claim the homestead exemption

Rentals allow:

- Depreciation

- More extensive business expense deductions

- Loss carryforwards (mostly long-term rental; short-term rental losses are deducted in the current year).

When you convert a primary to a rental, you start depreciating it at the adjusted basis value. And if you move back as a primary residence before selling, you may complicate the Section 121 capital gain exclusion.

Track use. Document everything. Treat each year correctly.

29. Can I deduct HOA fees and bank fees for rentals?

Absolutely.

If the expense is for your rental property, it is deductible. That includes:

- HOA dues

- Loan servicing fees

- Monthly maintenance charges

I once missed $800 in bank fees across three properties because they were not categorized correctly in my software. Now I review every fee monthly.

It is your money; do not give it away by accident.

30. What is the passive activity loss limitation?

The IRS says you cannot deduct rental losses against active income unless:

- Your income is below $150K (phases out from $100K)

- Or you qualify as a Real Estate Professional (REP)

Otherwise, losses carry forward until:

- You sell the property

- Or generate enough passive income to offset them

I now track my carryforwards on Form 8582 each year. They add up like a bank account, and become incredibly useful when I sell. When you change your CPA, make sure to tell him/her your current carryforward loss amount.

31. How do I track passive losses year to year?

The first time I sold a property, I had $28,000 in suspended losses I had forgotten about. Luckily, my accountant was on it and used Form 8582 to claim them all in one shot.

Now, I treat passive loss tracking like a savings account. Every year I:

- Update my passive loss worksheet

- Reconcile it with my tax return

- Label carryforwards by property

This helps me plan future sales and know which properties hold the biggest "tax refunds in waiting." Do not let those numbers go stale. Log them like you would your bank balances.

32. What is the best bookkeeping practice for landlords?

After years of Excel, shoeboxes, and forgetting to log mileage, I finally got serious.

I moved to the NEAT Receipt app and later paired it with QuickBooks Self-Employed for some short-term rentals. Now, I:

- Link each property to a separate bank account

- Reconcile monthly

- Save scanned receipts to Google Drive by property/year

I do a 10-minute review every Friday. And once a month, I run a "Profit & Loss Review" on each property. Good bookkeeping does not just save you time at tax season but it helps you make smarter investment decisions year-round. In addition, pay your teenage child $15 an hour to organize the business records for you, a wise business practice to teach and coach your child.

33. Can I deduct legal and professional fees?

Yes! If you are not doing this, you are overpaying the IRS.

I deduct fees paid to:

- Attorneys (lease reviews, evictions, contracts)

- CPAs and enrolled agents

- Bookkeepers

- Property managers and consultants

These fees are fully deductible if they are related to rental activity or real estate business. I once even deducted Zoom consultations with a 1031 exchange specialist—and yes, I saved the receipts.

34. What is the difference between repairs and capital improvements for tax purposes?

Repairs = deductible now. Improvements = depreciated over years.

But that line can be blurry.

So I created a rule-of-thumb flowchart for myself:

- Did I restore the original function? → Repair → Schedule E

- Did I upgrade beyond original value? → Improvement → Form 4562 with basis add-on

- Did I spend money with a blended nature? → Split into repair and improvement with a reasonable estimate

Example: Fixing a broken water heater = repair. Replacing it with a tankless, energy-efficient model = improvement.

Always label your invoices clearly. Write notes. Take before/after photos. If audited, I want my receipts to tell the story for me.

35. How do I handle rental property in multiple states?

At one point, I had rentals in Virginia (VA), Florida (FL), and North Carolina (NC).

Every year, I had to:

- File a nonresident return in NC

- Skip state tax in FL (no income tax!)

- File a full-year VA return and claim credits for taxes paid elsewhere

Pro tip: Get familiar with each state's e-file portal and recordkeeping expectations. In NC, I had to include lease summaries as part of a local tax assessment.

I use a spreadsheet called "State Split Tracker" with tabs for income, expenses, withholding, and estimated payments per state.

36. What are the tax implications of converting a primary residence to a rental?

When I moved out of my old townhouse and started renting it, I learned a valuable tax lesson:

Your depreciation schedule starts on the adjusted basis at the date of conversion, not the original purchase price.

Also:

- You may still qualify for the Section 121 gain exclusion if you sell within 3 years of moving out.

- You must switch from Schedule A deductions to Schedule E. If you move out in the middle of the year, split the taxes and mortgage interest pro rata into Schedule A and E.

I had my property appraised before converting. I also noted the exact date of change in use: with calendar logs, lease signing, and a mileage entry for the move-out.

37. Can I deduct insurance premiums for my rental property?

Absolutely. And it is more than just homeowners' insurance.

Here is what I deduct:

- Landlord policies (dwelling, liability)

- Umbrella liability covering rentals

- Flood insurance (when required)

- Business property riders

Just make sure that the policy is clearly associated with the rental, not your personal residence.

If it covers multiple properties, I allocate the premium proportionally by unit or square footage.

38. What is audit insurance and should I get it?

After hearing about a fellow landlord's $6,000 audit defense bill, I investigated IRS audit insurance, a policy that covers professional fees if you are audited.

I now carry it through my tax preparer. It does not cover extra taxes owed, but it does:

- Cover CPA or EA representation

- Help during IRS correspondence audits

- Provide peace of mind

For complex returns or REP claims, I think it is worth it. Just read the fine print: some plans have limits or exclusions for late filings.

39. How do I handle rental income if I have no receipts?

It has happened to me. A cash-paying tenant, a lost rent book, and a missing phone.

Here is what I did:

- Reconstructed payments using text messages and bank deposits

- Created a new digital rent ledger

- Wrote an affidavit summarizing payments

You must report all income, even cash. And you must do your best to document it. If audited, intentional omission = fraud, but honest reconstruction + documentation = survivable.

40. What are the most important lessons for continuous improvement in real estate tax filing?

Every year, I get better. And every year, I find a new mistake to avoid.

Here is my formula:

- Use the right tools (bookkeeping, cloud storage, and mileage tracker)

- Schedule a quarterly tax review, not just April panic

- Treat tax time like a business audit

- Create a "Lessons Learned" document every year with missed deductions, log gaps, or new ideas

I also take one course or seminar each year on real estate tax planning. The tax code changes. But my mindset stays the same:

Treat this like a business. File like a CFO. Think like the IRS.

Case Study 4

Real Estate Strategies

"The Tax-Smart Family: How Michael, Michelle, Jenny, and Justine Turned Everyday Life into Big Tax Wins"

Purpose of this case study

This case study illustrates how a family of four—Michael, Michelle, Jenny, and Justine—leveraged everyday decisions to unlock powerful tax advantages. By applying proactive planning, careful documentation, and strategic use of the tax code, they transformed routine family and business activities into opportunities for wealth building and multigenerational financial security. The goal is to provide practical, actionable insights for families seeking to maximize tax savings and turn ordinary life into extraordinary financial outcomes.

Situation

Michael and Michelle were a hardworking couple living in Virginia. Michael was a full-time realtor and entrepreneur. Michelle was a healthcare manager who dabbled in real estate rentals on the side. Their two daughters, Jenny (17) and Justine (19), were active, ambitious young women just beginning their adult lives.

Together, the family embarked on a journey not just to build wealth—but to play the tax game like pros.

Tasks

Here is how their real-life scenarios unfolded.

1. Michael and Michelle's rental property: The $2,450 HVAC question

Fact: Michelle needed a new HVAC system for her rental property.

Situation: Should they depreciate the HVAC over seven years—or expense it immediately?

Action: Michael advised using the *de minimis* safe harbor election because the item was under $2,500 per invoice.

Tax Result: Immediate full deduction under IRS safe harbor rules.

2. Jenny's teen labor: Helping the family rentals

Fact: Jenny, 17, helped the family business with property maintenance and recordkeeping.

Situation: They wanted to pay her fairly and teach real-world responsibility.

Action: Michael paid Jenny $25/hour for real work performed, logging her hours carefully.

Tax Result: Deductible on Schedule E as "outside labor"; advised to align pay rate closer to market norms.

3. Jenny's big move: Opening a Roth IRA

Fact: Jenny wanted to invest her earned income.

Situation: Could a 17-year-old open a Roth IRA?

Action: Michelle helped Jenny open a Roth IRA based on her W-2 earnings.

Tax Result: Roth IRA established legally; future tax-free growth locked in.

4. Deducting Jenny's work on Schedule E

Fact: The family needed to categorize Jenny's compensation correctly.

Situation: Could Jenny receive a 1099-NEC rather than a W-2?

Action: Deducted labor cost under "Outside Labor" on Schedule E. Issued a 1099-NEC if Jenny was 18+ and the payment was over $2,000.

Tax Result: Reduced rental income, legally minimizing taxes.

5. Michelle's business trip to NYC

Fact: Michelle traveled to NYC for expos, meetups, and visiting Justine.

Situation: Could she deduct her travel expenses?

Action: Anchored trip with business events on Friday, Monday, and Tuesday.

Tax Result: Most meals (50%), transportation, and hotels were deductible; personal sightseeing not deductible.

6. Michael's Tesla decision: Mileage vs. Actual expenses

Fact: Michael bought a Tesla Model Y for real estate work.

Action: After trial tracking, he chose the actual expenses method.

Tax Result: Higher deductions achieved with stricter recordkeeping required.

7. Michelle's backyard storage solution

Fact: Michelle stored rental supplies at home.

Action: Deducted shed-related costs as direct rental management expenses.

Tax Result: Full deduction without claiming the risky home office deduction.

8. Michelle's beach house: Mortgage and property tax questions

Fact: Michelle owned both a primary home and a Delaware rental.

Action: Allocated mortgage interest and property taxes carefully.

Tax Result: Partial deductions due to $750K mortgage limit and $10K SALT cap with AGI over $600,000.

9. Debra's business parties inspiring Michelle

Fact: Debra hosted business networking parties through her LLC.

Action: Michael and Michelle decided to follow a similar structure for client appreciation events.

Tax Result: Meals (50%) and venue rentals were deductible if structured through the LLC and documented.

10. Justine's flipping dreams

Fact: Justine planned to flip houses post-graduation.

Action: CPA advised setting up an LLC taxed as an S-Corp when profitable ($40,000+/year).

Tax Result: Avoided treating flips as passive and instead treated them as active business with self-employment tax planning.

Family tax lessons: Michael, Michelle, Jenny, and Justine's playbook

Topic	What They Did	Tax Outcome
HVAC expense	Used *de minimis* election	Immediate $2,450 deduction
Hiring teen labor	Paid Jenny for real work	Deductible labor + funded Roth IRA
NYC trip	Anchored with business days	Deducted meals, hotels, and transportation
Tesla use	Chose actual expense method	Higher deductions with strong records

Storage for rentals	Deducted as direct expense	No risky home office claim needed
Vacation home	Allocated interest and taxes	Partial deductions under new tax laws
Client events	LLC-routed business parties	Meals/venue deductible with proof
House flipping	Justine plans S-Corp setup	Minimized future SE tax

Closing reflection

The SMART Family did not just live ordinary lives. They planned. They documented fiercely. They treated everyday moves like business moves. And because of that, they did not just protect their income. They built a multigenerational advantage.

PART 5

SMART FAMILY FOUNDATION

Chapter 22

Building Our Family Foundation: How We Turned Giving into a Legacy of Love, Leadership, and Lasting Impact

It was a crisp autumn evening in Berry's Ferry, Virginia. While the leaves outside our kitchen window blazed red and gold, something even more beautiful was taking root inside.

Over dinner, my wife Olga, who had always had a heart for service, looked up thoughtfully and said, *"I wonder how much wealth we will leave behind to our children, and how much to the charities I love in my lifetime."*

The kids— Sasha (12), Kevin (14), and Olesia (18)—paused, forks mid-air. A flicker of curiosity passed between them.

And just like that, with one question, a seed was planted that would grow into something bigger than any of us: The SMART Family Foundation.

The Spark: A Legacy Beyond Wealth

I explained to them: *"Money fades. Businesses close. Fame passes. But impact... impact can ripple for generations."*

We were not just talking about leaving a few donations in our wills. We were talking about building a living, breathing legacy, one that would:

- Fund education for children who dreamed big but lacked resources.

- Support environmental projects to heal the planet Olga loved.

- Provide seed capital to help young entrepreneurs bring their ideas to life.

- Nurture art and beauty, passions that flowed through Sasha's creative heart.

And yes! Along the way, we would gain serious tax advantages. But this was bigger than taxes. This was about purpose.

Step 1: The Birth of a Foundation [1]

That very week, we rolled up our sleeves:

- We filed our Articles of Incorporation at the state level.
- We drafted our mission statement—together—over hot cocoa at the kitchen table.
- We submitted our IRS Form 1023-EZ application for 501(c)(3) status. [2]
- We built bylaws, elected a board (ourselves, at first), and chose a simple, memorable name: "The SMART Family Foundation." [3]

There was something sacred about those early meetings. Each decision, each signature, felt like laying a stone in a cathedral that would stand long after we were gone.

We were not just setting up a tax vehicle. We were setting up a family covenant—an agreement across generations to use our blessings wisely.

Step 2: Strategic Moves: The Power of Smart Giving

Lisa, our trusted CPA, guided us through some brilliant first moves:

1. Donate appreciated assets, not cash 4

Instead of writing checks, we gifted appreciated stocks (shares that had grown in value over the years).

- We avoided paying capital gains tax.
- The foundation sold the stock tax-free.
- We got a full fair-market-value deduction, up to 20% of our AGI.

That first year alone, we saved nearly $42,000 in combined federal and state taxes, just by being smarter with how we gave. Another tax benefit is that we brought down the marginal tax bracket from 32% to 24% so that we did a $50,000 Roth conversion at the 24% tax rate when the stock market dropped suddenly due to the Russia-Ukraine war. Smart move!

2. Plan around high-income years

We funded the foundation heavily in years when my business boomed, strategically reducing our taxable income and shifting ourselves into a lower bracket.

3. Create a "giving pipeline"

Rather than scrambling to give big donations every December 31st, we gave steadily to the foundation, which could then distribute grants carefully, thoughtfully, over many years. [5]

It was philanthropy on our terms, not Uncle Sam's. The heart of the foundation was family leadership. Here's where things got magical:

Each child claimed a corner of the mission.

- Olesia designed the scholarship program: setting application criteria, forming selection committees, even writing personal letters to winners.

- Kevin spearheaded the Young Entrepreneurs Fund: offering microgrants to local teens starting businesses.

- Sasha launched the Arts Alive Initiative: funding supplies, exhibits, and performance spaces for underserved young artists.

They did not just give away money but; they built programs, negotiated, and debated. They were trained to listen, learn, and lead.

Family meetings became board meetings. Disagreements became lessons in governance and diplomacy. Wins were celebrated together, tears wiped together, and dreams dreamed together.

It was not just charity. It was family bonding at its deepest, finest level.

Step 3: Trials by Fire and what the IRS Taught Us

Of course, it was not all smooth sailing.

⚠ The 5% distribution rule

Every year, we had to distribute at least 5% of the foundation's assets for charitable purposes. That included grants and administrative expenses. It meant we had to plan, not procrastinate.

⚠ The self-dealing trap

We learned (almost the hard way) that granting scholarships to a family member by the foundation was forbidden. Thank goodness, Lisa caught us before we signed anything. [6]

⚠ The paper trail

Every grant required meticulous documentation: Minutes, resolutions, receipts, and reports.

At first, it felt overwhelming. But over time, it taught us something powerful: True stewardship demands true diligence.

Step 4: The Silent Benefits We Never Expected

We entered into this for charity. What we got back was more than we ever imagined:

- **Confidence** blossomed in our children.

- **Financial literacy** deepened across the family.

- **Leadership skills** were honed, tested, and matured.

- **Global perspective** expanded as we funded refugee aid, environmental efforts, and more.

- **Family unity** grew stronger every quarter, every grant.

The foundation became our family's North Star: a reminder that life is not just about making money. It is about making meaning.

Step 5: Growing Wealth, Growing Purpose

Meanwhile, the financial benefits compounded:

💗 Our foundation's investments grew tax-free.

🤍 We paid just a tiny 1.39% excise tax on investment income.

🤍 Our estate size shrank (in a good way), lowering future estate taxes.

💗 Strategic donations offset Roth IRA conversions, maximizing our future tax-free income.

It was not just about saving taxes. It was about multiplying our impact.

Step 6: Our Family Foundation Playbook and Lessons Learned

Here is the expanded SMART Family Foundation blueprint: [7]

✔ Donate appreciated stock, not cash: Maximize deductions, avoid capital gains.

✔ Plan giving around income surges: Lower your taxable income when it matters most.

✔ Create a clear, inspiring mission: Everyone needs a "why."

✔ Involve every generation early: Kids, grandkids—everyone has a seat at the table.

✔ Build a pipeline, not a panic: Fund the foundation steadily; grant thoughtfully.

✔ Document everything meticulously: IRS loves good records.

✔ Prepare for succession now, not later: Leadership doesn't magically appear—it's trained.

✔ Think globally, act locally: Fund projects that matter both nearby and far away.

✔ Stay squeaky clean on self-dealing rules: The risk isn't worth it.

✔ Celebrate the wins often: Gratitude fuels the mission.

Our final reflection poem: *"What Legacy Really Means"*

When I see Olesia speaking at a scholarship dinner...
When I hear Kevin coaching a young entrepreneur...
When I see Sasha painting a mural funded by our grants...
I realize something profound:

We did not just create a family foundation.
We created a family tradition.
A way of living.
A way of giving.

One that will outlive us all.

One that will inspire us to do more.

When we build a family foundation, we are not just saving taxes.

We are building dreams. We are building the best practices.

Top 15 Family Foundation Tax Strategies

Strategy	Benefit
1. Donate appreciated stocks	Avoids capital gains, full FMV deduction
2. Fund in high-income years	Lowers AGI, lower tax brackets
3. Maximize 30% AGI limits	Gets full deduction benefit (up to 20% AGI if donating stocks)
4. Use lower tax bracket for Roth conversions	Lowers taxable income first
5. Invest for tax-free growth	Maximizes asset expansion
6. Keep meticulous records	Stays IRS-compliant and audit-proof
7. Pay reasonable salaries to family members	Tax-efficient wealth building by setting up Roth 401(k) with employer matching
8. Avoid self-dealing at all costs	Protects tax-exempt status
9. Think multi-generational	Trains future leadership
10. Celebrate small wins	Builds family morale
11. Fund international and domestic causes	Expands global outreach and influence
12. Integrate charitable planning with estate planning	Lowers future estate taxes
13. Carry over excess distributions	Builds a buffer for down years
14. Diversify foundation investments	Balances growth and liquidity
15. Lead with love and purpose	Keeps the true mission alive

Chapter 23

Hearts That Give–How to Turn Charitable Giving into a Legacy of Hope

It was a gray Sunday afternoon when it happened. Olesia, our eldest, was gluing posters for her youth group's disaster relief fundraiser. With the increased natural disasters caused by global warming and climate change, my family paid more attention to the struggling families thousands of miles away.

I asked myself if any of these actions changed anything. But when I saw Olesia looking happy and purposeful after the fundraising project, I realized that these contributions were a force for the better.

In that moment, I saw everything. The confusion. The hope. The yearning to believe that kindness mattered.

That single question launched a new chapter in our family's story, one where giving was not just spare change in a jar. It became an act of legacy. We did not just learn how to give.

We learned how to give intelligently, intentionally, and enduringly. This chapter tells that story—and shows you how to build your own.

Step 1: Giving is Not Charity—It is Engineering Hope.

We sat down at the kitchen table that night with the kids. No lectures. No guilt trips. Just real talk.

So how do we give?

- Because disasters do not ask permission.
- Because trauma leaves scars deeper than burnt homes.
- Because even when governments fail, communities rise.
- Because money is temporary, but kindness echoes forever.

We framed giving not as a loss, but as an investment—an investment in healing, dignity, and human possibility.

Key Mindset: You are not losing money when you give. You are planting hope—and hope multiplies.

Step 2: The Two Kinds of Giving—Why Only One Changes the World

Our family attorney taught us something profound:

- Emotional giving feels good, but often fades fast.

- Strategic giving changes lives permanently.

- Pledged giving transforms a community by improving itself year after year.

We decided to give differently: [1]

🤍 Focus on verified nonprofits (IRS 501(c)(3)s).
🤍 Prioritize groups with boots-on-the-ground operations.
🤍 Support causes aligned with our family's values (education, youth empowerment, disaster relief).

Every donation became a vote for the kind of world we wanted to build.

Key Shift: Give not just where your heart breaks, but where your values live.

Step 3: How Disasters Taught Us Precision Giving

When the Los Angeles wildfires devastated thousands, emotions ran high. Our phones buzzed with crowdfunding links, donation pleas, and heartbreaking images.

It was tempting to send money anywhere. But we paused and asked:

- Was the organization IRS verified?

- How much of our dollar would reach victims?

- Was there transparency in how funds were distributed?

We donated through: [2]

🤍 Chinese American Parent Association – Northern Virginia (CAPA-NoVa) wildfire relief fund.
🤍 National Youth Visionaries Association (NYVA) youth-led art fundraiser.
🤍 Salvation Army disaster response teams.

We skipped unverified GoFundMe pages, even when promoted by friends.

Key Rule: Give fast—but verify faster.

Step 4: Empowering the Next Generation—Youth Philanthropy in Action

We wanted our children to experience giving, not just watch us write checks. So, Olesia and Sasha launched their own project:

The Brave Art, Brave Heart initiative.

🖤 Three 90-minute art workshops.
🖤 Students painted canvases symbolizing resilience.
🖤 Artworks auctioned online to raise money for wildfire victims.

At the end of the project:

- They raised over $2,700.

- Earned 40+ community service hours.

- Inspired two neighboring schools to replicate the model.

The greatest gift was not the dollars raised.

It was the confidence born from realizing: *"We are not too young to make a difference."*

Key Principle: Teach children to be givers early—and they will grow into world-changers.

Step 5: Bunching Contributions—Tax Smarts for Bigger Impact

Lisa, our CPA, showed us a tax hack:

📖 **Bunching donations.**

Instead of giving $5,000 yearly (and missing itemized deduction thresholds), we:

- Donated $15,000 every third year.
- Took a sizable itemized deduction that year.
- Used Donor-Advised Funds (DAFs) to stretch grants over the next two years.

> 🔍 **Tax term:** A **Donor-Advised Fund (DAF)** is a charitable investment account that allows you to make irrevocable contributions, receive an immediate tax deduction, and recommend grants to your favorite charities over time.

> 💡 **Tax tip: Family foundation vs. DAF:** If you want the highest possible charitable deduction in a high-income year, a DAF allows you to deduct up to 60% of your AGI with cash contributions, doubling the 30% limit for private foundations.
>
> A private foundation gives you more control over how assets are invested, even allowing investments in alternatives or closely held businesses, while a DAF restricts you to the sponsor's platform and standard fund choices.

Bonus moves?

📖 Donated appreciated stock instead of cash, skipping capital gains tax!

Smart giving = Bigger gifts. Bigger impact.

Key tactic: Time your generosity wisely, tax law rewards strategic hearts.

Step 6: Avoiding the Pitfalls—Donor Scams and Emotional Traps

Heartbreak can make you reckless. We learned that:

✗ Many disaster donation sites are scams.

✗ Some nonprofits spend 90% on administration costs and compensation, not aid.

✗ Crowdfunding sites often eat up 7-12% in platform fees.

Lisa gave us a battle plan:

☑ Use the IRS Exempt Organization Search tool.

☑ Cross-reference Charity Navigator and GuideStar ratings.

☑ Demand official receipts with EIN numbers for donations over $260.

> 💡 **Tax tip:** The $260 **contemporaneous receipt** rule requires a receipt when donating to a qualified charity.[4] Such a written acknowledgment from the charity should be obtained before filing your tax return in order to claim a deduction. The receipt should clearly state that "No goods or services were provided in exchange for this contribution."

No guilt. No rushing.

Key Rule: In disasters, fraud spreads faster than fire. Stay vigilant.

Step 7: Building a Family-giving Blueprint

We formalized the SMART family giving manifesto. It said:

- Give 10% of side hustle/business income to causes we believe in.
- Prioritize disaster relief, youth leadership, and education programs.
- Review donations quarterly as a family.
- Require children to propose at least one nonprofit donation idea yearly.

It was not about the amounts.

It was about the *habit of intentional generosity.*

Key Practice: Build giving into your family constitution. Ritualize it. Celebrate it.

Step 8: Family Foundations—The Generosity Machine

Our next evolution? Launching the SMART **Family Foundation.**

Through it, we:

- 💜 Consolidated multiple small gifts into targeted annual grants.
- 💜 Empowered our children to serve as junior board members.
- 💜 Used the foundation to fund scholarships, microloans, and disaster rebuilding efforts.

Suddenly, our giving was not random.

It was orchestrated—like a symphony of kindness.

Key Strategy: Family foundations are not just for billionaires or millionaires, but for builders of legacy too.

Step 9: Documenting Giving for Taxes—No More Guesswork

To stay IRS-ready: [3]

- ☑ We saved every receipt and confirmation letter.
- ☑ Kept valuation guides for non-cash donations (e.g., used clothing donations to Salvation Army).
- ☑ Filed Form 8283 for non-cash gifts over $500.
- ☑ Archived appraisals for non-land, non-stock gifts valued over $5,000.

Tax time became a breeze.

And no more fear of losing deductions because of missing paperwork.

Key Habit: Audit-proof your generosity every single year.

Step 10: Case Studies— Case in Point

Story 1: The win

John donated $1,000 to CAPA-NoVA for wildfire victims.

- ☑ Clean IRS-approved receipt. [4]
- ☑ Exceeded standard deduction that year.
- ☑ Full deduction + massive community impact.

Story 2: The Painful Lesson

Jenny sent $500 to a friend's GoFundMe. [5]

- ☑ Good heart.
- ✗ No tax deduction.
- ✗ 10% loss to platform fees.

Story 3: The Legacy

Our foundation's $10,000 grant helped rebuild a rural library lost to fires.

☑ 300+ families regained access to books, computers, and hope.

☑ The library now hosts emergency workshops for disaster preparedness.

That is real change. Real legacy.

Top 20 Charitable-Giving Tax and Strategy Tips

Tip	Why It Matters
♥ 1. Give to IRS-qualified 501(c)(3)	Unlocks deductions and ensure impact.
♥ 2. Verify organizations before giving	Prevents fraud and waste.
♥ 3. Donate appreciated assets	No capital gains + full deduction at fair market value.
♥ 4. Bunch donations strategically	Maximizes tax itemization with the $40,000 SALT deduction
♥ 5. Launch a family foundation	Builds a platform for lasting change.
♥ 6. Document every donation over $260	IRS compliance made easy.
♥ 7. Use donor-advised funds (DAFs)	Flexibility and immediate deductions. Be careful of the asset management fee.
♥ 8. Cross-check ratings (Charity Navigator, GuideStar)	Trust but verify.
♥ 9. Encourage youth-led giving	Builds leadership and empathy.
♥ 10. Use disaster relief funds	Focuses on giving where it counts most.
♥ 11. Rotate causes to avoid fatigue	Broadens awareness and avoids burnout.
♥ 12. Watch for platform fees	Protects the full value of your gift.
♥ 13. Keep receipts organized	No scramble at tax time.
♥ 14. Plan giving meetings quarterly	Makes generosity a family ritual.
♥ 15. Pool donations with groups	Amplifies collective impact.
♥ 16. Celebrate giving anniversaries	Makes kindness memorable.
♥ 17. Learn AGI limits (60%, 30%, 20%)	Maximizes your allowable deductions.
♥ 18. Fund scholarships	Directly invests in futures.

Tip	Why It Matters
♥ 19. Track matched donations by employers	Doubles your giving power.
♥ 20. View giving as a legacy investment	Focuses on multi-generational impact.

> **Tax tip:** You can deduct up to (1) 60% of your AGI for public charities (e.g., churches, schools, hospitals, and donor-advised funds); (2) 30% of AGI in form of cash or appreciated assets such as stocks to public charities; (3) 30% of AGI in form of cash donation to a family foundation that you control; and (4) 20% of AGI in form of appreciated assets such as stocks to a family foundation.

Final Reflection in a Poem: "True Giving is Not Born of Guilt"

It's not just written in tax returns or IRS tax code.
It is a basket of giving and loving for hope.
A world we're building with respect and care.

A donation is our humble way of sharing.

In every dollar, there lives a story.
In every gift, we nurture a girl or boy.
In every act of kindness, a future is quietly blooming into greatness.

Chapter 24

Secrets Behind the 990-PF: 10 Dos and 10 Don'ts of Filing a Family Foundation Tax Return

The room buzzed with quiet energy as students logged into the Zoom workshop. I greeted them with a smile, my camera glowing in the warm Potomac evening. "Alright, class," I began, sharing my screen. "Welcome to Week Three of our Family Foundation Series. Tonight, we will dissect the 990-PF tax return, the most public document your private family foundation will ever file."

Behind me on the screen appeared a table of thousands of data points—foundation names, EINs, compensation figures, and asset values. "This," I told them, "is the IRS database. And once you submit your 990-PF, you enter this ecosystem forever."

Situation: A family in Maryland just launched a private foundation with $500,000 in appreciated stock. They intend to support refugee education and sponsor medical grants in Turkey. They're excited. They're generous. But they're unprepared.

Task: Their accountant emails: "It's time to file your first 990-PF."

Action: They take our workshop.

Result: They learn the 10 things to absolutely do and the 10 things to never, ever do when completing the 990-PF. [1]

Situation: The Smart Life Family Foundation, based in Fairfax County, Virginia, recently launched with $500,000 in appreciated stock and a mission to promote youth education, medical outreach, and global service learning. Like many new foundations, they were energized but uncertain about compliance.

Task: Their first Form 990-PF was due. The stakes were high, and the details mattered.

Action: They enrolled in our workshop and studied ten model scenarios to ensure IRS compliance.

Result: They built a robust, legally sound, and impact-focused foundation portfolio.

10 IRS-compliant case studies from Smart Family Foundation [2]

1. Youth leadership grant (education support)
   $5,000 scholarship awarded to a high school senior from a low-income household in DC, verified via FAFSA.

   o   Documentation: Application, award letter, 501(c)(3) school verification.

2. STEM workshop partnership
   Funded a $12,000 robotics summer program in partnership with a public charter school.

   o   Filed under qualified distributions to a registered nonprofit educational entity.

3. Medical aid donation (international)
   $20,000 to the Turkish Red Crescent for earthquake relief.

   o   Used expenditure responsibility letter, converted receipts, board resolution.

4. Board member compensation (reasonable)
   Paid $8,000/year part-time admin stipend to a family member with documented hours and market benchmarking.

   o   Reported on Schedule B Part VII-A; supported by timesheets.

5. 401(k) match for foundation manager
   Matched 20% of a $15,000 W-2 salary for their director.

   o   Aligned with retirement limits under IRC 415; reported on Part VIII.

6. Mission-aligned travel (tax deductible)
   $3,200 trip to San Diego for nonprofit leadership training and networking.

   o   Maintained receipts, agenda, post-event report, and photos.

7. Art Supply support for youth arts NGO
   $6,000 donation to Smart children Arts, with FMV documentation from Michaels and Costco.

   o   Claimed under program service expenses; verified with EIN.

8. Home office reimbursement
   Reimbursed $4,800 annual rent allocation for dedicated 10% office use.

   o   Documented square footage, written rental agreement, board approval.

9. Medical supplies purchased directly
   $2,500 in direct purchases of prenatal vitamins and first-aid kits for a clinic in rural Kenya.

   o   Tracked using receipt logs and customs declaration forms.

10. Foundation lounge and travel credit

    o   Used Amex Platinum for member airport lounge access during global outreach trips.

- Disclosed $695 membership as part of travel administration: board-approved expense policy.

The 10 DOs of filing a smart 990-PF [3]

1. DO track Fair Market Value (FMV) meticulously

   o Schedule B, Part II asks for FMV of all non-cash contributions. Use market quotes or qualified appraisals.

2. DO maintain a 3-to-1 Giving-to-Expense Ratio [4]

   o If you spend $10K on admin and travel, aim to give away $30K. That protects you from IRS scrutiny.

3. DO document reasonable compensation

   o If you pay family members a salary, make sure it matches the market. Median salary in small foundations was ~$10K/year.

4. DO take advantage of qualified distribution exceptions

   o Payments to schools, hospitals, and certain charities may bypass the 5% rule.

5. DO claim pension and health benefit deductions smartly

   o Foundations may contribute up to 25% of salary to 401(K). Add health premium reimbursements.

6. DO document international grants carefully

   o If you're supporting refugee projects in Turkey, keep records of receipts, purpose, and local partners.

7. DO deduct home office and launch travel expenses prudently

   o Reasonable rent, mileage, conference costs, and even Amex lounge memberships are deductible.

8. DO understand your Investment Income Tax (1.39%)

   o Net investment income is taxed at a flat 1.39%. This includes interest, dividends, and capital gains.

9. DO utilize the IRS Tax-Exempt Organization Search tool

   o Study how other similar foundations allocate their spending and write their mission.

10. DO file electronically and keep a digital archive

   o Use e-file systems, save PDFs, and double-check EINs, names, and codes before submission.

The 10 DON'Ts that invite trouble

1. DON'T inflate fair market values

    o   Overstated stock values or art appraisals are red flags.

2. DON'T pay outsized salaries to insiders

    o   A $60K salary from a $100K-revenue foundation is excessive.

3. DON'T forget to report compensation and benefits

    o   All W-2 amounts and retirement/health contributions must be listed.

4. DON'T claim excessive travel and dining expenses

    o   Travel is okay if program-related. A $100K annual "meeting" budget isn't.

5. DON'T delay your filings

    o   Late filings risk penalties and public flagging. Extensions must be requested properly.

6. DON'T miss the 5% minimum distribution rule

    o   You must distribute 5% of net investment assets each year, or face excise taxes.

7. DON'T omit grant recipient details

    o   Schedule B must include grantee names, addresses, EINs, and purposes.

8. DON'T hire unqualified preparers

    o   Many mistakes come from interns or tax staff who misunderstand Form 990-PF's nuance.

9. DON'T treat investment returns like donations

    o   Only true outside contributions count as charitable input. Sales of stock are not "gifts."

10. DON'T forget the mission statement and narratives

    o   Form 990-PF includes open text. Tell your foundation's story clearly and consistently.

Here are five strategic stories for Smart Life Family Foundation that align with IRS guidelines while fostering family bonds and community impact:

1. Intergenerational education initiative

Scenario: The foundation funds STEM scholarships for low-income students and partners with a local robotics nonprofit.

- Qualified expenses:

- $50,000 scholarship grants

- $15,000 program staff salaries

- $5,000 travel for family members to mentor scholarship recipients

- Family bonding: Three generations collaborate to review applications and host an annual "Innovation Day" for recipients.

- Impact: 25 students receive full tuition support, with mentorship improving college retention rates by 40%.

2. Disaster response family mission [5]

Scenario: The foundation organizes a disaster relief trip to rebuild homes after wildfires.

- Qualified expenses:

    - $30,000 construction materials donation to Habitat for Humanity

    - $8,210 travel/lodging for six family foundation board members

    - $2,050 safety gear purchases

- Family Bonding: Adult children lead volunteer teams while grandparents document the effort for grant reporting.

- Impact: 10 families regain permanent housing; IRS-safe 3:1 charitable/expense ratio maintained. [6]

3. Cultural heritage preservation project

Scenario: Funding oral history recordings with Indigenous elders.

- Qualified expenses:

    - $21,205 equipment/archiving costs

    - $12,000 stipends for tribal historians

    - $3,190 family travel to reservation ceremonies

- Family bonding: Teenage grandchildren train as interview technicians; family cooks meals for participants.

- Impact: 200+ hours of endangered language documentation preserved.

4. Health equity mobile clinic

Scenario: A converted RV provides free medical screenings in underserved areas.

- Qualified expenses:

    - $75,180 vehicle purchase

    - $45,000 clinician salaries

- $15,000 medical supplies

- Family bonding: Family members rotate as clinic greeters; teens create health education TikTok content.

- Impact: 1,200+ patients served annually; 10% of assets allocated to programming.

5. Sustainable agriculture fellowship

Scenario: Training program for refugee farmers paired with CSA shares for food-insecure families.

- Qualified expenses:

  - $40,950 farm equipment donations

  - $18,000 staff salaries

  - $7,258 family retreat at training farm

- Family bonding: Monthly "harvest dinners" where fellows and family share meals/strategies.

- Impact: 15 refugee families achieve food sovereignty; 100+ CSA boxes distributed weekly.

IRS Compliance Notes:

- All stories maintain <10% compensation/assets ratio

- Used "sandwich approach" for travel (charitable weekdays and weekend personal time)

- Documentation includes time logs, receipts, and conflict-of-interest policies

- Avoided self-dealing by partnering with 501(c)(3) organizations for direct services

End of Chapter Thought: The Power of Transparency

The general rule of thumb is to apply the 3-to-1 Rule: $3 donation vs. $1 foundation expenses. If you fly under the radar with clear purpose and sound math, the IRS has no reason to bother you. Your foundation is not just a tax vehicle. It's a mirror of your values, your family legacy, and your love. File the 990-PF not just with accuracy, but with a sense of honor.

Chapter 25

IRS Audit Red Flags–Real Stories from Family Foundations

Most family foundations start with good intentions. A scholarship here. A donation there. A board made up of siblings, kids, or maybe a cousin who's good with spreadsheets. But the IRS doesn't audit your intent. They audit your records.

So, what really triggers an IRS audit for private foundations? Here are ten story-driven case studies, fictionalized but based on real compliance patterns and audit outcomes. Each story includes a practical red flag, an IRS code reference, and an audit survival tip.

Story 1: "We were only approved on December 30th!"

Family: Carl & Min's Music Foundation
Red Flag: Missed first-year Form 990-PF filing
What Happened: They were approved by the IRS on December 30. "We hadn't done anything yet, so why file?" Carl shrugged. Nine months later: IRS letter citing a $2,000 penalty.

IRS Rule: IRC §6652—PFs must file even if formed for *one day* in the tax year.[1]

Survival Tip: Put May 15 on your calendar the day your EIN is approved. File Form 8868 if unsure.

Story 2: "Can I pay my brother to manage the property?"

Family: Stan's Robotics Scholarship Fund
Red Flag: Misunderstanding of disqualified persons under §4946 [2]
What Happened: Stan paid his brother (not a disqualified person) to oversee a vacant lot donated to the foundation. But later, Stan paid his daughter-in-law to design a website for the foundation.

IRS Rule: IRC §4941—Prohibits self-dealing with disqualified persons (spouses, ancestors, children, grandchildren, and their spouses).[3]

Survival Tip: Use a family tree chart and color-code disqualified parties before hiring or renting. Payment for service to disqualified persons must be well documented in a contract, and the compensation must be reasonable and comparable to the current market rate.

Story 3: "We bought bitcoin—just 5%!"

Family: The Smart Family Foundation
Red Flag: Jeopardizing investments
What Happened: We allocated 5% of the portfolio to BTC, backed by a detailed memo. An IRS agent flagged it but moved on after reviewing diversification logic.

IRS Rule: IRC §4944—Foundations must avoid speculative investments unless well-justified. [4]

Survival Tip: Draft a written Investment Policy Statement (IPS). Mention asset classes, caps, and intent. [5]

Story 4: "I flew to Malaysia to hand out scholarships."

Family: Carl and Mei's Global Scholars Fund
Red Flag: Unclear whether travel counts toward 5% payout
What Happened: Carl's travel ($3,000) was questioned by the IRS. But his documentation (photos, signed meeting logs, interviews) saved the day.

IRS Rule: Treas. Reg. §53.4942(a)-3. Grant-related expenses qualify as distributions.

Survival Tip: Use a 3:1 ratio: $3 of grants for every $1 of travel and charity related and supportive expenses. Include recipient lists and outcomes.

Story 5: "They never sent a receipt."

Family: Kevin & Juno's Cultural Exchange Trust
Red Flag: Donations of $260+ without acknowledgment letters
What Happened: Kevin donated $1,000 to an arts nonprofit in Turkey but had no formal receipt. The IRS disallowed the deduction.

IRS Rule: IRC §170—Deductions over $260 require a written statement saying, "no goods/services were received."

Survival Tip: Always get it in writing. Even an email with the right donation acknowledgment wording counts.

Story 6: "Are we... an operating foundation?"

Family: Turkish Robotics League Foundation
Red Flag: Activities resembling a business
What Happened: The foundation ran robotics tournaments and sold tickets. This exposed them to "operating foundation" classification.

IRS Rule: IRC §4942(j)(3)—Operating foundations face stricter audit rules and must pass 85% use tests.

Survival Tip: If you run frequent events, speak with an experienced board of directors or attorney. You may need a dual-entity structure.

Story 7: "I interviewed 12 students, but didn't pick any." [6]

Family: Carl's Mountain Hope Scholars Fund
Red Flag: Travel without awards
What Happened: If the IRS audits you over expenses without scholarships granted, you can provide documentation, such as interview notes, travel records and final decision notes.

IRS Rule: Reg. §53.4945-4(c)—Due diligence travel is allowed if documented.

Survival Tip: Keep photos, contact logs, and regional NGO referrals to justify expenses.

Story 8: "I paid my children $15/hour to file receipts."

Family: Lisa, my CPA's Admin Crew
Red Flag: Potential unreasonable compensation
What Happened: Lisa, my CPA, paid her two teenage children $15/hour to scan receipts and reconcile travel folders. She kept timesheets, hourly logs, and QuickBooks entries.

IRS Rule: IRC §4941(d)(1)(D)—Compensation to family must be "reasonable and necessary."

Survival Tip: Use a reasonable market hourly rate. Add weekly task checklists. The market rate of a bookkeeper ranges between $15 and $25 per hour.

Story 9: "We tried to donate to a friend's foundation."

Family: Smart Life Foundation
Red Flag: Donation to another private foundation without approval
What Happened: You planned a $10K grant to your friend's family-run nonprofit. It would cause IRS's concern over potential conflict of interest.

IRS Rule: IRC §4945(d)(4)—No grants to non-operating foundations without prior IRS approval.

Survival Tip: Search the grantee's EIN on IRS EO tool or GuideStar to verify status.

Story 10: "We store everything in a shoebox."

Family: The Paper Mountain Foundation
Red Flag: Poor recordkeeping
What Happened: During an audit, the foundation couldn't locate bylaws, didn't have minutes for two years, and had no 1099s for contractors.

IRS rule: TG 3-20—Maintain full financial, grant, and board records for 3–7 years minimum.

Survival tip: Use cloud storage (e.g., Dropbox), create folders by year, and scan everything. Audit readiness is peace of mind.

Red flag recap: Top 10 IRS audit triggers for private foundations

Red Flag	Related Code	Tips to Avoid Trouble
▶ 1. Late 990-PF filing	IRC §6033	Set reminders. File even with zero activity.
▶ 2. Hiring disqualified persons	IRC §4941	Chart your family tree. Use contracts.
▶ 3. Speculative investments	IRC §4944	Draft an IPS and limit exotic assets.
▶ 4. Travel without output	§53.4942(a)-3	Document outcomes and purpose. [7]
▶ 5. No gift receipts >$260	IRC §170	Always get a letter or email. [8]
▶ 6. Operating foundation risks	IRC §4942(j)(3)	Review event frequency. Avoid blurring with business. [9]
▶ 7. Scholarship due diligence	§4945(g)	Notes and interviews matter, even if no award is granted. [10]
▶ 8. Paying children	§4941(d)(1)(D)	Log hours. Use market rates. [11]
▶ 9. Grant to other private foundations	§4945(d)(4)	Confirm recipient's public charity status.
▶ 10. Poor records	TG 3-20	Use Dropbox. Label folders by year + type. [12]

🎓 Final Thought: Compliance is the Language of Legacy

You don't need to be perfect. But if you want to turn your family foundation into a legacy platform, not a liability, you must build viable systems. That means:

- **Clarity:** Know who's a disqualified person
- **Control:** Draft clear policies
- **Continuity:** Keep records that your children can understand and defend

Let the IRS see your generosity and your governance aligned.

"Tax shelter without soul is audit bait. Soul without structure is a missed opportunity. But together they build a legacy."

Chapter 26

❧

The Three-Legged Table: How We Built a Family Foundation Portfolio That Could Survive Anything

I still remember that Sunday morning when my wife and I sat down with our teenage son Kevin and our newly retired Uncle Fred. Coffee was brewing. Pages of Warren Buffett's annual letters were spread across the dining table. This wasn't just a money talk. It was a legacy meeting.

My Uncle Fred has been an experienced stock investor for decades. I consulted him about the wisest ways to invest. He sipped, smiled, and said, "Three things. Buffett. Broad market. Life insurance. That's your three-legged table."

That stuck. And it became our family's blueprint.

The Setup: From Zero to Stewardship

When we launched the Smart Life Family Foundation, we didn't start with millions. We started with a mission: to turn our tax dollars into scholarships and community grants. But managing the money? That was the hard part.

After months of research, trial, and error, we landed on a structure simple enough for a teenager to understand and solid enough for the IRS to respect:

- 70% in S&P 500 low-fee index funds (with annual expense ratio as low as 0.015%)

- 25% in cash value whole life insurance

- 5% in Bitcoin (just enough to keep the next generation curious)

We called it our "Three-Legged Table" portfolio. The three core legs provided balance: legacy investing (Buffett), diversification (S&P), and liquidity with safety (whole life). Bitcoin? That was the coaster—nice to have, but not essential.

How Each Leg Worked for Us

Berkshire Hathaway was our conviction piece. [1] We admired its leadership, discipline, and refusal to follow market fads. We told Kevin, "If Buffett's team runs out of ideas, the whole market's probably in trouble." [2]

We also framed it as a teaching tool. Kevin researched the top holdings every summer and presented a mini report to the family. He learned to look past stock tickers and into business models, dividends, and long-term value.

The S&P 500 Index Funds gave us exposure to the broad market with minimal cost. Fidelity's fund had such a low fee (1.5 basis points, i.e., $1.5 per year with $10,000 asset balance) that it was practically free. When we explained compounding fees to Kevin, he was shocked. "So, we're paying $150 a year on a $1 million investment? That's it?"

We smiled. "That's why fees matter."

Whole Life Insurance, owned by the foundation, was our secret weapon. [3] During down years, we borrowed from it instead of selling stocks. That one move saved our 2022 donation budget when the market tanked. We also used the policy as a cash reserve, earning consistent 4-5% returns while offering loan flexibility. It was our own line of credit, with no bank required.

Ten Mini-Stories, One Big Lesson

1. **The year of the dip:** In 2022, the market dropped. We needed to fund a $40,000 scholarship. Instead of selling stocks with a loss, we borrowed from our New York Life policy and repaid the loan when the market recovered.

2. **The youth music fund:** Our friend Karl used a policy on his 18-year-old daughter, owned by his foundation. In year 15, he borrowed money to support a rural orchestra. He also used this as a teaching example in his music class, inspiring young musicians to start thinking about money as rhythm and harmony, not just notes.

3. **The Aranya fellows:** A small $80K fund placed $10K into crypto and used the other 90% to support math education. It was diversified, mission-aligned, and bold. Aranya's foundation also partnered with a local school to develop a crypto-literacy module.

4. **The literacy leaders:** Cori invested 90% of her bank deposit into a whole life insurance policy in the form of paid-up addition. She used the statements to teach high school students how to build wealth patiently. She hosted monthly "Wealth Wednesdays" where students discussed compounding, policy dividends, and tax sheltering strategies.

5. **The Katrina outreach:** Katrina avoided stocks altogether, sticking with CDs and Fidelity income funds. Her reason? She wanted maximum liquidity to respond to urgent grants. One winter, when a fire struck a local art center, her foundation wired funds within 48 hours.

6. **The Zhan science fund:** Zhan was skeptical until he saw whole life returns compared to his CD rates. Now he uses it as a buffer. He also used the policy to fund a science camp's robotics lab, without selling a single share.

7. **Smart youth scholars:** We let our son manage the 5% BTC portfolio under close IPS oversight. It became a lesson in volatility and responsibility. Kevin even wrote a paper titled "Bitcoin, Buffett, and Balance Sheets" that he submitted to a high school competition—and won.

8. **The Gandy transfer:** We helped Abel transfer a personal life policy into the foundation. We documented everything for the IRS. It passed the audit with flying colors. The audit agent even complimented the clarity of the documentation.

9. **Gabe DAF:** Gabe, a college student, used a donor-advised fund (DAF) with 60% CDs and 40% S&P. He skipped insurance due to age and underwriting. He later added a micro-grant program for first-generation college students.

10. **The Fred hackathons:** Uncle Fred invested conservatively but funded civic tech challenges every year, showing that low-risk does not mean low-impact. In 2023, his foundation awarded a $5,000 prize for an app that connects veterans to local health clinics.

Audit Proofing and Annual Rituals

Every January, we hold a family retreat. We:

- Review our Investment Policy Statement (IPS)

- Check if our 5% payout is met

- Rebalance the portfolio

- Write down the "why" behind every investment change

- Review the loan schedule on life insurance

- Update our strategic donation list

We call it our Foundation's Annual Report—to ourselves. And yes, we keep minutes.

During one retreat, we caught ourselves over allocating to Bitcoin, as it was creeping up to 8%. Kevin suggested a rebalance himself. "We're investors, not gamblers," he joked. Proud parent moment.

Top 20 Tax Tips for Family Foundation Investment

1. **Use whole life insurance owned by the foundation:** Contributions may be deductible and cash value growth is tax-deferred. Loans are tax-free if structured properly. Employer owned life insurance triggers a special IRS form to file with your 990 PF. Seek a tax pro for advice.

2. **Rebalance with purpose:** Every rebalance should be documented in meeting minutes to show fiduciary duty and avoid IRS scrutiny.

3. **Use life insurance loans instead of selling in down markets:** Preserve appreciated assets and avoid locking in paper losses.

4. **Write an investment policy statement (IPS):** Define allocation, philosophy, risk tolerance, and documentation standards.

5. **Add a cryptocurrency allocation sparingly:** Consider a capped allocation to crypto if it aligns with mission and your younger trustees are involved.

6. **Transfer personal policies into the foundation carefully:** Get professional help, document ownership change, and update the insurer.

7. **Consider DAFs for a simpler setup:** Donor-advised funds may be better than private foundations for smaller families or families with no record-keeping discipline.

8. **Teach youth with real roles:** Let teens manage a small sub-account to learn IPS, diversification, and stewardship.

9. **Avoid real estate in foundations:** UBIT (Unrelated Business Income Tax) and depreciation recapture make it complex. [4]

10. **Treat the foundation like a business:** Use payroll, ADP, board minutes, and quarterly reports to stay professional.

11. **Use loans for liquidity without triggering capital gains:** Life insurance loans provide liquidity without needing to sell securities or stocks.

12. **Hold quarterly mini-retreats to stay on track:** These regular check-ins can reinforce discipline, correct drift, and teach accountability.

13. **Rotate investment responsibilities among trustees:** Give each family member a chance to manage a piece and report back annually.

14. **Use insurance policy values to secure loans or grants:** Many banks accept these as collateral, helping extend the impact.

15. **Fund scholarships using loan proceeds strategically:** Allows you to keep your portfolio intact while still fulfilling the 5% payout.

16. **Document everything with precision:** Keep digital folders labeled by year and topic. Use templates for consistency.

17. **Outsource admin tasks smartly:** Use tech like ADP and cloud accounting to simplify reporting and reduce compliance risk.

18. **Introduce monthly learning themes:** For example, "April is Audit Month" or "November is IPS Review Month." Keeps things fun and intentional.

19. **Track dividends, fees, and policy loans on a dashboard**: Visual tools help everyone, from teens to trustees, see performance clearly.

20. **Celebrate successes publicly within the family**: Send newsletters, take pictures at retreats, print mini annual reports.[5] Make legacy visible.

Final Word

A family foundation isn't just a tax strategy. It's a conversation. A classroom. A compass.

With our balanced approach (S&P 500, and cash value whole life), we built something that could stand steady through storms and raise future generations with clarity and purpose.

Every January, when we gather around our little round table, we remember that it's not about having millions. It's about wisely doing millions of good things with the little we steward.

Case Study 5

The BrightPath Family Foundation Annual Report-2024

Family Background

Dr. Marcus Zhang and his wife, Lydia, run the "BrightPath Family Foundation," a private family philanthropy focused on education and faith-based giving. Every year since 2018, Marcus has documented their family's progress through a personal vision board, blending biblical reflection with financial, spiritual, and physical milestones.

In 2024, their family spread their roots across the globe; through giving, growing, and glowing.

Vision Board Pillars

1. Familial Balance

- The BrightPath Foundation donated over $47,000 to charitable projects in the U.S., Nepal, Iceland, and China.

- Their daughters Lena (a university pre-health major and choir member) and Tessa (a young environmental advocate) volunteered abroad and deepened cross-cultural friendships.

- Their son Brandon, at just 20, became one of the youngest Certified Flight Instructor-Instrument (CFII) holders at a top aviation university.

- Their youngest, Nathan, navigated college applications under the family's guiding prayer and support.

- Lydia's private music studio saw record enrollment, with one student declaring a music major.

Tax tip: Build charitable giving into your family's mission; use a private foundation to teach children stewardship early.

2. Financial Balance

- The family retirement portfolio returned 16.2%, beating their 12% target.

- Of 24 life insurance policies, 18 outperformed benchmarks; underperforming IULs were actively rebalanced.

- Each child held at least one tax-advantaged account: Roth IRAs, 401(k)s, HSAs, 529 plans, and rental properties.

- Family discussions included budgeting, compounding, and the "latte effect."

Tax tip: Use family dinners as a launchpad for teaching Roth conversions, cost segregation, and smart gifting.

🔍 **Tax term: Indexed Universal Life Insurance (IUL)** is a type of permanent life insurance that combines a death benefit with a cash value component that earns interest based on the performance of a market index (like the S&P 500), but without direct market investment.

💡 **Tax tip: The Latte Effect, or Matcha Effect,** is a personal finance concept that shows how small, routine daily expenses, like a $6 latte or matcha, can add up to significant sums over time, especially when that money is instead invested and compounded. It was coined by David Bach in "The Automatic Millionaire."

---

3. Spiritual Balance

- Marcus began each day with four Bible translations using a parallel Bible (NIV, KJV, NASB, Amplified).

- Each night, he journaled "10 things I'm grateful for," cultivating a gratitude-rich mindset and restful sleep.

Tax tip: Merge Bible study with mental health—gratitude journaling is both a spiritual and neurological boost.

4. Physical Balance

- Marcus shed 18 lbs—from 169 to 151—and maintained his weight through:

  o A 90-day sobriety challenge

  o 300 hot yoga sessions with Lydia (affectionately called "Hot Lydia")

  o National qualification in the USA Yoga Championship for the 7th year in a row

- The family gave up red meat and leaned into warm oat-based dinners.

Tax tip: Pair fitness challenges with family accountability—make wellness a legacy, not a task.

5. Professional Balance

- Marcus earned 300+ CPE credits from industry leaders (CFP Board, AICPA, Drake, CFA Institute).

- He led a regulatory team through complex audits and tax updates, continuously improving systems knowledge.

Tax tip: Track CPEs as part of your vision board. Celebrate knowledge, not just income.

Final Reflection: The Zhang Family Motto

"One generation shall commend your works to another, and shall declare your mighty acts." (Psalm 145:4)

Their 2024 success wasn't accidental; it was vision-driven, habit-built, and faith-anchored.

---

10 Takeaway tax tips for your family vision board

1. Use a private foundation to teach multi-generational giving.
2. Gift rental properties into family trusts and leverage depreciation.
3. Open Roth IRAs for minors with earned income.
4. Track IUL and whole life policies with annual benchmarks.
5. Pair 529 plan contributions with tax-credit state strategies.
6. Use parallel Bibles for deeper scripture reflection.
7. Schedule quarterly CPE audits to stay tax smart.
8. Plan family sabbaticals with tax-deductible charitable components.
9. Replace red meat with heart-healthy alternatives, even in tax season.
10. Capture your year in writing—your future self and children will thank you.

Afterword

My Family, My Finance, and My Future

As I reflect on the journey chronicled in these pages, one truth stands above all: family is the foundation upon which every financial plan is built. My story is not just about numbers, strategies, or even the pursuit of financial independence. It is about the people I love, the lessons we have learned together, and the future we are building, one decision at a time.

Family First

Every financial milestone, every tax-saving tactic, and every investment decision has been shaped by the needs and dreams of my family. Whether it was opening a Roth IRA for my children, writing our annual family financial letter, or teaching them the value of patience and resilience, these moments have been about much more than money. They have been about creating a legacy of wisdom, discipline, and shared purpose.

Finance as a Tool, Not a Goal

Over the years, I have come to see finance not as an end, but as a means, a tool for unlocking opportunities, reducing stress, and empowering each family member to pursue their passions. The rituals we have built (vision boards, gratitude ledgers, and our annual family report) are not just about wealth accumulation. They are about clarity, communication, and building confidence for the road ahead.

Looking to the Future

The world is changing faster than ever. Artificial intelligence, new tax laws, and shifting economic landscapes mean tomorrow's challenges will not look like yesterday's. But I am confident that the habits, values, and strategies we have built as a family will endure. We will continue to adapt, to learn, and to support each other, no matter what comes our way.

My hope is that the stories and lessons in this book inspire you to see your own family as the greatest asset in your financial life. May you build not just wealth, but wisdom. Not just security, but freedom. And may your future be as bright and resilient as the love that binds your family together.

Thank you for joining me on this joyful journey. Be SMART!

About the Author:

Mike Nie is a Christian father, tax strategist, and financial educator with over 25 years of experience helping families turn everyday decisions into lifelong opportunities. His experience includes: (1) Audit and Advisory Director at PricewaterhouseCoopers LLC (PwC, 10 years); (2) Audit Inspection Leader at the PCAOB (4 years); and (3) Staff Accountant at a federal financial regulatory agency (11+ years).

His credentials include Certified Public Accountant (CPA), Certified Financial Planner (CFP®), Chartered Financial Analyst (CFA®), and Enrolled Agent (EA). Other credentials include Financial Risk Manager (FRM®), Sustainability and Climate Risk (SCR®), and Distinguished Toastmasters (DTM®).

Mike and his wife Olga live in the DC Metro area with four adult children: a blended and blessed family.

As the Owner of Smart 1040 LLC (www.Smart1040.us), Mike specializes in faith-based, family-centered tax planning—with a focus on proactive strategy, not just tax filing. He can be reached at Help@Smart1040.us.

Author's children wrote their personal experience of how the book author installed and instilled financial wisdom into their daily life. Enjoy!

****

Money has always shaped the decisions our family makes. From a young age, I watched my father's wise financial habits in action - habits that have since taken root in both my brother and me. One quality that stands out most is his frugality. While he never hesitates to spend wisely on meaningful investments, he has always remained deeply mindful of costs. Perhaps it comes from the classic Asian father figure he embodies, but my father has consistently been a thoughtful and intentional money manager.

As I grow older and step further into independence, my father's advice lingers in the back of my mind with every purchase. While I may indulge a bit more than he would prefer, he instilled in me the belief that every dollar has a purpose and that how we choose to spend it matters. He has modeled restraint in everyday purchases that offer only short-term satisfaction, always emphasizing the difference between a 'need' and a 'want.' Yet, when it comes to opportunities with lasting value, such as education, property, or global travel, he has never hesitated to act decisively.

These lessons have guided me in my own journey. When I began operating a rental property in Daytona Beach, I felt my father's influence at every step, even in the small things, like keeping the porch light off to save on electricity. For me, the property wasn't just about securing an asset, but it was about adopting a mindset that views money as a tool for stability and growth. Managing tenants, covering repairs, and navigating the ups and downs of ownership forced me to apply his principles in real time.

Younger me was always annoyed by the constant financial lessons during family dinners and endless financial podcasts on long road trips. Truthfully, even now I would find them tedious. But I now recognize the significance of his insights and feel fortunate to have him as my father.

Chris

Ever since a young age, my father and I have had the end goal of becoming financially independent. It all started right before Covid, when the world faced a new dilemma. My father, being very hardworking and money driven, explored and learned about the financial world in the present and future. He learned all about many different investment ideas ranging from ROTH IRA, 529 Plan for college, and real estate. My dad has always been money driven and my brother and I are fortunate enough to be under his wing. His knowledge, commitment, and hard work influence our lives so much. He constantly strives to learn more and more everyday, how to invest money in stocks for the future and how to ensure that my brother and I are millionaires in the near future.

Out of all the topics that my dad has taught me, the two that stick out the most are life insurance and real estate. My dad has a few life insurance policies himself. Across our family (my dad and wife Olga, my step sisters, Chris and I), we have several life insurance policies each person, mostly worth $1,000,000 each. My father teaches me that life insurance is very important in life, ensuring that the family is taken care of in case of an emergency. To me, life insurance is very important because I believe that life is very unpredictable. With life insurance, our family is taken care of.

The other topic is real estate. My dad himself has influenced my family so much about real estate. My current house that I live in is located in VA. He lives in Maryland with Olga. He also has an active investment of a condo located in VA near a popular shopping center. Here, a couple rents out his studio apartment. This constant money coming in gives him great financial freedom.

He has spread this wisdom to my brother and me. My brother attends school at a university located in Florida. He himself has a brand new condo in which he stays in while renting out the other two rooms to tenants. Similar to him, I recently invested and purchased a brand new condominium in Manassas, Virginia. Manassas is a growing area for industries and cyber security. The most important thing about where the residence is located is how important the location is to you. Whether the house is located near a major university or a major attraction, this attracts people.

Overall, my father is a wise and influential individual not only to my family, but to many people around him. He constantly strives to learn more and more on how to save money and to be financially smart and independent. Ranging from our family bank (The Nie Family Bank), 529 Plans, real estate and properties, life insurance, ROTH IRA, Warren Buffet stocks, SMART Life Foundation, my personal Gym Operator and Moving LLC, and many more.

My father will continue to spread his kindness and wisdom to my family and enjoys learning more and more to teach the youth, and that means people of all ages. I am forever grateful for the impact that he has left in my life. Thank you dad, and let us work on becoming financially independent.

Kevin

When I think back on the financial lessons my stepfather taught me that shaped my life, one of the earliest and simplest ideas that stuck with me was the Latte Effect. The principle is straightforward: small, everyday expenses add up over time, and if you redirect those dollars into savings or investments, you can build something substantial. I learned quickly that financial discipline isn't about never enjoying yourself, but about making intentional choices—knowing when a short-term pleasure is worth it, and when it's wiser to let that money work for you.

This mindset carried me into college, where budgeting became less of an option and more of a survival skill. Learning how to track expenses, plan for textbooks and utilities, and resist the temptation of spending money I didn't really have taught me the value of financial independence. I realized just how important college budgeting was and how it became one of the first real lessons in preparing myself for adulthood.

Along the way, I explored the often-overlooked world of life insurance and even earned my license to sell it in the future. Beyond the obvious safety net it provides, I discovered its less talked-about benefits: the ability to borrow against its value, the tax advantages, and the security of knowing the money you put into it grows quietly in the background. It's a tool that, when used wisely, gives families both protection and flexibility.

Investing, in all its forms, has always been a cornerstone of my stepfather's philosophy—and it is steadily becoming my own. Whether through a 401(k), life insurance, or an IRA, the key lesson was always the same: start early, stay consistent, and trust in compounding. I've come to deeply believe in my stepfather's favorite principle: the power of letting money work for you, rather than constantly working for money.

If there's a single takeaway from my stepfather's financial lessons and my personal financial journey, it's that discipline and foresight—applied to the small choices as well as the big ones—can completely change the trajectory of a life.

Olesia

If you ask me to describe my stepfather, Mike, he is a servant-hearted, loving, dedicated man, always seen with a pen and a new tax book in hand. Mike is constantly learning and aiming to discover how to be the most effective and efficient with money. This is why his professional credential abbreviations don't fit on his business card. His drive to expand his knowledge of money by learning about taxes, life insurance, retirement savings, and even environmental sustainability built his elaborate skillset and understanding of all things related to maintaining wealth in the smartest way possible. Mike inspires me to seize opportunities to become an expert in a range of topics, because an interdisciplinary mind proposes the smartest and most creative solutions to complicated problems.

Mike enjoys sharing his inquiries with others, frequently talking about a new financial tip at the dinner table or working with numerous clients, professors, or non-profit organizations, in which the leaders often join our assumed "family dinners" out. We roll our eyes, but Mike smiles, because business meeting over meal may make the meal expenses deductible. He discovers ways to knit smart-saving-tips in our daily life, especially when it comes to traveling. "Travel with purpose", Mike says, as he unravels the SMART Life Family Foundation flag to take a picture in front of an international non-profit logo. Through the SMART Life Family Foundation, Mike reinvented traveling by finding local organizations to donate to throughout our trip, and in return, we received meaningful connections and memorable experiences.

By choosing less conventional paths on the road to financial success, Mike demonstrates what it means to wholeheartedly support the people he loves. He teaches his children that creativity, connection, and continuous learning are the keys to building a prosperous future.

Sasha

Acknowledgements

This book would not have come to life without the wisdom, support, and inspiration of several extraordinary individuals.

I am deeply grateful to **Coach Lucy Chen**, whose unwavering lessons on resilience helped shape not only the content of this book, but also the perseverance behind its creation. Her voice reminded me that every challenge is an opportunity to grow stronger.

Special thanks to **Dr. Frances Chiu**, whose relentless focus on clarity, brevity, and specificity pushed me to distill complex tax strategies into language that speaks directly and powerfully to families. Her mentorship sharpened my message and made every word count.

I also want to thank **Dr. Cindy Cui**, whose thoughtful eye for readability and flow helped transform technical concepts into something any reader could digest and apply. Her feedback reminded me that accessibility is the first step toward empowerment.

Finally, my heartfelt appreciation to **Rev James Webb**, whose quiet strength and unwavering emphasis on faith and family served as a constant anchor throughout this journey. His example reminds me that true wealth is measured in love, legacy, and service.

This chapter lists all friends, families and supporters who make this book more reader friendly. Thank you all. Again, I am accountable for all errors in both content and grammar.

To each of you: this book carries your fingerprints. Thank you for believing in its purpose. Any omissions or errors are my fault.

Dr. Maxwell Adekoje – Goldmine Realty	Xiaoying Li	Anna Wang
Lian An		Acton Wang
Lara Atella, Director of Hot Yoga Capitol Hill	Xiaoling Li	Jing Williams
James Barber – Life Insurance Expert, Oregon Cash Flow Pro	Enyou Li	Min Wu
Sabrina Barcus	Zhengqing Li	Ming Wu
Haitao Cao		
Ting Chau	Yan Liang	Dr. Jiang Wu
Jean Chen		
Lucy Chen	Xin Lin	Yuhua Xiang
Hui Lun Chen	Davy Ling	Yanhong (Lucy) Xie
Xin Chen	Patrick Liu	Rongtao Xu
Haifeng Henry Chen	Zhan Liu	
Yin Cheng	Jia Liu	Vivian Xu – President, CAPA MC
Ben Cheng	Cong Liu	Shuli Xia – President, CAPA BC

Lori Correa – Ex-Training Program Manager, Drake Software, Professional Tax Solutions

Abdulvahid Coskun

Randy Culpepper

Yuqin Ding

Deanna Echols

Suzanne S. Elliott, MA, Ed. – Owner, H.O.T. Yoga on the Island; USA Yoga Board Member

Judy Fu

Ted Gancayco

Fan Gong

Fred, Nancy and Andy

Yutao Guo

Alice Guo – Impact Speaking Academy

Yaoyu Guo

Molly Guo, XPerf Inc.

Mei Han

Jinjie Hu

Wenlei Jiang

Wei Jiang

Xiaoli Jiang

Brittany Jiang

Sizhang Jiang

Jongling Jie

Kari Jin

Katina Ketchem

Zhipeng Liu

Grace Liu

Kevin Liu

Lili Liu

Song Lu

Lei Luo

Na Luo

JunJun Malatesta

Songan Mao

Jun Meng

Cori Minton

LyudmMila Nemtsov, MD

Stan Niu

Sandy Ni – NEAT Future Family Foundation

Tian Olson

Lisa Pafe

Steve Parisi – President, IBC Global, LLC

Faye Qu

Debbie (Rappoport) Bigman, CPA, Retired PwC Partner

Zach Ruff – Home Insurance Claim Specialist

Stanley Sawtelle

Wendy Shi

Linna Su

Lily Yang

Karl Yap

George Yu, The Yu Family Foundation

David Yu

Tracy Yuan, CPA

John Yuan

Fanny Yuan

Jenny Yi – YEE Patriotic Products, Yeepatriot.com

Alexander and Lincoln – New Gen Restoration LLC

Crystal Zhang

Cathy and Sophie Zhang

Beixun Zhang

Hao Zhang, P.E., Environmental Remediation Engineer

Xuejuan Zhang

Lucy Zhang

Hongwei Zhang

Qiang Zhang

Yan Michelle Zhang

Tim Zhao, National Youth Visionaries Association

Jian Lina Zhen

Yin Zheng

Jian Zhong

Brett Korade – Co-Founder, LAB Realty Group; Captain, USN (Ret)

Zhicheng Lai – AZ Tax & Insurance Agency, Tax Practitioner
Cheyenne Lepler
Chi Wellness LLC

Jenny Li

Beverly Li

Jaikumar Subramani

Judin Sukri
Ed Tate, Owner, Ed Tate & Associates LLC World Champion of Public Speaking
Jennifer Vanmeter, Executive Coach
Xiuping Wang
Diana Wang
Xiaolin Wang

Yuyan Zhou, President, CAPA NoVA

Weiyu Zhou

Changqong Zhu

Appendix 1

Commonly Used Cover Letters to the IRS

Real estate professional grouping letter

[Your Name]

[Your Address]

[Taxpayer Identification Number]

Pursuant to Treasury Regulation § 1.469-9(g), I hereby elects to treat all interests in rental real estate as a single activity for purposes of determining material participation under the passive activity loss rules of IRC § 469. I am a qualifying real estate professional under IRC § 469(c)(7).

The rental real estate activities grouped into this single activity include:

1. [Property Address 1]

2. [Property Address 2]

3. [Property Address 3]

[Add additional properties as needed]

Rental property 2% cost basis safe harbor election

Subject: Safe Harbor Election under § 1.263(a)-3(h) – Real Estate Expenses

Taxpayer: [Your Name or Entity Name]

Taxpayer Identification Number: [SSN or EIN]

Tax Year: [e.g., Calendar Year Ending December 31, 20xx]

Form Attached: [e.g., Form 1040 with Schedule E or Form 1120S]

To Whom It May Concern:

In accordance with Treasury Regulation § 1.263(a)-3(h), I hereby elect the Safe Harbor for Small Taxpayers for the following property(ices) for the tax year ending [Insert Tax Year End Date].

As the taxpayer's average annual gross receipts for the preceding three tax years were less than $10 million, and the unadjusted basis of each building is under $1 million, the taxpayer qualifies for this safe harbor.

The aggregate number of repairs, maintenance, improvements, and similar costs incurred for each building listed below did not exceed the lesser of 2% of the unadjusted basis of the building or $10,000, and the expenses were paid to improve property used in a trade or business.

Properties Covered by This Election:

1. [Property Address 1], Unadjusted Basis: $[XXX,XXX]
   - Total improvement/repair costs: $[X,XXX]
   - % of basis: [e.g., 1.8%]
2. [Property Address 2], Unadjusted Basis: $[XXX,XXX]
   - Total improvement/repair costs: $[X,XXX]
   - % of basis: [e.g., 1.2%]

Election Statement: The taxpayer hereby elects the Safe Harbor for Small Taxpayers under § 1.263(a)-3(h) to deduct the above-listed expenses related to eligible building property(ies). This election is being made on a timely filed original federal income tax return, including extensions, for the applicable year.

Thank you for your attention to this matter.

Sincerely,

[Signature]

[Name of Taxpayer or Authorized Representative] [Phone Number] [Date]

De minimis **safe harbor election (Section 1.263(a)-1(f))**

Note: This election allows businesses to deduct certain tangible property costs up to $2,500 per item (or $5,000 if you have an applicable financial statement) instead of capitalizing them.

Subject: Section 1.263(a)-1(f) *De Minimis* Safe Harbor Election

Content of the statement:

[Your Name]

[Your Address]

[Taxpayer Identification Number]

The taxpayer is hereby making the *de minimis* safe harbor election under § 1.263(a)-1(f).

This election is made annually and is not a change in accounting method, so no Form 3115 is required.

Sincerely,

[Signature]

[Name of Taxpayer or Authorized Representative]

[Phone Number]

[Date]

Election to Deduct Start-Up and Organizational Costs—IRC §195 and §259

Smart 3-D Printing LLC
[Your Address]
[Taxpayer Identification Number]

To whom it may concern:

Pursuant to **Internal Revenue Code Section 195 (Start-Up Costs)** and **Section 259 (Organizational Costs)**, the taxpayer **Smart 3-D Printing LLC** hereby elects to deduct qualifying start-up ($x,xxx) and organizational expenses ($x,xxx) incurred in connection with the creation and launch of the business.

This election is being made for the tax year in which Smart 3-D Printing LLC begins active business operations, in accordance with IRS guidelines. The total start-up expenses and organizational expenditures, up to $5,000 each, are being deducted as allowed, with any excess amounts over $50,000 reduced dollar for dollar and the remainder to be amortized over 180 months.

This election is made as part of the initial income tax return for the business year in which operations commenced.

Sincerely,

[Signature]
[Name of Authorized Representative or Managing Member]
[Phone Number]

Self-rental safe harbor election (under Treas. Regs. § 1.469-4(c))

[Taxpayer Name]
[Taxpayer Address] [City, State ZIP]
[Taxpayer Identification Number]
[Date]

Internal Revenue Service
[Appropriate IRS Service Center Address]

RE: Disclosure of Grouping of Activities under Treas. Regs. § 1.469-4(c) – Self-Rental Arrangement

To Whom It May Concern:

Pursuant to the requirements of Treas. Regs. § 1.469-4 and Rev. Proc. 2010-13, this letter serves as the taxpayer's written statement disclosing the grouping of activities for purposes of section 469 of the Internal Revenue Code for the tax year ending [Year].

Description of Activities and Grouping

The taxpayer, [Taxpayer Name], owns [describe rental property, e.g., "a commercial building located at 123 Main Street, Anytown, State"] (the "Rental Property"). The Rental Property is leased to [describe commonly controlled trade or business, e.g., "ABC, Inc."], a trade or business in which the taxpayer holds a [describe ownership interest, e.g., "100% ownership interest"]. The trade or business activity conducted by [ABC, Inc.] is [describe business, e.g., "a retail grocery store"].

For the current tax year, the taxpayer is grouping the following activities as a single activity for purposes of section 469:

- The rental activity involving the Rental Property; and
- The trade or business activity conducted by [ABC, Inc.].

Legal Basis for Grouping

Under Treas. Regs. § 1.469-4(c), one or more trade or business activities or rental activities may be treated as a single activity if the activities constitute an appropriate economic unit for the measurement of gain or loss for purposes of section 469. The determination of whether activities constitute an appropriate economic unit is based on all relevant facts and circumstances, including similarities and differences in types of businesses, common control, common ownership, geographical location, and interdependencies between the activities.

In this case, the rental activity and the trade or business activity are closely interrelated:

- The Rental Property is used exclusively by [ABC, Inc.] in its trade or business.
- The taxpayer owns [100%] of both the rental activity and the trade or business activity, resulting in identical ownership and common control.
- The activities are located at the same address and are economically interdependent, as the rental activity exists solely to support the trade or business activity.

Accordingly, the taxpayer has determined that these activities constitute an appropriate economic unit under Treas. Regs. § 1.469-4(c).

Self-Rental Arrangement and Section 469 Treatment

Treas. Regs. § 1.469-4(d)(1) generally limits the grouping of rental activities with trade or business activities. However, grouping is permitted if (A) the rental activity is insubstantial in relation to the trade or business activity, (B) the trade or business activity is insubstantial in relation to the rental activity, or (C) each owner of the trade or business activity has the same proportionate ownership interest in the rental activity, in which case the portion of the rental activity involving the rental of property for use in the trade or business may be grouped with the trade or business activity.

In this case, the taxpayer is the sole owner of both the rental activity and the trade or business activity. Therefore, the grouping is permitted under Treas. Regs. § 1.469-4(d)(1)(i)(C), provided the activities constitute an appropriate economic unit, as described above.

Conclusion

This statement is submitted in compliance with the disclosure requirements of Rev. Proc. 2010-13 and Treas. Regs. § 1.469-4(e). The taxpayer will continue to use this grouping in subsequent taxable years unless a material change in facts and circumstances occurs that makes the original grouping clearly inappropriate.

If you have any questions or require additional information, please contact [Taxpayer or Representative Name] at [phone number or email address].

Sincerely,

[Signature]
[Taxpayer Name, Title, if applicable]

Enclosures:

- [List any supporting documentation, if applicable]

Appendix 2

IRS Safe Harbors Used in the Book

Safe Harbor Rule	Chapter	IRS Code/Notice	Description
1. *De minimis* safe harbor for tangible property	Chapter 17: Real Estate Game	IRC §1.263(a)-1(f)	Allows expense items up to $2,500 ($5,000 with audited FS) rather than capitalizing.
2. Safe harbor for small taxpayers (SHST)	Chapter 17: Real Estate Game	IRC §1.263(a)-3h	Allows certain building-related costs to be deducted if under $10,000 or 2% on an unadjusted basis.
3. Home office simplified safe harbor	Chapter 12: Home Office	IRS Revenue Procedure 2013-13	Simplifies method for home office deduction: $5/sq ft up to 300 sq ft.
4. Real estate professional grouping election safe harbor	Chapter 17: REP Strategies	IRC §1.469-9(g)	Allows grouping all rental activities into one for material participation.
5. Safe harbor for QBI wages and property test	Chapter 8: Small Biz Tax	IRC §199A	Applies to limitations on QBI deduction for higher-income filers.
6. Safe harbor for rental real estate as a trade or business	Chapter 17: Real Estate Game	IRS Notice 2019-07	Allows rentals to qualify for §199A deduction if certain requirements are met.

7. Safe harbor for accounting method changes (Form 3115)	Chapter 19: Depreciation Masterclass	IRC §446 and Rev. Proc. 2015-13	Streamlines process for changing depreciation methods.
8. Safe harbor for deducting repairs vs. improvements	Chapter 18: Real Estate Mastery	IRC §1.162-4 and §1.263(a)-3	Guidelines to distinguish deductible repairs from capital improvements.
9. $5,000 Start-Up and Organization Cost Safe Harbor	Chapter 11: Business Foundations	IRC §195 and §259	Allows immediate deduction of up to $5,000 each for qualifying start-up and organizational costs in the first year.

Note: The IRS safe harbor is a provision in tax law that allows taxpayers to avoid penalties and reduce audit risk if they meet specific criteria outlined by the IRS. It provides a "safe zone" where the IRS agrees not to challenge or penalize a certain tax position, even if the outcome would otherwise be uncertain or subject to interpretation.

Appendix 3

IRS Code Referenced in the Book

Chapter	IRS Publication	Publication Description	Code Description
Chapter 1: Buffett's lessons	Pub 590-B	Distributions from IRAs	Roth IRA rules
Chapter 2: Vision board	Pub 590, Pub 969	IRA and HSA benefits overview	Tax-advantaged accounts and life insurance definitions
Chapter 3: FIRE journey	Pub 590-A/B, Pub 969	IRA rules and HSA guidance	Early withdrawal rules, 401(K) limits, Roth conversion rules
Chapter 4: Layoff strategy	Pub 4128	Tax impact of job loss	Severance pay, unemployment compensation and retirement plan distributions
Chapter 5: Education Planning	Pub 970	Tax benefits for education, including 529s and credits	529 Plans, American Opportunity Tax Credit, Coverdell ESA rules
Chapter 6: Artificial Intelligence and Tax Planning	IRS Strategic Plan (2023–2031)	How to use AI to improve tax efficiency	IRS AI governance.
Chapter 7: Retirement mindset	Pub 590-B	IRA distributions	Qualified retirement plan rules
Chapter 8: 401(K) mastery	Pub 560	Retirement plans for small businesses	Deferral limits and catch-up rules
Chapter 9: Whole life legacy	Pub 525	Taxable and nontaxable income	Life insurance exclusions and definitions

Chapter 10: Family trust setup	Pub 559	Survivors, executors, and administrators guidance	Grantor trust rules
Chapter 11: Small Business Tax	Pub 334	Tax guide for small business	QBI deduction and ordinary expenses
Chapter 12: Home office	Pub 587	Business use of your home	Home office deduction requirements
Chapter 13: Auto deduction	Pub 463	Travel, gift, and car expense deductions	Ordinary business expenses and documentation requirements
Chapter 14: Business travel	Pub 463	Travel, gift, and car expense deductions	Business expense deductions
Chapter 15: Medical Expense	IRS Code: §162(l)	Self-employed health insurance deduction	Health insurance premiums
Chapter 16: Business retirement plan	Pub 560	Retirement plans for small businesses	Limits and structures for retirement contributions
Chapter 17: Real estate game	Pub 527	Residential rental property guidance	Home sale exclusion and like-kind exchange rules
Chapter 18: Real estate and rental	Pub 527, Pub 544, Pub 551	Residential rental property, basis of assets, sales of property	Rental income and expenses, depreciation rules, basis calculation, gain or loss recognition, and exclusion rules for home sales
Chapter 19: Depreciation masterclass	Pub 946	How to depreciate property	Depreciation, capital improvements, and recapture rules
Chapter 20: REP strategies	Pub 925	Passive activity and loss rules	Real estate professional qualification for loss deductions
Chapter 21: Real estate FAQs	Pub 527	Residential rental property guidance	Hobby loss rules and home use restrictions
Chapter 22: Family foundation	Pub 578	Private foundations	Excise taxes and charitable deduction rules
Chapter 23: Charitable Giving	Pub 526	Charitable contribution rules	Deductions for donations
Chapter 24: 990-PF filing	Form 990-PF Instructions	How to file private foundation return	Excise tax on investment income, self-dealing, minimum distribution

Chapter 25: Non-profit audit red flags	Pub 557	Tax-Exempt Status for Your Organization	Revocation and Penalties
Chapter 26: Portfolio management	Pub 4228-PF	Jeopardizing Investments	Investment to carry out its exempt purpose (e.g., risky, speculative investments)

Appendix 4

IRS Forms or Schedules Referenced in the Book

Form or Schedule	Access Link
Form 1040	U.S. Individual Income Tax Return. The primary form for filing personal federal income taxes. https://www.irs.gov/forms-pubs/about-form-1040
Form 1099	Used to report various types of non-employment income, such as interest, dividends, and contractor payments. https://www.irs.gov/forms-pubs/about-form-1099
Form W-2	Reports wages and tax withholding for employees. https://www.irs.gov/forms-pubs/about-form-w-2 Schedule A
	Used to itemize deductions such as medical expenses, taxes, mortgage interest, and charitable gifts. https://www.irs.gov/forms-pubs/about-schedule-a-form-1040
Schedule A	About Schedule A (Form 1040), Itemized Deductions | Internal Revenue Service
Schedule B	About Schedule B (Form 1040), Interest and Ordinary Dividends | Internal Revenue Service
Schedule C	Used to report income or loss from a sole proprietorship or single-member LLC. https://www.irs.gov/forms-pubs/about-schedule-c-form-1040
Schedule D	https://www.irs.gov/instructions/i1040sd 2024 Instructions for Schedule D (2024) | Internal Revenue Service
Schedule E	Reports income and loss from rental real estate, royalties, partnerships, S corps, estates, and trusts. https://www.irs.gov/forms-pubs/about-schedule-e-form-1040
Form 3115	Application for Change in Accounting Method, often used for cost segregation catch-up depreciation. https://www.irs.gov/forms-pubs/about-form-3115
Form 4562	Instructions for Form 4562 (2024) | Internal Revenue Service

Form 4797	Instructions for Form 4797 (2024)	Internal Revenue Service
Form 5329	Additional Taxes on Qualified Plans
Form 5500-SF	https://www.dol.gov/sites/dolgov/files/EBSA/employers-and-advisers/plan-administration-and-compliance/reporting-and-filing/form-5500/2024-sf-instructions.pdf
Form 8283	Used to report noncash charitable contributions over $500. https://www.irs.gov/forms-pubs/about-form-8283
Form 8582	Instructions for Form 8582 (2024)	Internal Revenue Service
Form 8606	Used to report nondeductible contributions to traditional IRAs and conversions to Roth IRAs. https://www.irs.gov/forms-pubs/about-form-8606
Form 8822-B	About Form 8822-B, Change of Address or Responsible Party - Business	Internal Revenue Service
Form 8863	Used to claim education credits like the American Opportunity and Lifetime Learning Credits. https://www.irs.gov/forms-pubs/about-form-8863
Form 8889	Reports HSA contributions, deductions, and distributions. https://www.irs.gov/forms-pubs/about-form-8889
Form 8960	Calculates the Net Investment Income Tax for high-income earners. https://www.irs.gov/forms-pubs/about-form-8960
Form 8868	Application for Extension of Time To File an Exempt Organization Return https://www.irs.gov/instructions/i8868
Form 8941	Instructions for Form 8941 (2024)	Internal Revenue Service Credit for Small Employer Health Insurance Premiums
Form 990-PF	Return for private foundations reporting assets, income, and grants. https://www.irs.gov/forms-pubs/about-form-990-pf

Appendix 5

The Ten Tax Books That Changed My Life—A Family Story

If you told me 20 years ago that reading dusty tax books would change my family's destiny, I would have laughed. I thought taxes were just a necessary evil, something to survive each spring. But as a husband, father, business owner, and mentor to others, I realized tax planning could be a powerful tool for building wealth, security, and freedom.

The transformation began with books, one by one, page by page. Each book became a stepping stone. Here are the ten books that not only taught me but also changed me.

1. The Snowball: Warren Buffett and the Business of Life by Alice Schroeder [1]

I picked this up expecting a biography and found a blueprint for patience, simplicity, and discipline. Buffett taught me that real wealth is not built overnight. I stopped chasing hot stocks and built a boring but big, beautiful portfolio of well-diversified index funds such as S&P 500 (with fees as low as 0.015% per year). More importantly, I started thinking in decades, not days.

Inspired, I opened UTMA accounts for my kids, teaching them to invest long-term. Today, our "family compound" strategy (a mix of simple, durable investments) keeps growing quietly, just like Buffett's snowball.

2. Money: Master the Game by Tony Robbins [2]

Tony's book jolted me awake. His breakdown of hidden 401(k) fees made me furious and determined.

I pored over a small business 401(k) plan ($260 monthly administrative fees, $5 per participant, and layers of fund fees). That day, I moved everything to Vanguard IRAs. Simple, transparent, powerful, and no fees. I have since helped dozens of friends cut fees. One client cried when she realized she was saving $4,200 a year.

3. The Retirement Savings Time Bomb by Ed Slott [3]

Ed Slott became my "retirement sensei." His wisdom about Roth conversions, avoiding rollover traps, and maximizing tax-free growth shaped my entire strategy.

When my wife accidentally triggered a taxable distribution, Ed's guidance helped us craft an appeal letter and saved us $7,000 of penalties. Today, I convert small chunks of our IRAs to Roth every time the market (measured by S&P 500) dips 10% or more.

4. Family Trusts by Hartley Goldstone [4]

This was not just about legal documents. It was about vision.

After reading this, I did not just create a trust; I also wrote a legacy letter to my kids. Every year, we hold "trustee meetings" over pizza and pasta, reviewing our mission, goals, and dreams. When tragedy struck our extended family, we saw firsthand how trust clarity preserved relationships and legacies.

5. Family Banking with Life Insurance by David Phillips [5]

This little-known book opened my eyes to whole life insurance as a personal banking system. I started small: One policy for me, then one for each child.

Today, we have over 20 policies across our family. We have borrowed against them to buy rentals, pay medical bills, and invest in businesses, all tax-free. It has been like having a financial safety net that grows stronger every year. In addition, policy loan interest may be deductible as a business interest expense if the fund is used in profit-making businesses.

6. Tax Deductions Big Time by Sandy Botkin [6]

This book was like finding a treasure map.

From home office deductions to paying my children legitimately through my business, it turbocharged our tax returns. I paid my son $7,000 for real work, funded his Roth IRA, and watched him build retirement wealth before he turned 15.

7. J.K. Lasser's Small Business Taxes by Barbara Weltman [7]

Barbara Weltman became my annual guide.

In every new edition, I highlighted and implemented new strategies: deducting our family board meetings at beach rentals, documenting mileage, and meals the right way, maximizing business deductions. I have gifted this book to over 30 clients, and every single one found hidden gold.

8. The Case for IBC by L. Carlos Lara & Nelson Nash [8]

This slim book drastically changed how I saw banking.

Why borrow from banks when we can borrow from ourselves? Using loans from our life insurance policies, we have funded real estate, cars, and tuition, earning back the "banker's profit" ourselves. It has been transformational for my family.

9. The Win-Win Wealth Strategy by Tom Wheelwright [9]

Tom taught me that the IRS is not out to get us but encourages us. The government rewards entrepreneurs, real estate investors, and energy innovators with tax breaks.

His insights on deducting life insurance loan interest and structuring real estate deals completely reshaped my playbook. I now view the tax code as an investment manual.

10. The Tax and Legal Playbook by Mark J. Kohler [10]

Mark made asset protection and tax planning feel simple. His "trifecta" strategy—LLC for rentals, S Corp for business, trust for wealth transfer—became our foundation.

Today, thanks to his teachings, our family structure is robust, protected, and prepared to weather any storm. If you want a high quality tax consult, seek a good accountant from the Certified Tax Advisor Network created and maintained by Mark J. Kohler and his company.

Top 10 Tax Planning Strategies These Books Inspired

1. Roll over 401(k)s to low-fee IRAs (Tony Robbins)

2. Convert to Roth IRA during market dips (Ed Slott)

3. Use whole life insurance as a tax-free family bank (Living Wealth, Lara & Nash)

4. Employ children through your business (Sandy Botkin)

5. Deduct family retreats as business meetings (Barbara Weltman)

6. Use the Augusta rule to rent your home to your business (Mark Kohler)

7. Deduct life insurance loan interest for investments (Tom Wheelwright)

8. Create a family trust to avoid probate (Hartley Goldstone)

9. Document everything for maximum deductions (Multiple authors)

10. Start a side business to unlock deductions (Collective wisdom from all)

Glossary

- **1040** – Main U.S. individual income tax return.
- **1099** – Forms for non-employment income such as freelance, dividends, and interest.
- **5% Rule (Foundation Payout Rule)** – Private foundations must distribute 5% of assets annually.
- **529 Plan** – Tax-free education savings account for qualified expenses.
- **AGI (Adjusted Gross Income)** – Total income minus specific deductions; used to calculate taxable income.
- **AMT (Alternative Minimum Tax)** – Ensures high-income earners pay a minimum tax, even with deductions.
- **AMT Credit** – Offsets regular tax for AMT paid in prior years.
- **Backdoor Roth IRA** – Strategy to bypass Roth IRA income limits via conversion.
- **Basis** – Value of an asset used for tax calculations.
- **Bonus Depreciation** – Immediate deduction of eligible property costs.
- **C-Corp** – A corporation taxed separately from its owners under Subchapter C.
- **Capital Gains Tax** – Tax on profit from asset sales.
- **Cost Segregation** – Accelerated depreciation strategy for real estate.
- **CYA Letter** – Cover letter to document and justify tax positions.
- **Depreciation Recapture** – Tax on previously claimed depreciation when asset is sold.
- **Form 3115** – Used to change accounting methods.
- **Form 8606** – Tracks non-deductible IRA contributions and Roth conversions.
- **Form 990-PF** – Annual IRS return for private foundations.
- **FSA (Flexible Spending Account)** – Pre-tax account for health or dependent care expenses.
- **HELOC** – Home Equity Line of Credit; interest may be deductible on business tax return if the fund is used in profit-seeking business.
- **HSA (Health Savings Account)** – Tax-advantaged savings for health expenses with triple tax benefits.
- **IRA (Individual Retirement Arrangement)** – A tax-advantaged account established for the exclusive benefit of an individual or their beneficiaries, designed to encourage retirement savings.
- **IRS Audit Flag** – Deductions or patterns that raise audit risk.
- **IRS Pub** – IRS publications providing official guidance.
- **LLC (Limited Liability Company)** – Flexible legal entity with liability protection and pass-through taxation.
- **Mega Backdoor Roth** – Uses 401(K) after-tax contributions to allow larger Roth conversions.
- **NOL (Net Operating Loss)** – Business loss that can be carried forward to offset future income.
- **QBI (§199A Qualified Business Income)** – Deduction of up to 20% of pass-through business income.

- **QCD (Qualified Charitable Distribution)** – IRA donation satisfying RMD and reducing taxable income.
- **REP (Real Estate Professional)** – Status allowing rental losses to offset active income.
- **RMD (Required Minimum Distribution)** – Mandatory retirement withdrawals starting at age 73 (or other number depending on your birth year).
- **Roth IRA** – After-tax retirement account with tax-free withdrawals.
- **S-Corp** – A pass-through entity where income is taxed at the shareholder level.
- **Safe Harbor Rules** – Simplified IRS procedures offering protection and clarity.
- **SBLOC (Securities-Backed Line of Credit)** – Loan secured by investments to avoid capital gains. Interest may be deductible on business tax return if the fund is used in profit-seeking business.
- **Schedule A** – Itemized deductions for individuals.
- **Schedule C** – Reports income/loss from a sole proprietorship.
- **Schedule E** – Reports rental, royalty, partnership, and S-Corp income.
- **Section 1031 Exchange** – Defers capital gains tax by reinvesting in similar property.
- **Section 121 Exclusion** – Excludes up to $500,000 of capital gain on sale of a primary residence.
- **SEP IRA** – Retirement plan for self-employed/small business owners with higher contribution limits.
- **Short-Term vs. Long-Term Gain** – Short-term (≤1 year) taxed higher than long-term (>1 year).
- **Solo 401(k)** – High-limit retirement plan for self-employed individuals with no employees.
- **Traditional IRA** – Tax-deductible retirement account with taxable withdrawals.
- **UGMA/UTMA** – Custodial accounts for minors with income or capital gain taxed as the kiddie tax.
- **W-2** – Form reporting annual wages and tax withholdings.

BONUS

100 SMART Family Tax Planning Tips Under the One Big Beautiful Bill Act

The passage of the One Big Beautiful Bill Act marks a transformative moment for American families seeking to maximize their financial well-being. With sweeping reforms that make the 2017 tax cuts permanent, expand the child tax credit, boost the standard deduction, and introduce innovative savings tools like Trump Accounts, this legislation delivers unprecedented opportunities for families to keep more of what they earn and build lasting wealth.

From eliminating taxes on tips and overtime pay to enhancing 529 education savings and providing new incentives for estate planning, the Act empowers families at every stage of life to make smarter, more strategic tax moves. This bonus chapter unveils 100 actionable, family-focused tax strategies, each designed to help you navigate the new landscape, reduce your tax burden, and secure a brighter financial future under the One Big Beautiful Bill Act.

Disclaimer: Many of the tax forms and schedules will be released by the IRS and other agencies in a few months. You are advised to visit IRS.gov for more updates. Some states may choose not to amend the state tax codes to reflect the federal level tax law changes. Seek tax advice from the CPAs that are licensed in your state(s).

Unless otherwise noted, AGI thresholds are for 2025 and may be indexed for inflation in future years. For married couples, joint filing is often advantageous for phase-out thresholds. Taxpayers should consider timing income, deductions, and major purchases to maximize benefits under any phase-out rules. Consult a tax advisor for personalized planning, especially if your AGI is near a phase-out threshold.

1. Permanent Tax Changes

No.	Permanent Tax Change	Description	Tax Planning Tips
1	Permanent extension of reduced individual tax rates	The lower individual tax rates from the TCJA are made permanent; the sunset after 2025 is repealed. IRC §1(j), Sec. 70101	Review income acceleration/deferral strategies, as rate increases are no longer a concern. Consider Roth conversions or capital gain recognition without fear of higher future rates.
2	Permanent increase and enhancement of standard deduction	The increased standard deduction is made permanent and further increased ($23,625 for heads of household, $15,750 for singles, and $31,500 for joint, indexed). IRC §63(c)(7), Sec. 70102	Taxpayers who previously itemized may now benefit more from the standard deduction. Bunch charitable contributions or deductible expenses in alternate years to maximize itemization when possible.
3	Permanent suspension of personal exemptions (except for seniors)	Personal exemptions remain suspended, but a $6,000 deduction is allowed for seniors (65+) through 2028, phased out at higher incomes. IRC §151(d)(5), Sec. 70103	Seniors should ensure their SSNs are reported to claim the deduction. Plan income to avoid phase-out thresholds. Apply "buy, borrow and build" strategy in retirement.
4	Permanent increase and enhancement of child tax credit	The child tax credit is permanently increased to $2,200 per child, with inflation adjustments and stricter SSN requirements. IRC §24(h), Sec. 70104	Ensure all qualifying children have valid SSNs. Consider timing of births/adoptions to maximize credits.
5	Enhancement of qualified business income (QBI) deduction	The phase-in threshold for QBI deduction limitations is increased to $75,000 ($150,000 joint), and a $400 minimum deduction is established for active business income, with inflation adjustments.	Owners of pass-through entities should review aggregation and wage/property strategies. Ensure material participation to qualify for the minimum deduction.

No.	Permanent Tax Change	Description	Tax Planning Tips
		IRC §199A(b)(3), §199A(i), Sec. 70105	
6	Permanent increase in estate and gift tax exemption	The exemption is permanently increased to $15 million (indexed), effective for estates/gifts after 2025. IRC §2010(c)(3), Sec. 70106	Consider gifting strategies to utilize higher exemption. Review and update estate plans to reflect the new limits.
7	Permanent increase in AMT exemption and phaseout thresholds	The increased AMT exemption and phaseout thresholds are made permanent, with modified inflation adjustments and phaseout rates. IRC §55(d)(4), Sec. 70107	Fewer taxpayers will be subject to AMT. Review incentive stock option exercise strategies and other AMT-sensitive transactions.
8	Permanent limitation on mortgage interest deduction	The $750,000 cap on mortgage interest deduction is made permanent, and mortgage insurance premiums are treated as interest. IRC §163(h)(3)(F), Sec. 70108	Consider paying down mortgage balances to maximize deductibility. Evaluate the impact of mortgage insurance premiums on total deductions.
9	Permanent limitation on casualty loss deduction	Casualty loss deduction is expanded by including both federally and state-declared disasters. IRC §165(h)(5), Sec. 70109	Ensure proper documentation for losses. Consider insurance coverage adequacy, as non-disaster losses are not deductible.
10	Permanent full expense for business property	100% bonus depreciation for qualified business property is made permanent. IRC §168(k), Sec. 70301	Accelerate purchases of eligible property to maximize deductions. Consider the impact on taxable income and potential for NOLs. Coordinate with Section 179 expensing.
11	Miscellaneous itemized deductions	Permanent termination of miscellaneous itemized deductions other than	The educator expenses are now deductible as itemized deductions. In addition, educators include

No.	Permanent Tax Change	Description	Tax Planning Tips
		educator expenses (Sec. 70110)	interscholastic administrators or coaches.
12	Bicycle commuting reimbursements	Permanent treatment of bicycle commuting reimbursements as qualified transportation fringe benefits for employees (Sec. 70112)	Part of the White House effort to make Americans healthy again.
13	Moving expenses	Permanent expanded the moving expense deduction from members of the armed forces on active duty to intelligence community defined by the National Security Act who move on job duty (Sec. 70113)	What can be deducted? Only reasonable expenses of: (1) Moving household goods and personal effects from the former residence to the new residence; (2) Traveling (including lodging, but not meals) from the former residence to the new place of residence.

2. Tax Code Changes that are Only Effective Between 2025 and 2028, and May Sunset Afterwards

#	Tax Change/Provision	Description	IRC/OBBB Section Reference	Tax Planning Tip
1	No tax on tips	Excludes up to $25,000 in qualified tips per year, phased out at higher income.	New IRC §231; Sec. 70201	Ensure all tips are properly reported and documented to maximize the exclusion before 2029.
2	No tax on overtime	Excludes up to $12,500 ($25,000 joint) in qualified overtime pay per year, phased out at higher income.	New IRC §232; Sec. 70202	Track and report overtime separately; consider timing overtime work to maximize annual exclusions.
3	Temporary deduction for car loan interest	Deduction of up to $10,000/year for interest on loans for new U.S.-assembled passenger vehicles.	IRC §163(h)(4); Sec. 70203	If planning to buy a new car, do so before 2029 and ensure it meets U.S. assembly requirements.
4	Trump accounts and contribution pilot program	New tax-advantaged savings accounts for children under 18, with a $5,000 annual contribution limit and $1,000 government-	New IRC §530A, §6434; Sec. 70204	Open and fund Trump Accounts for eligible children as early as possible to maximize compounding and government match.

#	Tax Change/Provision	Description	IRC/OBBB Section Reference	Tax Planning Tip
		funded pilot for newborns.		
5	Employer contributions to Trump Accounts	Employers can contribute up to $2,500 per employee (indexed) to Trump Accounts, excluded from employee income.	New IRC §128; Sec. 70204(b)	Encourage employer contributions and coordinate with your employer to maximize this benefit.
6	Certain contributions to Trump Accounts excluded from gross income	Qualified general contributions to Trump Accounts are excluded from the beneficiary's income.	New IRC §139J; Sec. 70204(c)	Seek out eligible contributions from charities or government programs for children's Trump Accounts.
7	Trump Accounts contribution pilot program	$1,000 government-funded contribution for newborns (2025–2028) via election by a parent.	New IRC §6434; Sec. 70204(d)	For children born in 2025–2028, file the election promptly to secure the $1,000 government contribution.
8	Deduction for car loan interest allowed to non-itemizers	Non-itemizers can claim the car loan interest as an above-the-line deduction.	Sec. 70203(b)	Even if you do not itemize, claim the deduction for qualifying car loan interest to lower taxable income.

3. Tax Code Changes Affecting Small Business Owners

No.	Tax Change/Provision	Description	Tax Planning Tip
1	Full expense of domestic research and experimental expenditures (Sec. 70302)	Domestic research and experimental expenditures can be fully expensed immediately (new IRC §174A). A taxpayer may elect to capitalize and amortize these costs ratably over a period of at least 60 months. Foreign R&D remains amortized over 15 years.	Track and document all qualifying R&D expenditures related to business projects to ensure full expense. If the new small business incurs losses in its inception period, the 60-month amortization may be more tax beneficial than the full depreciation.
2	Increase in Section 179 expensing limits (Sec. 70306)	Section 179 expense limit increased to $2.5 million, phaseout at $4 million, with inflation adjustments (IRC §179(b)). SUV limit remains unchanged at $31,300.	Time purchases of qualifying property to stay under the phaseout threshold and maximize deductions.
3	Modification of limitation on business interest (Sec. 70303)	Reinstates EBITDA limitation for tax years beginning after December 31, 2024.	Increased deductibility: The EBITDA add-back increases the adjusted taxable income, which in turn increases the amount of business interest expense that can be deducted.

No.	Tax Change/Provision	Description	Tax Planning Tip
			Taxpayers with significant depreciation and amortization deductions (e.g., capital-intensive businesses) will benefit most.
4	Full expensing for certain business property (Sec. 70301)	100% bonus depreciation for property acquired and placed in service after January 19, 2025.	Consider electing out if you want to spread deductions over future years (e.g., to avoid creating or increasing a net operating loss, or to better match deductions with income over the years).
5	Extension and enhancement of paid family and medical leave credit (Sec. 70304)	Permanently extends the credit. Allows credit to be claimed for premiums paid for insurance policies providing paid and family leave for employees.	Employers who do not want to self-insure paid family and medical leave can purchase qualifying insurance policies and claim the credit for premiums paid, provided the policy meets the statutory requirements for leave duration and wage replacement.

No.	Tax Change/Provision	Description	Tax Planning Tip
			This can simplify administration and risk management, especially for smaller employers.
6	Special depreciation allowance for qualified production property (Sec. 70307)	100% deduction for qualified production property: (1) nonresidential real property; (2) used for manufacturing, production, or refining; and (3) construction period and place in service period requirements. Segregate costs: For mixed-use buildings, perform a cost segregation study to allocate costs between qualifying production areas and non-qualifying areas.	Maintain detailed records: (1) construction start and placed-in-service dates; (2) documentation of the property's use as an integral part of a qualified production activity; and (3) allocation of property between qualifying and non-qualifying uses (e.g., production vs. office space)
7	Enhancement of employer-provided childcare credit (Sec. 70401)	Increases credit percentage from 25% to 40% (50% for eligible small businesses) for amounts paid or incurred after December 31, 2025. Increases maximum credit from $150,000 to $500,000 ($600,000 for eligible small businesses). Eligible small businesses meet the gross receipts test under IRC Section 448(c) for the previous five years (rather than three years).	Qualified childcare expenditures can include amounts paid to outside vendors to provide childcare services. Qualified childcare facilities may include facilities that are jointly owned or operated by the

No.	Tax Change/Provision	Description	Tax Planning Tip
			taxpayer and other parties.
8	Expansion of qualified small business stock gain exclusion (Sec. 70431)	Phased increase in exclusion for gain from qualified small business stock (i.e., section 1202 stocks): | Years stock held	Applicable %
---	---
Three	50
Four	75
Five+	100		Stock acquired from another shareholder (not original issuance) does not qualify. Failure to maintain C corporation status or active business requirements can disqualify stock. Inadequate documentation can result in loss of exclusion.
9	1099-K *de minimis* rule (Sec. 70432)	Form 1099-K requirement for third-party settlement organizations to $20,000 on more than 200 transactions. Applies retroactively to calendar years beginning after December 31, 2021.	Small sellers, gig workers, and casual users of platforms such as eBay, Etsy, PayPal, and Venmo who do not exceed both $20,000 in payments and 200 transactions in a year will generally not receive a Form 1099-K. Individuals selling personal items (e.g., used furniture, clothing) in small amounts are less

No.	Tax Change/Provision	Description	Tax Planning Tip
			likely to be reported.
10	Increased reporting threshold for 1099-NEC and 1099-MISC (Sec. 70433)	$2,000 for tax years beginning after December 31, 2025 (indexed for inflation).	The prior threshold ($600) has not been adjusted for inflation since 1954.

4. Tax Code Changes Affecting Retirees

No.	Tax Change/Provision	Description & Impact for Retirees	Tax Planning Tips
1	Permanent extension of reduced individual tax rates	The lower individual tax rates from the TCJA are made permanent, preventing a rate increase for retirees with taxable income.	Retirees with taxable income should continue to benefit from lower rates, making Roth conversions and other income acceleration strategies more attractive. Use rental losses (up to $25,000) to further reduce the AGI.
2	Permanent increase and enhancement of standard deduction	The increased standard deduction is made permanent and further increased.	Retirees should compare itemized vs. standard deduction annually.
3	Termination of personal exemptions except for seniors	Personal exemptions remain eliminated for most, but a new $6,000 deduction is allowed for each taxpayer and spouse age 65+ (through 2028). This deduction phases out when modified AGI exceeds $75,000 (single) or $150,000 (joint).	Retirees with AGI below the phaseout threshold should claim the deduction. Those near the threshold may benefit from income deferral or other planning to maximize the deduction.

Defer social security benefits to 70 if feasible. Delay traditional 401(k) withdrawal is possible.

Use the "buy, borrow and retire" strategy during the retirement age. |
| 4 | Permanent increase in estate and gift tax exemption | The estate and gift tax exemption is permanently increased to $15 million (indexed), reducing estate tax exposure for wealthy retirees. | Retirees with large estates should review gifting and estate plans to maximize use of higher exemption.

Unused estate exclusion amounts can be ported to the surviving spouse, so-called deceased spousal unused exclusion. Seek a tax pro. |

5. Tax Code Changes Affecting Real Estate Investors and Homeowners

No.	Tax Change/Provision	Description	Impact on Real Estate Investors/Landlords	Tax Planning Tip
1	Permanent Increases SALT deduction to $40,000 in 2025	State and Local Taxes (SALT) increased by 1% starting in 2027, and reverts back to $10,000 in 2030 (Sec. 70120)	SALT deduction reduced by 30% of excess modified adjusted gross income over the threshold amount. Back to $10,000 if AGI (joint) is over $600,000.	By paying the property taxes in December rather than waiting until January of Year 2, the taxpayer increases total deductions. This is especially true in the year 2029. SALT can include your second home (or vacation home).
2	Permanent full expensing for business property	100% bonus depreciation for qualified business property is made permanent (IRC §168(k)).	Real estate investors can immediately expense the full cost of eligible property (e.g., certain improvements, personal property) rather than depreciate over several years, improving cash flow.	Accelerate acquisitions and improvements of qualifying property to maximize immediate deductions; consider cost segregation studies to identify eligible assets.
3	Exception to percentage-of-completion for residential construction	Exceptions from the percentage-of-completion method expanded to include residential construction	Real estate developers of residential properties may use the completed contract method, deferring income recognition	Structure contracts and project timelines to qualify for the exception and

No.	Tax Change/Provision	Description	Impact on Real Estate Investors/Landlords	Tax Planning Tip
		contracts with a 3-year completion test (IRC §460(e)).	until project completion.	defer taxable income.
4	Permanent limitation on mortgage interest deduction	$750,000 cap on mortgage interest deduction is made permanent; mortgage insurance premiums are treated as interest (IRC §163(h)(3)(F)).	Investors and landlords with leveraged properties face a permanent cap on deductible mortgage interest, potentially increasing taxable income.	Consider optimizing debt structure and exploring alternative financing to maximize deductible interest.
5	Permanent limitation on casualty loss deduction	Casualty loss deduction limited to federally and state-declared disasters (IRC §165(h)(5)).	Losses from property damage are only deductible if the event is a declared disaster, limiting deductions for other losses.	Maintain comprehensive insurance coverage and document all losses for potential deduction if a disaster is declared.
6	Permanent renewal and enhancement of opportunity zones (Sec. 70421)	New decennial designations, expanded reporting, new rural opportunity funds, and extended/modified benefits (IRC §1400Z-1, §1400Z-2).	Investors can continue to defer and potentially exclude capital gains by investing in qualified opportunity funds, with new zones and reporting requirements.	Monitor new zone designations and reporting rules; consider both urban and rural opportunities for tax-advantaged investments. Invest in opportunity zones close to coal mines, shipyard and other natural

No.	Tax Change/Provision	Description	Impact on Real Estate Investors/Landlords	Tax Planning Tip
				resource locations where OBBB supports.
7.	Permanent enhancement of low-income housing tax credit (LIHTC) (Sec. 70422)	State credit ceiling increases are made permanent; bond financing requirements are relaxed (IRC §42(h)(3)).	Developers and investors in affordable housing projects benefit from increased and more accessible LIHTC allocations, improving project feasibility.	Explore new affordable housing projects or expansions to take advantage of increased credits and relaxed financing rules.

6. Tax Code Changes Affecting Gen Z (Tips, overtime, child credit, and more)

No.	Tax Change/Provision	Description	Impact on Gen Z	Tax Planning Tip
1	Deduction for qualified tips	Allows a deduction of up to $25,000 per year for cash tips received in occupations that customarily received tips before 2025, subject to income phaseouts and reporting requirements.	Gen Z workers in service industries (restaurants, salons, etc.) can reduce taxable income by excluding tips, lowering their tax bill.	Keep detailed records and ensure all tips are properly reported to maximize the deduction and avoid IRS issues.
2	Deduction for overtime pay	Permits a deduction of up to $12,500 ($25,000 joint) per year for overtime compensation required under the Fair Labor Standards Act, with income phaseouts.	Young workers putting in extra hours can reduce taxable income, making overtime more financially rewarding.	Track overtime hours and ensure employers report overtime pay separately on W-2s for deduction eligibility.
3	Enhanced standard deduction	Increases the standard deduction, effective 2025.	Most Gen Z filers will benefit from a higher standard deduction, reducing taxable income even if they don't itemize.	Compare itemized deductions to the new standard deduction each year to choose the most beneficial option.
4	Expanded child tax credit	Increases the child tax credit to $2,200 per child, with inflation adjustments and stricter SSN requirements.	Young parents in Gen Z will receive a larger credit per child, increasing refunds or	Ensure both you and your child have valid SSNs and file early to claim the credit.

No.	Tax Change/Provision	Description	Impact on Gen Z	Tax Planning Tip
			reducing tax owed.	
5	Permanent above-the-line student loan interest deduction	Makes the deduction for up to $2,500 of student loan interest permanent and subject to inflation adjustments. AGI $200,000 (joint) phase-out applies.	Gen Z graduates repaying student loans can continue to reduce taxable income, lowering their tax bill.	Make at least the minimum payments on student loans to maximize the deductible interest each year.
6	Employer student loan repayment exclusion	Makes permanent the exclusion from income for up to $5,260 per year in employer-paid student loan repayments, with inflation adjustments.	Gen Z employees can receive tax-free student loan payments from employers, reducing both tax and debt.	Seek out employers offering this benefit and coordinate with HR to ensure payments are structured for tax-free treatment. Parents' businesses can hire children via payroll so that children and other employees equally enjoy such tax-free fringe benefits.
7	Expanded 529 plan qualified expenses	Broadens 529 plan distributions to cover more K-12 (including home schooling) and postsecondary credentialing expenses and increases the	Gen Z students and parents can use 529 funds for a wider range of educational expenses,	Use 529 funds strategically for both college and qualifying non-degree programs

No.	Tax Change/Provision	Description	Impact on Gen Z	Tax Planning Tip
		annual K-12 limit to $20,000.	including job training and certifications.	to avoid taxes and penalties.
8	Refundable portion of adoption credit	Up to $5,000 of the adoption credit is now refundable, with inflation adjustments.	Gen Z individuals adopting children can receive a cash refund even if they owe no tax, easing the financial burden of adoption.	File for the adoption credit once eligible and keep all documentation to support the claim.
9	Increased dependent care assistance exclusion	Raises the exclusion for employer-provided dependent care assistance to $7,500 ($3,750 MFS).	Gen Z parents can receive more tax-free assistance for child or dependent care, reducing out-of-pocket costs.	Enroll in employer dependent care programs early in the year to maximize the exclusion.
10	Creation of Trump Accounts for children	Establishes new tax-advantaged savings accounts for children under 18, with a $5,000 annual contribution limit and a $1,000 government-funded pilot for newborns (2025–2028).	Gen Z parents can jumpstart savings for their children's future, with tax-deferred growth and potential government contributions.	Open a Trump Account for your child once eligible to maximize contributions and potential government funding.

7. Tax Planning Tips Around the Trump Accounts (Sec. 70204)

No.	Tax Change/Provision	Description	Tax Planning Tips
1	Accounts must be created before the beneficiary reaches age 18. The beneficiary must have an SSN.	The account beneficiary must be an individual who has not attained age 18 before the close of the calendar year in which the account is established.	If your child has not yet reached the age of 18 by the end of the calendar year, you can still establish and fund a Trump Account for them up to the annual contribution limit for that year.
2	Treated as a Traditional IRA under IRC Section 408(a).	The withdrawal after 18 has no other age limitation (e.g., 59.5), more flexible than 401(K) and IRA; and has no usage limitation (can pay tuition, car, house or even wedding), more flexible than 529 plan.	Liquidate the assets during the stock market peak time. Take advantage of the zero or low long term capital gain tax rate by selling stocks from the Trump Account when your AGI is below a certain threshold.
3	$5,000 contribution limit in 2026, adjusted for inflation starting in 2028	The limit does not include certain exempt contributions (such as qualified rollovers, qualified general contributions, or contributions under the Trump Accounts Contribution Pilot Program)	Contributions to Trump Accounts are not treated as gifts for the purpose of the annual gift tax exclusion under section. Such money can come from any family or nonfamily member.
4	Contributions to other retirement plans are not	There is no minimum age to	You child can have a few funded tax preferential

No.	Tax Change/Provision	Description	Tax Planning Tips
	limited before the beneficiary reaches age 18 (e.g., minor Roth IRA).	contribute to a Roth IRA, provided the individual has earned income. A Trump Account contribution can be earned income or gifted money, whereas a Roth IRA contribution must be earned income.	accounts before age 18: (1) Coverdell education savings account; (2) minor Roth IRA; (3) Roth 401(K), (4) UTMA; (5) 529 plan, (6) teen brokerage account; (7) cash value in whole life insurance; and (8) Trump Account.
5	Employers can contribute up to $2,500 to employees (or their dependents under 18). Not taxable to the employee.	Employer contribution counts towards the $5,000 annual contribution limit.	Employer contributions must be made under a separate written plan (a "Trump Account contribution program") for the exclusive benefit of employees. The plan must meet requirements similar to those for dependent care assistance programs, including nondiscrimination and eligibility rules.
6	Account funds must be invested in mutual funds or exchange-trade funds that track a qualified index (e.g., S&P 500 index).	Annual fees must be less than 0.1% of assets. No sector or industry funds. Does not use leverage.	You cannot apply the "buy, borrow and build" strategy against the Trump Account.
7	$1,000 contribution by Treasury deposited into Trump Account for children born between 2025 and 2028	Children must meet SSN and dependency test requirements.	The $1,000 government contribution is not counted against the $5,000 annual contribution limit for Trump Accounts. It is

No.	Tax Change/Provision	Description	Tax Planning Tips
			considered an "exempt contribution."

8. Tax Code Changes with AGI Phase Out Clauses

No.	Tax Change/Provision	Description	AGI Phase Out Thresholds	Tax Planning Tip
1	Child tax credit (CTC) enhancement (Sec. 70104)	Increases CTC to $2,200 per child, with inflation adjustments and stricter SSN requirements.	Phase out begins at $200,000 (single), $400,000 (joint); credit reduced by $50 per $1,000 over threshold.	Max out traditional IRA and 401(k) contributions. Fully fund HSA. Use real estate strategies (such as short term rental) to bring down the AGI.
2	State and local tax (SALT) deduction cap (Sec. 70120)	Raises SALT deduction cap to $40,000 ($20,000 MFS) for 2025, with phase-down for high AGI.	Phase-down: Cap reduced by 30% of AGI over $500,000 (single or joint), $505,000 in 2026, but not below $10,000.	If near the threshold, accelerate or defer SALT payments to maximize deduction in a favorable year.
3	Deduction for qualified tips (Sec. 70201)	Allows deduction up to $25,000 for qualified tips, phased out at higher AGI.	Deduction reduced by $100 for each $1,000 AGI over $150,000 (single), $300,000 (joint).	One spouse has high W-2 income, and the other can be a sole proprietor (with legitimate business loss) and tip income.
4	Deduction for qualified overtime compensation (Sec. 70202)	Allows deduction up to $12,500 ($25,000 joint) for overtime pay, phased out at higher AGI.	Deduction reduced by $100 for each $1,000 AGI over $150,000 (single), $300,000 (joint).	Coordinate overtime work and other income to avoid phase-out; consider joint filing if married.
5	Deduction for car loan interest (Sec. 70203)	Allows deduction up to $10,000 for interest on new U.S.-assembled car loans, phased	Deduction reduced by $200 for each $1,000 AGI over $100,000	Time vehicle purchases and loan payments with years with lower AGI;

No.	Tax Change/Provision	Description	AGI Phase Out Thresholds	Tax Planning Tip
		out at higher AGI.	(single), $200,000 (joint).	consider joint filing if married.
6	Senior personal exemption (Sec. 70103)	$6,000 deduction for each taxpayer/spouse age 65+, phased out at higher AGI.	Deduction reduced by 6% of AGI over $75,000 (single), $150,000 (joint).	If near the threshold, manage AGI through retirement plan contributions or timing of income. Delay social security benefits till 70, if feasible.
7	Itemized deduction limitation (Sec. 70111)	Reduces itemized deductions by 2/37 of the lesser of deductions or income above the 37% bracket threshold.	Reduction applies to income above the 37% bracket threshold (approx. $609,350 single, $731,200 joint for 2025, indexed).	Max out traditional IRA and 401(K) contributions. Fully fund HSA. Both can bring down the AGI.
8	Child and dependent care credit (sec. 70405)	Increases credit to 50% of eligible expenses, phased down to 35% at $15,000 AGI, then to 20% at $75,000 (single)/$150,000 (joint).	50% rate reduced by 1% per $2,000 over $15,000 (to 35%), then by 1% per $2,000 ($4,000 joint) over $75,000 ($150,000 joint) to 20%.	Max out traditional IRA and 401(K) contributions. Fully fund HSA. Both can bring down the AGI.
9	Above-the-line charitable deduction (Sec. 70424)	Increases above-the-line charitable deduction to $1,000 ($2,000 joint), subject to AGI floor.	Only contributions exceeding 0.5% of AGI are deductible.	Bunch charitable contributions in a single year to exceed the floor and maximize deduction.

No.	Tax Change/Provision	Description	AGI Phase Out Thresholds	Tax Planning Tip
10	Adoption credit (Sec. 70402)	Up to $5,000 of the adoption credit is refundable, with inflation adjustments.	Refundable portion phased out for AGI above $259,000 (single/joint, 2025, indexed).	Time adoption expenses with years with lower AGI; consider income deferral strategies if near the threshold.

9. Tax Code Changes Affecting Healthcare and Medical Expenses

No.	Tax Change/Provision	Healthcare and Medical Matters	Tax Planning Tip
1	Allowance of bronze and catastrophic plans in connection with health savings accounts (Sec. 71307)	Bronze and catastrophic plans treated as high-deductible health plans. Effective by the month after December 31, 2025.	Statutory language specifically treats these plans as HDHPs, regardless of whether or not they meet the usual minimum deductible and maximum out-of-pocket requirements for HDHPs under section 230(c)(2)(A). More people can benefit from the HSA account.
2	Revising home equity limit for determining eligibility for long-term care services under the Medicaid program (Sec. 71108).	Increases the home equity limit to $1 million.	Review your home equity, state law, and overall Medicaid planning strategy with a qualified professional to take advantage of the new rules while avoiding unnecessary transfers or tax consequences.
3	Requirement for states to establish Medicaid community engagement requirements (Sec. 71119)	The 80-hour per month rule, including work hours, community service hours, education program hours, or the combination of the three.	Employers with low-wage workers should be aware that employees may need documentation of hours worked to satisfy Medicaid requirements. Providing pay stubs and employment verification promptly can help employees maintain coverage.
4	Requiring verification of eligibility for premium tax credit (Sec. 71303)	Effective tax years beginning after December 31, 2027.	Delays the advance payment of the premium tax credit until an individual's eligibility for enrollment in a qualified health plan has been verified by an Exchange.

No.	Tax Change/Provision	Healthcare and Medical Matters	Tax Planning Tip
5	Extension and enhancement of paid family and medical leave credit (Sec. 70304)	Permanently extends the credit. Allows credit to be claimed for premiums paid for insurance policies providing paid and family or medical leave for employees.	If feasible, increasing the payment rate above 50% can increase the credit percentage.\n\nOptimize leave duration: The credit is available for up to 12 weeks per employee per year; structuring leave policies to maximize this period can increase the total credit.

10.   Tax code Affecting Student Loan Programs, 529 Plans and Education

No.	Tax Change/Provision	Impact on Taxpayers	Tax Planning Tip
1	Permanent exclusion for employer payments of student loans: IRC §127(c)(1)(B) exclusion for employer-paid student loan principal/interest is made permanent and indexed for inflation (Sec. 70412).	Employees can receive up to $5,260 (indexed after 2026) per year in tax-free student loan repayment assistance from employers.	If your employer offers this benefit, maximize participation to pay down student loans tax-free. Consider negotiating for this benefit if not offered.
2	Expansion of 529 qualified expenses: IRC §529(c)(7) expanded to include K-12 curriculum, tutoring, testing, and therapies; annual limit increased to $20,000 (Sec. 70413).	529 plan funds can now be used for a broader range of K-12 expenses, not just tuition, up to $20,000 per year.	Families with K-12 students should consider using 529 plans for eligible non-tuition expenses, but check state conformity to federal law.
3	529 plans cover postsecondary credentialing: IRC §529(e)(3), (f) now include expenses for recognized postsecondary credential programs, including fees, testing, and continuing education (Sec. 70414).	529 funds can be used for vocational training, certifications, and required testing, not just traditional college.	If pursuing a non-degree credential, use 529 funds to cover these costs tax-free. HVAC, plumber, electrician, and acupuncture are good licenses to obtain.
4	Exclusion for student loan discharge due to death or disability: IRC §108(f)(5) exclusion for student loan forgiveness on account of death or disability is made permanent (Sec. 70119).	Discharged student loan amounts due to death or total/permanent disability are not taxable income.	If eligible for discharge, ensure proper documentation is provided to avoid unexpected tax liability.
5	529 plan rollovers to ABLE accounts: IRC §529(c)(3)(C)(i)(III) allows rollovers from 529 plans to ABLE accounts for the	Families can transfer 529 funds to ABLE accounts (for individuals with disabilities)	If a beneficiary becomes disabled, consider rolling over unused 529 funds to an ABLE account for

No.	Tax Change/Provision	Impact on Taxpayers	Tax Planning Tip
	beneficiary or family member (Sec. 70117).	without tax or penalty, up to the annual ABLE contribution limit.	broader qualified expense coverage.
6	Exemption of certain assets from the FAFSA filing (Sec. 80001)	These assets are excluded from the student aid index computation: (1) family farm on which the family resides; and (2) a small business with not more than 100 full-time employees.	It is not clear whether College Board Scholarship Service (CSS), a program private college uses to decide financial aid, would exclude these family assets.

11. Tax Code Changes Affecting Charitable Giving and Non-Profit Organization

No.	Tax Change/Provision	Description	Tax Planning Tip
1	Permanent reinstatement of partial deduction for charitable contributions (Sec. 70424)	Apply to taxpayers with standard deduction. $2,000 for joint return ($1,000 for other taxpayers), starting in 2026.	Only contributions exceeding 0.5% of AGI are deductible. Bunch charitable contributions in a single year to exceed the floor and maximize deduction. If AGI is over $500,000, using itemized deduction to track charity giving will give you more deductions.
2	Tax credit for contributions of individuals to scholarship granting organizations (Sec. 70411)	Nonrefundable tax credit up to $1,700 for contributions made to scholarship granting organizations for tax years beginning after December 31, 2026	The nonprofit organization cannot be a family foundation. However family foundations can make qualified donations to these scholarship granting nonprofits.
3	0.5% floor on deduction of charitable contributions made by individuals (Sec. 70425)	For taxpayers who itemize, only charitable contributions in excess of 0.5% of the AGI are deductible	Taxpayers may find it more efficient to make a large charity contribution to their family foundation, which in turn gives charitable donations.
4	1% floor on deduction of charitable contributions made by corporations (Sec. 70426)	Only charitable contributions in excess of 1% of the corporation's adjusted taxable income are deductible for tax years beginning after December 31, 2025.	Taxpayers may find it more difficult to use business entities to make donations.
5	Modification of excise tax on investment income of certain	Tiered excise tax rate applies based on student-adjusted	Private colleges may face fiscal challenges, leading to lower student aid. Families

No.	Tax Change/Provision	Description	Tax Planning Tip
	private colleges and universities (Sec. 70415)	endowment up to 8%.	should seek self-funding resources in advance, including the newly funded Trump Account.

12. Tax Code Changes Affecting EV Credit or Clean Energy Homeowners

No.	Tax Change/Provision	Impact on EV Owners	Tax Planning Tip
1	Termination of clean vehicle credit (§30D) for new EVs (Sec. 70502)	The federal tax credit for new clean vehicles (up to $7,500) is eliminated for vehicles acquired after September 30, 2025.	If considering a new EV purchase, complete the acquisition before October 1, 2025 to claim the credit.
2	Termination of previously-owned clean vehicle credit (§25E) (Sec. 70501)	The credit for previously owned (used) clean vehicles (up to $4,000) is eliminated for vehicles acquired after September 30, 2025.	Purchase a qualifying used EV before October 1, 2025 to take advantage of the credit.
3	Termination of qualified commercial clean vehicles credit (§45W) (Sec. 70503)	The credit for commercial clean vehicles is eliminated for vehicles acquired after September 30, 2025.	Businesses should accelerate purchases of qualifying commercial EVs before the deadline.
4	Termination of alternative fuel vehicle refueling property credit (§30C) (Sec. 70504)	The credit for installing EV charging stations ends for property placed in service after June 30, 2026.	Install home or business EV charging equipment before July 1, 2026 to claim the credit.
5	Termination of clean electricity production and investment credits for wind/solar (affects EV charging infrastructure) (Sec. 70508)	Credits for wind/solar facilities (often used for EV charging) end for property placed in service after December 31, 2027, with new restrictions on foreign content.	Complete installation of renewable energy systems for EV charging before 2028 and ensure compliance with domestic content rules.

13.   Tax Code Changes Affecting Disabled Individuals

No.	Tax Change/Provision	Description	Tax Planning Tip
1	Extension and enhancement of increased limitation on contributions to ABLE Accounts (Sec. 70115)	Permanently allows the designated beneficiaries who work to contribute the least of their taxable compensation or the amount equal to the poverty line for a one-person household. The poverty line for a one-person household for the preceding year (for 2025: $15,060 in the continental U.S.).	The beneficiary (or their representative) is responsible for tracking and ensuring compliance with these limits and must maintain adequate records. Distributions for qualified disability expenses are tax-free. Maximizing contributions allows for greater tax-free growth and more resources for disability-related needs.
2	Extension and enhancement of increased limitation on contributions to ABLE accounts (Sec. 70115)	Makes the increased annual contribution limit permanent. The annual contribution limit to an ABLE account was generally the annual gift tax exclusion amount under IRC §2603(b) (e.g., $19,000 in 2025) and indexed with inflation rate afterward.	Rollovers from Trump Accounts to ABLE accounts do not count toward the annual or aggregate contribution limits, allowing for additional funding flexibility.
3	Extension and enhancement of savers credit allowed for ABLE contributions (Sec. 70116)	Credit allowed for contributions made by the disabled individual. Maximum credit increased from $2,000 to $2,100, effective for tax years beginning after December 31, 2026	The individuals with disabilities who earn income should continue to receive a tax credit for a portion of the contributions they make to their own ABLE accounts.
4	Extension of rollovers from qualified tuition programs to ABLE	60 days for rollover. Rollovers count toward the ABLE account annual contribution limit.	Family member rollovers: Rollovers can be made for the benefit of a family member of the original 529 beneficiary, provided

	accounts permitted (Sec. 70117)		the recipient is an eligible individual under ABLE rules. This can be useful if the original 529 beneficiary does not need the funds, but a sibling or another family member with a disability does.
5	Trump Account qualified ABLE rollover contributions (Sec. 70204)	Direct rollovers of the entire Trump Account balance to ABLE accounts at age 17 are not taxable.	Be aware of the annual ABLE contribution limit: The amount rolled over counts toward the annual ABLE account contribution limit for the year. For 2025, this is $19,000. Excess contribution may be subject to a 6% excise tax.

14.   Tax Code Changes Affecting All Other Topics

No.	Tax Change/Provision	Description	Tax Planning Tip
1	Excise tax on remittance transfers (Sec. 70604)	Impose a 1% tax on remittance transfers made after 2025.	The tax applies only to remittance transfers for which the sender provides: cash, money order, and cashier's check. A fund with a debit card or credit card is not taxed.
2	Enforcement provisions with respect to COVID-related employee retention credits (ERC) (Sec. 70605)	Increases penalties on ERC promoters. Disallows ERC refund claims filed after January 31, 2024. Extends statute of limitations for assessment to six years.	Taxpayers should use caution for audit readiness when ERC was filed by the promoters.
3	SSN requirement for American opportunity and lifetime learning credits (Sec. 70606)	Requires SSN for taxpayer (and spouse, if married). No credit is generally allowed for married taxpayers filing separately.	To claim the American Opportunity Tax Credit (AOTC), the taxpayer must provide the educational institution's EIN on Form 8863. This information is typically found on Form 1098-T, which the institution provides to the student.
4	Task force on the replacement of direct file (Sec. 70607)	Creation of a task force to design a public-private partnership to provide free tax filing to replace Free File and Direct File. The goal is to provide free tax filing for up to 70% of all taxpayers calculated	Retirees should manage their AGI below the 70% national level to avoid the filing fee and audit risk. Pre-retirement planning includes Roth conversion, HSA funding, and buy-borrow-retire strategy.

No.	Tax Change/Provision	Description	Tax Planning Tip
		by adjusted gross income.	
5	Educator expenses (Sec. 70110)	Removes educator expenses as a 2% miscellaneous itemized deduction. Instead, these expenses deductible are part of the itemized deductions. Adds interscholastic administrator or coach as an eligible educator.	More professional coaches in sports, arts, music, and other fields will benefit more deductions.
6	Wagering losses (gambling loss) (Sec. 70114)	90% of wagering losses are deductible but limited to wagering gains, effective for tax years beginning December 31, 2025.	Gambling community grows these days, including sport gambling, election gambling, racing car gambling, and more.
7	Savers credit expansion (Sec. 70116)	This credit is allowed for ABLE contributions made by the disabled individual. Maximum credit increased to $2,100, effective after the year 2026.	More disability benefits provided by the tax code.

Endnotes

Chapter 1:

1. Berkshire Hathaway Inc. (n.d.). *Shareholder letters* [Annual letters archive]. Retrieved June 2025, from https://www.berkshirehathaway.com/letters/letters.html

2. Vitucci, N. (2025, May). *Every Berkshire Hathaway shareholder letter 1977–2024* [PDF]. Retrieved from https://Sashavitucci.com/wp-content/uploads/2025/05/Berkshire-Hathaway-Letters-to-Shareholders_to2024.pdf

3. Sarwa. (2025, November). *90 Warren Buffett quotes on investing, business, and life.* Retrieved June 2025 from https://www.sarwa.co/blog/warren-buffett-quotes

Chapter 2:

1. Webb, J. (2022). *Create Your Self-Manifesting Vision Board* [e-book]. Soul of Prosperity series.

2. Berkshire Hathaway Inc. (2025). *Annual & interim reports.* https://berkshirehathaway.com/reports.html

3. S&P Dow Jones Indices. (n.d.). *S&P 500 index overview.* S&P Global. https://www.spglobal.com/spdji/en/indices/equity/sp-500/#overview

4. Internal Revenue Service. (2024). *Health savings accounts (HSAs).* U.S. Department of the Treasury. https://www.irs.gov/publications/p969

5. Berkley, T. (2024). *HSA Owner's Manual, Fourth Edition: What every accountholder, employer, and benefits consultant needs to know about Health Savings Accounts—and how to use them strategically.* Independently published

6. Internal Revenue Service. (2024). *Roth IRAs.* U.S. Department of the Treasury. https://www.irs.gov/retirement-plans/roth-iras

7. Department of the Treasury & Internal Revenue Service. (2008, March 3). *Notice of Proposed Rulemaking—UGMA/UTMA and 529 Accounts* (IRB 2008–9). https://www.irs.gov/pub/irs-tege/a2008_17.pdf

Chapter 3:

1. Rieckens, S. (2019). *Playing with FIRE (Financial Independence Retire Early): How far would you go for financial freedom?* New World Library.

2. Parisi, S. (2025, April 10). *How Whole Life Insurance Works & How to Maximize Your Cash Value* [Video]. YouTube. https://www.youtube.com/watch?v=CPEUB4oAnBk

3. Langley, K. (2023, November 22). *Warren Buffett talks stock donations—and his will—in Thanksgiving note. The Wall Street Journal.* Warren Buffett Talks Stock Donations—and His Will—in Thanksgiving Note

4. Kim, H. (2025, June 11). *Understand your 529 state tax benefits: Should you stay in-state or shop around for an out-of-state 529 plan?* Morningstar. https://www.morningstar.com/personal-finance/how-do-your-states-529-tax-benefits-stack-up

5. Slott, E. (2024). *The Retirement Savings Time Bomb Ticks Louder: How to Avoid Unnecessary Tax Landmines, Defuse the Latest Threats to Your Retirement Savings, and Ignite Your Financial Freedom* (Revised ed.). Penguin Books

6. Internal Revenue Service. (2025, January 2). *Retirement topics – Exceptions to tax on early distributions* (Topic No. 558). https://www.irs.gov/retirement-plans/plan-participant-employee/retirement-topics-exceptions-to-tax-on-early-distributions

7. Internal Revenue Service. (2025, May 27). *One-participant 401(K) plans* [Webpage]. https://www.irs.gov/retirement-plans/one-participant-401k-plans

8. Internal Revenue Service. (n.d.-a). *Like-kind exchanges – Real estate tax tips.* IRS. https://www.irs.gov/businesses/small-businesses-self-employed/like-kind-exchanges-real-estate-tax-tips

Chapter 4:

1. Federal News Network. (2025, April). *What federal workers should consider before accepting deferred resignation.* Retrieved June 2025, from https://federalnewsnetwork.com/workforce/2025/04/what-federal-workers-should-consider-before-accepting-deferred-resignation/

2. Internal Revenue Service. (2025, May 27). *Substantially equal periodic payments.* Retrieved June 12, 2025, from https://www.irs.gov/retirement-plans/substantially-equal-periodic-payments

3. Internal Revenue Service. (2024). *Form 8606: Nondeductible IRAs* [PDF]. U.S. Department of the Treasury. Retrieved June 12, 2025, from https://www.irs.gov/pub/irs-prior/i8606—2024.pdf

4. Kaiser Family Foundation. (2024, May 28). *Deductibles in ACA Marketplace Plans, 2014–2025.* Retrieved June 12, 2025, from https://www.kff.org/affordable-care-act/issue-brief/deductibles-in-aca-marketplace-plans/

5. Internal Revenue Service. (2025, April 24). *Gig economy tax center* [Web page]. U.S. Department of the Treasury. Retrieved June 12, 2025, from https://www.irs.gov/businesses/gig-economy-tax-center

6. Burgard, D. (n.d.). *How to appeal financial aid award packages.* Finaid.org. Retrieved June 12, 2025, from https://finaid.org/financial-aid-applications/financial-aid-appeal/

7. Chen, L. (2024). *Build Resilience: Live, Learn, and Lead.* Manuscripts LLC.

8. Gelb, A. (2022, November 16). *A Layoff Playbook. Medium.* Retrieved June 12, 2025, from https://medium.com/@gelbamanda/a-layoff-playbook-8b7cbec6ee69

Chapter 5:

1. Internal Revenue Service. The *529 plans: Qualified tuition programs (QTPs).* U.S. Department of the Treasury. https://www.irs.gov/taxtopics/tc313

2. Tanabe, G., & Tanabe, K. (2025). *The Ultimate Scholarship Book 2026: Billions of Dollars in Scholarships, Grants and Prizes* (18th ed., Kindle ed.). SuperCollege.

3. Internal Revenue Service. *AOTC – American Opportunity Tax Credit.* IRS. https://www.irs.gov/credits-deductions/individuals/aotc

4. Internal Revenue Service. (2025, January 2). *Topic No. 310: Coverdell education savings accounts.* https://www.irs.gov/taxtopics/tc310

5. U.S. Department of Education, Federal Student Aid. (2024). *School-Determined Requirements* (Volume 1, Chapter 1, p. 232) in *FSA Handbook 2024-2025.* U.S. Department of Education. https://fsapartners.ed.gov/knowledge-center/fsa-handbook/2024-2025/vol1/ch1-school-determined-requirements

Chapter 6:

1. Thomson Reuters Tax & Accounting. (2025, January 30). *How AI will impact the tax and accounting profession.* https://tax.thomsonreuters.com/blog/the-future-of-professionals-how-ai-is-the-catalyst-for-reshaping-every-aspect-of-tax-and-accounting-work/

2. Internal Revenue Service. (2025). *General instructions for forms W-2 and W-3 (2025)* [PDF]. U.S. Department of the Treasury. https://www.irs.gov/pub/irs-pdf/iw2w3.pdf

3. Internal Revenue Service. (2024). *Form 8863: Education Credits (American Opportunity and Lifetime Learning Credits)* [PDF]. U.S. Department of the Treasury. https://www.irs.gov/pub/irs-pdf/f8863.pdf

4. Internal Revenue Service. (2024, December). *Publication 551: Basis of Assets* [PDF]. U.S. Department of the Treasury. https://www.irs.gov/publications/p551

5. Internal Revenue Service. (2025, May 27). *Retirement topics – 401(K) and profit-sharing plan contribution limits* [Webpage]. https://www.irs.gov/retirement-plans/plan-participant-employee/retirement-topics-401k-and-profit-sharing-plan-contribution-limits

6. Internal Revenue Service. (2025). *Credits for new clean vehicles purchased in 2023 or after* [Webpage]. https://www.irs.gov/credits-deductions/credits-for-new-clean-vehicles-purchased-in-2023-or-after

7. Ovaska, S. (2025, June 1). *Agentic AI poised to change the way CPAs work. Journal of Accountancy.* https://www.journalofaccountancy.com/issues/2025/jun/agentic-ai-poised-to-change-the-way-cpas-work/

Chapter 7:

1. Investment Company Institute. (2012). *The success of the U.S. retirement system* https://www.ici.org/pdf/ppr_12_success_retirement.pdf

2. Internal Revenue Service. (2024). *Publication 590-A: Contributions to individual retirement arrangements (IRAs)* (2024 ed.). U.S. Department of the Treasury. https://www.irs.gov/pub/irs-pdf/p590a.pdf

3. Internal Revenue Service. (2024, October 9). *Family employees.* In *Small Business & Self-Employed.* U.S. Department of the Treasury. Retrieved [date you accessed it], from https://www.irs.gov/businesses/small-businesses-self-employed/family-employees

4. Internal Revenue Service. (2025, May 29). *Health Reimbursement Arrangements (HRAs).* U.S. Department of the Treasury. Retrieved August 7, 2025, from https://www.irs.gov/newsroom/health-reimbursement-arrangements-hras

5. MarketWatch / The Wall Street Journal. (2021, January 22). *Vision boarding in a year of uncertainty.* Retrieved June 2025, from https://www.wsj.com/lifestyle/relationships/vision-boarding-in-a-year-of-uncertainty-11611323077

6. Benz, C. (2024). *How to Retire: 20 Lessons for a Happy, Successful, and Wealthy Retirement.* Harriman House.

Chapter 8:

1. Hegna, T. (2020). Don't worry, retire happy: Seven steps to retirement security *(2nd ed.).* Tom Hegna, Inc.

2. Internal Revenue Service. (2025, May 27). *One-participant 401(K) plans.* U.S. Department of the Treasury. Retrieved June 28, 2025, from https://www.irs.gov/retirement-plans/one-participant-401k-plans

3. Tergesen, A., & Adedoyin, O. (2024, August 4). *The 401(K) investors convinced that target-date funds miss the mark. The Wall Street Journal.* Retrieved June 28, 2025, from https://www.wsj.com/personal-finance/retirement/401k-savers-target-date-funds-alternatives-6e4e6f75

4. Davies, S., & Brown, D. C. (2021, October 8). *For investors who miss their retirement targets, fees in target-date funds may be to blame.* Leeds School of Business, University of Colorado Boulder. Retrieved June 2025, from https://www.colorado.edu/business/news/2021/10/08/research-davies-target-date-funds

5. Lasker, R. (2025, April 16). *Backdoor Roth IRA: Advantages and tax implications explained.* Investopedia. https://www.investopedia.com/terms/b/backdoor-roth-ira.asp

6. Kohler, M. J. (2023). *Choosing best retirement plan* [PowerPoint slides]. Mark J. Kohler. Retrieved June 28, 2025, from Mark J. Kohler's website: https://www.markjkohler.com/wp-content/uploads/2023/01/Choosing-best-retirement-plan.pptx.pdf

7. Internal Revenue Service. *(2019, September 24)*. *Revenue Procedure 2019-38: Safe harbor for rental real estate as a trade or business under section 199A [PDF]*.

Chapter 9:

1. Phillips, D. T. (2015). *The Family Bank Strategy: How to create your own personal tax-free bank and protect your estate from creditors and predators*. CreateSpace Independent Publishing Platform.

2. New York Life Insurance Company. (2025). *2024 Report to Policy Owners* [PDF]. Retrieved June 12, 2025, from https://www.newyorklife.com/report-to-policy-owners

3. The Northwestern Mutual Life Insurance Company. (2025). *2024 Statutory Annual Statement* [PDF]. Retrieved June 12, 2025, from https://www.northwesternmutual.com/2024-annual-report/

4. The Guardian Life Insurance Company of America. (2024). *2024 Annual Report* [PDF]. Retrieved June 12, 2025, from The Guardian Annual 2024

5. Massachusetts Mutual Life Insurance Company. (2024). *2024 Annual Report* [PDF]. Retrieved June 12, 2025, from https://www.massmutual.com/global/media/shared/doc/financial-documents/annual-reports/2024_annual_report.pdf

6. Foundation Source. (2022). *Insuring a private foundation's financial future* [White paper]. Foundation Source. Retrieved from https://foundationsource.com/resources/white-papers/insuring-a-private-foundations-financial-future/

7. Thompson, J. (2024). *Money. Wealth. Life Insurance: How the Wealthy Use Life Insurance as a Tax-Free Personal Bank to Supercharge Their Savings*.

8. Nash, R. N. (2000). *Becoming your own banker: Unlock the infinite banking concept* (Rev. ed.). R. Nelson Nash.

9. Yellen, P. (2009). *Bank on yourself*. BenBella Books.

10. Gunderson, G. B., & Isom, M. (2016). *What Would the Rockefellers Do?: How the wealthy get and stay that way*. Wiley.

Chapter 10:

1. Tallgrass Estate Planning. (2023, September 18). *The family bank: Protect assets, reduce taxes, and create generational wealth*. Tallgrass Estate Planning. https://www.tallgrassestateplanning.com/post/the-family-bank-protect-assets-reduce-taxes-and-create-generational-wealth.

2. IRS. (2025). *Estates and trusts: Form 1041 and filing requirements* [Web page]. U.S. Department of the Treasury. Retrieved June 2025 from https://www.irs.gov/e-file-providers/estates-and-trusts

3. Griffiths-Hamilton, E. (2014). *Build Your Family Bank: A Winning Vision for Multigenerational Wealth.*

4. Internal Revenue Code, 26 U.S.C. § 7702 (2025). *Definition of life insurance contract.* United States Code. Retrieved June 12, 2025, from https://www.law.cornell.edu/uscode/text/26/7702

5. Internal Revenue Code, 26 U.S.C. § 72(e), § 72(s) (2025). *Rules for life insurance and annuity contract distributions.* United States Code. Retrieved June 12, 2025, from https://www.law.cornell.edu/uscode/text/26/72

6. Internal Revenue Code, 26 U.S.C. §§ 671–679 (2025). *Grantors and others treated as substantial owners.* United States Code. Retrieved June 12, 2025, from https://www.law.cornell.edu/uscode/text/26/subtitle-A/chapter-1/subchapter-J/part-I/subpart-E

7. Internal Revenue Code, 26 U.S.C. §§ 2601–2664 (2025). *Tax on generation-skipping transfers.* United States Code. Retrieved June 12, 2025, from https://www.law.cornell.edu/uscode/text/26/subtitle-B/chapter-13

8. Gorman, T. (2024). *Family-Proof Your Wealth: Prepare your heirs, avoid conflicts, and build a legacy for generations.* FamilyWealthWays.

9. LegalZoom. (2024, October). *How to make a do-it-yourself living trust.* Retrieved June 13, 2025, from https://www.legalzoom.com/articles/do-it-yourself-living-trust

Chapter 11:

1. Internal Revenue Service. (2025, March 4). *Small business and self-employed tax center.* U.S. Department of the Treasury. Retrieved June 13, 2025, from https://www.irs.gov/businesses/small-businesses-self-employed

2. Weltman, B. (2024). *J.K. Lasser's 1001 deductions & tax breaks 2025: Your complete guide to everything deductible* (Includes small business and self-employed deductions). Wiley.

3. Watson, J. (2024). *Taxpayer's comprehensive guide to LLCs and S corps: 2025 edition.* WCG CPAs & Advisors.

4. Kohler, M. J. (2024, December 10). *How to pay your children in your business.* Retrieved June 13, 2025, from https://markjkohler.com/how-to-pay-your-kids-in-your-business/

5. Foote, T. (2007). *The Kid's Roth IRA Handbook: Securing tax-free wealth from a child's first paycheck* (1st ed.). TracyTrends Publishing.

6. Internal Revenue Service. (2024, December 3). *Topic No. 511: Business travel expenses.* U.S. Department of the Treasury. Retrieved June 13, 2025, from https://www.irs.gov/taxtopics/tc511

7. 26 C.F.R. § 1.263(a)-1 *(2025). Capital expenditures; general regulation including de minimis election.* Retrieved June 13, 2025, from 26 CFR § 1.263(a)-1 - Capital expenditures; in

general. | Electronic Code of Federal Regulations (e-CFR) | US Law | LII / Legal Information Institute

8. Forbes Advisor. (2025, June). *Top business credit cards of 2025*. Retrieved June 13, 2025, from https://www.forbes.com/advisor/credit-cards/best/business/

Chapter 12:

1. National Association of Tax Professionals. (2021, October 26). *Navigating home office deductions.* NATP Blog. https://blog.natptax.com/article?articleId=4l7IhpbXSx5W9jqDuAVrrx

2. *Commissioner v. Soliman*, 506 U.S. 168 (1993). United States Supreme Court. Retrieved June 13, 2025, from https://caselaw.findlaw.com/court/us-supreme-court/506/168.html

3. Internal Revenue Code, 26 U.S.C. § 280A(d) (2025). *Disallowance of certain expenses in connection with business use of home, rental of vacation homes, etc.* United States Code. Retrieved June 13, 2025, from https://uscode.house.gov/view.xhtml?req=granuleid:USC-prelim-title26-section280A

4. Kohler, M. J. (2024, December 3). *Maximizing your S-Corp home office tax deduction: Tips and tricks.* Mark J. Kohler Blog. Retrieved June 13, 2025, from https://markjkohler.com/maximizing-home-office-tax-deduction/

Chapter 13:

1. Internal Revenue Service. (2025, January 2). *Standard mileage rates* [Webpage]. https://www.irs.gov/tax-professionals/standard-mileage-rates

2. Internal Revenue Service. (2024). *Publication 587: Business Use of Your Home (Including Daycare)* [PDF]. U.S. Department of the Treasury. https://www.irs.gov/pub/irs-pdf/p587.pdf

3. Internal Revenue Service. (2025, May 22). *Clean vehicle tax credits* [Webpage]. U.S. Department of the Treasury. https://www.irs.gov/clean-vehicle-tax-credits

4. Internal Revenue Service. (2025, April 10). *Alternative Fuel Vehicle Refueling Property Credit* [Webpage]. U.S. Department of the Treasury. https://www.irs.gov/credits-deductions/alternative-fuel-vehicle-refueling-property-credit

5. Peterson, L. (2025, January 10). *Section 179 deduction: Limits, how it works in 2025.* NerdWallet. Retrieved June 12, 2025, from https://www.nerdwallet.com/article/taxes/section-179-deduction

6. Internal Revenue Service. (2024, August 20). *Topic No. 510: Business use of car*. Retrieved June 12, 2025, from https://www.irs.gov/taxtopics/tc510

7. Prvulovic, A. (2025, April 29). *5 Best mileage tracking apps in 2025: Tested and compared.* Timeero. Retrieved June 12, 2025, from https://timeero.com/post/best-mileage-tracking-apps

Chapter 14:

1. TurboTax Expert. (2025, April 29). *Tax deductions for business travelers.* TurboTax. Retrieved June 13, 2025, from https://turbotax.intuit.com/tax-tips/jobs-and-career/tax-deductions-for-business-travelers/L83DdTEZ8

2. National Association of Tax Professionals. (2022, August 30). *Taxpayer's right to deduct travel expenses for a side gig upheld by Tax Court.* NATP Blog. Retrieved June 13, 2025, from https://blog.natptax.com/article?articleId=1q86KOkaHBMJs6F3lOQQWT

3. Han, A. (2025, May 6). *Why not have the IRS help pay for part of your travel costs?* [LinkedIn post]. LinkedIn. https://www.linkedin.com/posts/amandayhan_tax-savings-toolkit-activity-7315116561420193793-5iag

4. Treasury Regulation § 1.274-12 (2025). *Final regulations on business meals and entertainment.* U.S. Dept. of the Treasury. Retrieved June 13, 2025, from https://www.irs.gov/newsroom/heres-what-businesses-need-to-know-about-the-enhanced-business-meal-deduction

5. Cicalese, J. D. (2023, November 1). *Navigating around limits on meals and entertainment.* The Tax Adviser. Retrieved June 13, 2025, from https://www.thetaxadviser.com/issues/2023/nov/navigating-around-limits-on-meals-and-entertainment.html

6. IRS Topic on spousal travel. (2024). *Spousal travel.* U.S. Department of the Treasury. Retrieved June 14, 2025, from https://www.irs.gov/government-entities/federal-state-local-governments/spousal-travel

7. Weiss & Company LLP. (2022, November 17). *International business travel: The ins and outs of tax deductions.* Weiss CPA News. Retrieved June 14, 2025, from https://weisscpa.com/news/international-business-travel-the-ins-and-outs-of-tax-deductions/

8. Internal Revenue Service. (2023, May 15). *Business travelers should check out these deductions before hitting the road.* U.S. Department of the Treasury. Retrieved June 14, 2025, from https://www.irs.gov/newsroom/business-travelers-should-check-out-these-deductions-before-hitting-the-road

Chapter 15:

1. U.S. Code. (2024). *26 U.S.C. § 162(l): Special rules for health insurance costs of self-employed individuals.* Legal Information Institute, Cornell Law School. https://www.law.cornell.edu/uscode/text/26/162

2. Fidelity Investments. (2023). *HSA guidance: Understanding health savings accounts for employers and individuals.* https://www.fidelity.com/go/hsa

3. IRS. (2024). *Publication 969: Health savings accounts and other tax-favored health plans.* U.S. Department of the Treasury, Internal Revenue Service. https://www.irs.gov/publications/p969

4. Devenir. (2023). *The HSA opportunity for Gen Z and young professionals.* https://www.devenir.com

5. IRS. (2024). *Form 8941 and instructions: Credit for small employer health insurance premiums.* U.S. Department of the Treasury, Internal Revenue Service. https://www.irs.gov/forms-pubs/about-form-8941

Chapter 16:

1. *Pensions disappearing for new employees at big firms: study.* (2025, June 7). *The Wall Street Journal.* Retrieved June 13, 2025, from https://www.wsj.com/articles/BL-CFOB-2779

2. Kohler, M. J. (2023, August). *401(K) options for small business owners* [PDF]. Retrieved June 13, 2025, from https://markjkohler.com/wp-content/uploads/2023/08/401k-Options-for-Small-Business-Owners.pdf

3. Internal Revenue Service. (2025, May 29). *Tax treatment for family members working in the family business.* U.S. Department of the Treasury https://www.irs.gov/newsroom/tax-treatment-for-family-members-working-in-the-family-business

4. Internal Revenue Service. (2024, October 9). *Family employees.* U.S. Department of the Treasury. Retrieved June 13, 2025, from https://www.irs.gov/businesses/small-businesses-self-employed/family-employees

5. Urbach & Avraham, CPAs. (2021, November 18). *Schedule C vs S-Corporation.* Retrieved June 13, 2025, from https://www.ua-cpas.com/blog/index.php/2021/11/18/schedule-c-vs-s-corporation/

6. Fidelity Investments. (n.d.). *What is a mega backdoor Roth?* Retrieved June 13, 2025, from https://www.fidelity.com/learning-center/personal-finance/mega-backdoor-roth

7. Internal Revenue Service. (2024). *Instructions for Schedule C (Form 1040), Profit or Loss From Business* [PDF]. U.S. Department of the Treasury. Retrieved June 13, 2025, from https://www.irs.gov/pub/irs-pdf/i1040sc.pdf

8. Internal Revenue Service. (2024). *Instructions for Form 1120-S (2024)* [PDF]. U.S. Department of the Treasury. Retrieved June 13, 2025, from https://www.irs.gov/pub/irs-pdf/i1120s.pdf

Chapter 17:

1. Internal Revenue Service. (2014, July 11). *Section 121 — Exclusion of gain from sale of principal residence* (Revenue Ruling 2014-02) [PDF]. U.S. Department of the Treasury. https://www.irs.gov/pub/irs-drop/rr-14-02.pdf

2. Han, A., & MacFarland, M. (2018). *The Book on Tax Strategies for the Savvy Real Estate Investor: Powerful Techniques Anyone Can Use to Deduct More, Invest Smarter, and Pay Far Less to the IRS!* BiggerPockets Publishing.

3. Han, A., & MacFarland, M. (2020). *The Book on Advanced Tax Strategies: Cracking the Code for Savvy Real Estate Investors* (2nd ed.). BiggerPockets Publishing.

4. Internal Revenue Service. (2024). *Instructions for Schedule E (Form 1040), Supplemental Income and Loss* [PDF]. U.S. Department of the Treasury. https://www.irs.gov/pub/irs-pdf/i1040se.pdf

5. Botkin, S. C. (2006). *Real Estate Tax Secrets of the Rich: Big-Time Tax Advantages of Buying, Selling, and Owning Real Estate*. McGraw-Hill Education.

6. Internal Revenue Service. (2024). *Instructions for Form 8824: Like-Kind Exchanges (and section 1043 conflict-of-interest sales)* [PDF]. U.S. Department of the Treasury. https://www.irs.gov/pub/irs-pdf/i8824.pdf

7. Richard, D. G. (2013). *Smart Essentials for College Rentals: Parent and investor guide to buying college-town real estate*. Inkspiration Media.

8. Sorensen, M. N. (2018). *The Self-Directed IRA Handbook: An Authoritative Guide for Self-Directed Retirement Plan Investors and Their Advisors* (2nd ed.). SOKOH Publishing.

9. Internal Revenue Service. (2024). *Publication 527: Residential Rental Property (Including Rental of Vacation Homes)* [PDF]. https://www.irs.gov/pub/irs-pdf/p527.pdf

Chapter 18:

1. Internal Revenue Service. (n.d.). *Real estate (taxes, mortgage interest, points, other property expenses)*. https://www.irs.gov/faqs/itemized-deductions-standard-deduction/real-estate-taxes-mortgage-interest-points-other-property-expenses/real-estate-taxes-mortgage-interest-points-other-property-expenses-5

2. Internal Revenue Service. (n.d.). *Topic No. 503: Deductible taxes*. https://www.irs.gov/taxtopics/tc503

3. Internal Revenue Service. (2025). *Instructions for Form 4562 (2024): Depreciation and Amortization (including Section 179)* [PDF]. https://www.irs.gov/instructions/i4562

4. Internal Revenue Service. (2022, February). Cost Segregation Audit Techniques Guide (Publication 5653) [PDF]. U.S. Department of the Treasury. https://www.irs.gov/pub/irs-pdf/p5653.pdf

5. Internal Revenue Service. *(2022, December). Instructions for Form 3115 (Rev. December 2022): Application for Change in Accounting Method [PDF].* U.S. Department of the Treasury. https://www.irs.gov/pub/irs-pdf/i3115.pdf

6. Internal Revenue Service. (2024). *Publication 925: Passive Activity and At-Risk Rules* [PDF]. https://www.irs.gov/publications/p925

7. *The Tax Adviser. (2017, March). Navigating the Real Estate Professional Rules.* https://www.thetaxadviser.com/issues/2017/mar/navigating-real-estate-professional-rules/

8. Godwin, T., & McKinley, J. (2024, January). *The self-rental rules: Risks and opportunities. The Tax Adviser.* https://www.thetaxadviser.com/issues/2024/jan/the-self-rental-rules-risks-and-opportunities/

Chapter 19:

1. Internal Revenue Service. (2024). *Publication 946: How to Depreciate Property* [PDF]. https://www.irs.gov/forms-pubs/about-publication-946

2. Rohde, J. (2021, March 15). *The Rules Around Deducting Closing Costs on Rental Property.* Stessa Blog. https://www.stessa.com/blog/are-closing-costs-tax-deductible-on-rental-property/

3. Internal Revenue Service. (n.d.). *Additional First-Year Depreciation Deduction (Bonus) – FAQ.* https://www.irs.gov/newsroom/additional-first-year-depreciation-deduction-bonus-faq

4. Adams, H. (2025, February 14). *Understanding depreciation recapture on rentals.* Schwab. https://www.schwab.com/learn/story/understanding-depreciation-recapture-on-rentals

5. Rogers, L. J. (2025). *Section 1031 exchange: How to Swap Till Ya' Drop—Building Family Wealth While Minimizing Taxes.* Davro Press.

6. Internal Revenue Service. (n.d.). *Topic No. 409: Capital gains and losses.* https://www.irs.gov/taxtopics/tc409

7. Internal Revenue Code, 26 U.S.C. § 469(c)(7) (2025). *Passive activity loss rules: Real estate professionals.* https://www.law.cornell.edu/uscode/text/26/469

Chapter 20:

1. Lau, C. (2023, September). *Passive loss limitations on rental real estate. Journal of Accountancy,* 234(9), 20–28. https://www.journalofaccountancy.com/issues/2023/sep/passive-loss-limitations-on-rental-real-estate/

2. Internal Revenue Service. (2024). *Publication 583: Starting a Business and Keeping Records* [PDF]. U.S. Department of the Treasury. https://www.irs.gov/pub/irs-pdf/p583.pdf

3. Internal Revenue Service. (n.d.). *Audit Technique Guide : Passive Activity Losses* [PDF]. Bradford Tax Institute: https://bradfordtaxinstitute.com/Endnotes/ATG_Passive_Activity_Guide.pdf

4. Internal Revenue Service. (2025, March 6). *Recordkeeping.* https://www.irs.gov/businesses/small-businesses-self-employed/recordkeeping

5. U.S. Department of the Treasury. (2024). *Treas. Reg. § 1.469-5T(a)(1)–(7)* (Material participation tests). In *Internal Revenue Code* (26 C.F.R. § 1.469-5T(a)(1)–(7)). https://www.law.cornell.edu/cfr/text/26/1.469-5T

6. Internal Revenue Service. (2024). *Publication 463: Travel, Gift, and Car Expenses* [PDF]. U.S. Department of the Treasury. https://www.irs.gov/pub/irs-pdf/p463.pdf

Chapter 21:

1. Field, M. (2023). *Every Landlord's Tax Deduction Guide* (15th ed.). Nolo
2. Luxon, B. (2023, October 12). *Schedule C vs. Schedule E for rental property.* Landlord Studio Blog. Retrieved June 12, 2025, from https://www.landlordstudio.com/blog/schedule-c-vs-schedule-e
3. Hall, B. (2022, January 15). *The Real Estate CPA Explains: Repairs vs. Improvements. Azibo Academy.* Retrieved June 12, 2025, from https://www.azibo.com/academy/repairs-vs-improvements-explained
4. REI Hub. (2023, March 15). *Reporting rental income: IRS red flags for property owners.* Retrieved June 12, 2025, from https://www.reihub.net/resources/reporting-rental-income-irs-red-flags-for-property-owners/
5. Business News Daily. (2023, February 1). *The 7 best small business accounting apps.* Business News Daily. Retrieved June 15, 2025, from https://www.businessnewsdaily.com/5709-android-accounting-finance-apps-small-business.html
6. Kohler, M. J. (2011). *What your CPA isn't telling you: Life-changing tax strategies.* Entrepreneur Press.
7. Internal Revenue Service. (2025). *Instructions for Form 4797: Sales of Business Property* [PDF].https://www.irs.gov/pub/irs-pdf/i4797.pdf
8. Gibbs, S. (2024, February 16). *Homestead exemptions by state: Complete guide with comparison charts.* Insurance & Estates. Retrieved June 2025, from https://www.insuranceandestates.com/homestead-exemptions-by-state-with-charts/

Chapter 22:

1. Internal Revenue Service. (n.d.). *Private foundations.* U.S. Department of the Treasury. Retrieved June 14, 2025, from https://www.irs.gov/charities-non-profits/private-foundations
2. Internal Revenue Service. (2024, December). *Instructions for Form 1023-EZ, Streamlined Application for Recognition of Exemption Under Section 501(c)(3) of the Internal Revenue Code.* U.S. Department of the Treasury. Retrieved June 14, 2025, from https://www.irs.gov/pub/irs-pdf/i1023ez.pdf
3. Internal Revenue Service. (2025, June 4). *Life cycle of a private foundation – Starting out.* U.S. Department of the Treasury. Retrieved June 15, 2025, from https://www.irs.gov/charities-non-profits/private-foundations/life-cycle-of-a-private-foundation-starting-out
4. Internal Revenue Service. (n.d.). *Charitable contribution deductions.* U.S. Department of the Treasury. Retrieved June 14, 2025, from https://www.irs.gov/charities-non-profits/charitable-organizations/charitable-contribution-deductions

5. Internal Revenue Service. (n.d.). *Private foundations — Required distributions (IRC § 4942).* U.S. Department of the Treasury. Retrieved June 14, 2025, from https://www.irs.gov/charities-non-profits/private-foundations/taxes-on-failure-to-distribute-income-private-foundations

6. Internal Revenue Service. (n.d.). *Private foundations – Self-dealing (IRC 4941(d)(1)(C))* . U.S. Department of the Treasury. Retrieved June 15, 2025, from https://www.irs.gov/government-entities/private-foundations-self-dealing-irc-4941d1c

7. Hopkins, B. R. (2008). *Private foundation law made easy.* Wiley.

Chapter 23:

1. Internal Revenue Service. (n.d.). *Charitable organizations providing disaster relief — Questions and answers.* U.S. Department of the Treasury. Retrieved June 15, 2025, from https://www.irs.gov/charities-non-profits/charitable-organizations/charitable-organizations-providing-disaster-relief-questions-and-answers

2. Internal Revenue Service. (n.d.). *Disaster relief: Charitable contributions to U.S. organizations for international relief* [Web page]. U.S. Department of the Treasury. Retrieved June 15, 2025, from https://www.irs.gov/charities-non-profits/charitable-organizations/disaster-relief-contributions-to-us-organizations-for-international-relief

3. Internal Revenue Service. (n.d.). *Charitable organizations: Substantiation and disclosure requirements.* U.S. Department of the Treasury. Retrieved June 15, 2025, from https://www.irs.gov/charities-non-profits/charitable-organizations/charitable-organizations-substantiation-and-disclosure-requirements

4. Internal Revenue Service. (n.d.). *Charitable contributions: Written acknowledgments.* U.S. Department of the Treasury. Retrieved June 15, 2025, from https://www.irs.gov/charities-non-profits/charitable-organizations/charitable-contributions-written-acknowledgments

5. Internal Revenue Service. (n.d.). *Grants to individuals* [Private foundations]. U.S. Department of the Treasury. Retrieved June 15, 2025, from https://www.irs.gov/charities-non-profits/private-foundations/grants-to-individuals

Chapter 24:

1. Internal Revenue Service. (2024, November 20). *Instructions for Form 990-PF (2024)* [PDF]. U.S. Department of the Treasury. Retrieved June 15, 2025, from https://www.irs.gov/pub/irs-pdf/i990pf.pdf

2. FoundationSource. (2022, April 18). *10 things you didn't know you could do with a private foundation* [White paper]. Retrieved June 15, 2025, from https://foundationsource.com/resources/white-papers/10-things-you-didnt-know-you-could-do-with-your-foundation/

3. Internal Revenue Service. (2016). *Private foundations audit technique guide* (Publication No. IRS–TEGE–ATG–2016–1) [PDF]. U.S. Department of the Treasury. Retrieved June 15, 2025, from https://www.irs.gov/pub/irs-tege/atg_private_foundations.pdf

4. Internal Revenue Service. (2025, May). *Statistics of income: Domestic private foundations and charitable trusts* [Data set]. U.S. Department of the Treasury. Retrieved June 15, 2025, from https://www.irs.gov/statistics/soi-tax-stats-domestic-private-foundation-and-charitable-trust-statistics

5. Rockefeller Philanthropy Advisors. (n.d.). *Crafting your foundation's mission and vision*. Retrieved June 15, 2025, from https://www.rockpa.org/guide/crafting-your-foundations-mission-and-vision/

6. Internal Revenue Service. (n.d.). SOI Tax Stats - Annual Extract of Tax-Exempt Organization Financial Data. U.S. Department of the Treasury. https://www.irs.gov/statistics/soi-tax-stats-annual-extract-of-tax-exempt-organization-financial-data

Chapter 25:

1. Internal Revenue Service. (2024). *Internal Revenue Code §6033 – Returns by exempt organizations*. U.S. Department of the Treasury. Retrieved June 15, 2025, from https://www.law.cornell.edu/uscode/text/26/6033

2. Internal Revenue Service. (2024). *Internal Revenue Code §4946 – Definitions and special rules*. U.S. Department of the Treasury. Retrieved June 15, 2025, from https://www.law.cornell.edu/uscode/text/26/4946

3. Internal Revenue Service. (2024). *Internal Revenue Code §4941 – Taxes on self-dealing*. U.S. Department of the Treasury. Retrieved June 15, 2025, from https://www.law.cornell.edu/uscode/text/26/4941

4. Internal Revenue Service. (2024). *Internal Revenue Code §4944 – Taxes on investments which jeopardize charitable purpose*. U.S. Department of the Treasury. Retrieved June 15, 2025, from https://www.law.cornell.edu/uscode/text/26/4944

5. Internal Revenue Service. (n.d.). *Private foundations: Grants to individuals*. U.S. Department of the Treasury. Retrieved June 15, 2025, from https://www.irs.gov/charities-non-profits/private-foundations/grants-to-individuals

6. National Council of Nonprofits. (n.d.). *Investment policies for nonprofits*. Council of Nonprofits. Retrieved June 15, 2025, from https://www.councilofnonprofits.org/running-nonprofit/administration-and-financial-management/investment-policies-nonprofits

7. U.S. Department of the Treasury. (2025). *Treas. Reg. § 53.4942(a)-3 – Grant-related expenses qualifying as charitable expenditures*. Retrieved June 15, 2025, from https://www.ecfr.gov/current/title-26/chapter-I/subchapter-F/part-53/section-53.4942(a)-3

8. Internal Revenue Service. (2025). *26 U.S.C. § 170 – Charitable, etc., contributions and gifts.* U.S. Department of the Treasury. Retrieved June 15, 2025, from https://www.law.cornell.edu/uscode/text/26/170

9. Internal Revenue Service. (2025). *26 U.S.C. § 4942(j)(3) – Operating foundations.* U.S. Department of the Treasury. Retrieved June 15, 2025, from https://www.law.cornell.edu/uscode/text/26/4942

10. U.S. Department of the Treasury. (2025). *Treas. Reg. § 53.4945-4(c) – Grants to individuals: Travel and due diligence.* Electronic Code of Federal Regulations. Retrieved June 15, 2025, from https://www.ecfr.gov/current/title-26/chapter-I/subchapter-F/part-53/section-53.4945-4

11. Internal Revenue Service. (2025). *26 U.S.C. § 4941(d)(1)(D) – Acts of self-dealing: Compensation to disqualified persons.* U.S. Department of the Treasury. Retrieved June 15, 2025, from https://www.law.cornell.edu/uscode/text/26/4941

12. U.S. Department of the Treasury. (2024, August 1). *IRS Exempt Organizations Technical Guide TG 3-20: Introduction to private foundations and special rules under IRC 508* [PDF]. U.S. Department of the Treasury. Retrieved June 15, 2025, from https://www.irs.gov/charities-non-profits/audit-technique-guides-atgs-and-technical-guides-tgs-for-exempt-organizations

Chapter 26:

1. Buffett, W. E. (2024, November 26). *Warren Buffett to donate $1.1 billion of Berkshire stock to 4 family foundations. ABC News.* Retrieved June 15, 2025, from https://abcnews.go.com/Business/warren-buffett-donate-11-billion-berkshire-stock-4/story?id=116232411

2. Howard G. Buffett Foundation. (2024). *Form 990-PF return of private foundation* (Cal. yr. end Dec. 2023). Retrieved from https://projects.propublica.org/nonprofits/organizations/470825856

3. Internal Revenue Service. (1980). *Rev. Rul. 80-133, 1980-1 C.B. 258* (private foundation investment in life insurance). Retrieved June 15, 2025, from https://www.irs.gov/pub/irs-tege/rr80-133.pdf

4. Internal Revenue Service. (2025, April 8). *Unrelated business income tax.* U.S. Department of the Treasury. Retrieved June 15, 2025, from https://www.irs.gov/charities-non-profits/unrelated-business-income-tax

5. National Center for Family Philanthropy. (2006). *Principled planning: A guide for family foundation retreats* [PDF]. Retrieved June 15, 2025, from https://www.ncfp.org/wp-content/uploads/2018/09/Principled-Planning-A-Guide-for-Family-Foundation-Retreats-COF-2006-principled-planning-a-guide-for-family-foundation-retreats.pdf

Appendix 5:

1. Schroeder, A. (2008). *The snowball: Warren Buffett and the business of life.* Bantam Books.

2. Robbins, A. (2014). *Money: Master the game: 7 simple steps to financial freedom.* Simon & Schuster.

3. Slott, E. (2024). *The retirement savings time bomb ticks louder: How to avoid unnecessary tax landmines, defuse the latest threats to your retirement savings, and ignite your financial freedom.* Penguin Books.

4. Goldstone, H., Hughes, J. E., & Whitaker, K. (2015). *Family trusts: A guide for beneficiaries, trustees, trust protectors, and trust creators.* Bloomberg Press.

5. Phillips, D. T. (2015). *The family bank strategy: How to create your own personal tax-free bank and protect your estate from creditors and predators.* CreateSpace Independent Publishing Platform.

6. Botkin, S. C. (2022). *Lower Your Taxes – BIG TIME! 2023–2024: Small Business Wealth Building and Tax Reduction Secrets from an IRS Insider* (9th ed.). McGraw Hill Professional.

7. Weltman, B. (2024). *J.K. Lasser's small business taxes 2025: Your complete guide to a better bottom line* (27th ed.). Wiley.

8. Nash, R. N., Lara, L. C., & Murphy, R. P. (2018). *The case for IBC* (2nd ed.). Sheridan Books.

9. Wheelwright, T. (2022). The win-win wealth strategy: 7 investments the government will pay you to make. Wiley.

10. Kohler, M. J. (2019). The tax & legal playbook: Game-changing solutions to your small-business questions (2nd ed.). Entrepreneur Press.

Index

Numbers

401(K), 10, 142-158, 192, 256-260

- catch-up contributions, 158
- employer match as free money, 10, 142, 146
- mega backdoor Roth, 158
- Rule of 50, 51
- Solo 401(K), 155-161, 256-262
- split between Traditional and Roth, 143-144

529 Plans, 34, 93-95, 99, 192

- education expenses, 94
- state tax benefits, 94-95
- strategic funding during market dips, 34

72(t) Distributions (SEPP), 37, 52

A

Accountability, 70-71, 232-241

Adaptability, 108-116

AGI (Adjusted Gross Income), 19, 67, 74, 194

- phase-out limits, 95, 194
- rental loss limitations, 206
- strategic timing for tax credits, 46

AI and Tax Planning, 108-116

- ChatGPT for tax scenarios, 109
- Blue Tax AI for audit risk prediction, 110
- document reconstruction tools, 111

AMT (Alternative Minimum Tax), 67, 108

- family bank concept implementation, 179, 185

- trustee selection strategy, 183

- generation-skipping tax planning, 182

V

Vehicle Deductions, 124, 134-139, 217

- standard mileage vs. actual expense method, 217

- business use percentage calculations, 135

- depreciation for vehicles over 6,000 lbs, 134

- EV credit and installation deductions, 135

- parking and toll deductibility, 217

Vision Board Tax Integration, 14-21, 69-87, 232-241

- family engagement in financial planning, 70-71

- tax strategy visualization, 19-20

- quarterly progress reviews, 21

www.ingramcontent.com/pod-product-compliance
Lightning Source LLC
Chambersburg PA
CBHW051207200326
41519CB00025B/7032